BRITISH SUPREMACY IN SOUTH AFRICA
1899-1907

BRITISH SUPREMACY IN SOUTH AFRICA 1899-1907

by

G. H. L. Le May

*Professor of Political Studies
in the University of the
Witwatersrand, Johannesburg*

CLARENDON PRESS · OXFORD
1965

Oxford University Press, Amen House, London E.C.4

GLASGOW NEW YORK TORONTO MELBOURNE WELLINGTON
BOMBAY CALCUTTA MADRAS KARACHI LAHORE DACCA
CAPE TOWN SALISBURY NAIROBI IBADAN ACCRA
KUALA LUMPUR HONG KONG

PRINTED IN GREAT BRITAIN BY
BLACKIE AND SON LTD., BISHOPBRIGGS, GLASGOW

To
BASIL LE MAY

PREFACE

I must record my gratitude to the Council of the University of the Witwatersrand, which allowed me a sabbatical year in 1960, and to the Nuffield Foundation which, by the award of a Nuffield Dominion Travelling Fellowship, made it possible for me to spend that year in the United Kingdom.

Many friends and colleagues have helped me with advice and criticism. In particular, I should like to thank Professor Asa Briggs, Dr. J. E. Butler, Sir Keith Hancock, Mr. David Fieldhouse, Professor Stanley Jackson, Mr. F. W. Deakin, Mrs. Phyllis Lewsen, Professor Julius Lewin, Mr. R. B. McCallum, Professor Kenneth Robinson, Professor Michael Roberts, Professor L. H. Samuels and Mr. A. W. Stadler. I hope that their criticisms have been heeded; but the responsibility for the views which I have expressed is my own. In particular, I should like to thank Penelope, my wife, but for whose discipline this book would never have been finished.

To Professor J. S. Marais, who read every word of the manuscript, I have a special debt of gratitude.

I should like, further, to express my gratitude to the Warden and Fellows of New College, Sir Winston Churchill and the Chartwell Literary Trust, the Marquess of Salisbury, and the Librarians of the University of Birmingham, the London School of Economics and Political Science, Christ Church, the Colonial Office and the War Office.

My thanks are due to Mrs. Audrey Lawrie, who made the index.

CONTENTS

CHAPTER ONE

SIR ALFRED MILNER'S WAR

> I should much prefer to leave [South Africa] and to
> rest any claim to credit in connexion with it on the fact
> that I precipitated a crisis which was inevitable before
> it was altogether too late.
>
> *Milner to Lord Roberts, June 1900*

In 1877 Britain annexed the Transvaal. In 1881, after the victory of
the Boers at the battle of Majuba, Britain withdrew from the
Transvaal and accorded to its inhabitants 'complete self-government,
subject to the suzerainty of Her Majesty, her heirs and successors'.[1]
Suzerainty was a vague word. As it was interpreted by its author
Lord Kimberley, the British Colonial Secretary of the time, it drew
attention to certain limitations upon the independence of the
Transvaal state which were enumerated in the Convention of
Pretoria of August 1881.[2] The most important of these were the
British control of the Transvaal's foreign policy and the right of the
Crown to impose a veto upon legislation affecting Natives. In 1884
the Convention of Pretoria was replaced by the Convention of
London, which made no mention of suzerainty, removed the veto on
native legislation, and contained only one explicit prohibition:
'The South African Republic will conclude no treaty or engagement
with any State or nation other than the Orange Free State, nor with
any native tribe to the eastward or westward of the Republic until
the same has been approved by Her Majesty the Queen'.[3]

In 1886 the discovery of gold attracted to the Witwatersrand a
diverse and expanding population; a census of 1896 showed that

---

[1] Preamble to the Convention of Pretoria.

[2] Cf. Kimberley's statement in the House of Lords on 17 October 1899 (4th
Parl. Deb., lxxvii, 13): 'The only interpretation I ever attached to it was that it
was thought by us—I think wrongly—to be a convenient mode of expressing
generally that certain stipulations existed in the Convention which limited the
sovereignty of the Transvaal State, and that to the extent of those limitations
contained in this particular provision of the Convention of 1881 there was what
constituted what might be called generally a suzerainty.'

[3] Convention of London, Article IV.

there were 50,907 Whites living in and around Johannesburg, of whom only 6,205 were Transvaalers and the rest aliens.[1] The Uitlanders (as the aliens came to be called) brought with them customs and aspirations that were far removed from the traditional Boer way of life as it had hitherto been practised in President Kruger's republic. The Transvaal Government found itself suddenly charged with novel problems of administration arising from the rapid growth of an industrial community. Johannesburg swiftly acquired some of the less attractive features of a frontier boom town. Many of the Uitlanders regarded themselves not as sojourners in a foreign land but as the potential owners of a country that was being transformed by their money and their energies; they looked on the Transvaal burghers as uncouth, uneducated, and obstructive and on the Transvaal Government as grasping, exclusive, and oppressive. The quotation that follows was published after the war had begun, but expressed sentiments held by an important part of the mining community of the Witwatersrand in the 1890s. Writing of 'Kruger's exhortations', one of the magnates complained that these were

both innumerable and intolerable, comprising exorbitant taxation, Government grants to private monopolies, corrupt administration and legislation, the denial of personal rights . . . and the denial of representation upon reasonable conditions of franchise, for interests representing more than two-thirds of the population, more than one-half the land, more than nine-tenths of the assessed property, and more than nine-tenths the taxes paid in the Transvaal.[2]

With equal exaggeration, some fundamentalist Boers were of the opinion that Johannesburg was a City of the Plain.

President Kruger's dominating purpose was to retain the qualified independence that his country had regained in 1881 and to enlarge this, through persevering pressure, into full sovereignty. He had, in addition, certain territorial ambitions, notably to obtain for the landlocked Transvaal an outlet to the sea[3]. He represented an obstacle in the path of British imperial advancement. Joseph Chamberlain, who had become Colonial Secretary in 1895, was determined immediately to assert the paramountcy of British

[1] J. S. Marais, *The Fall of Kruger's Republic* (1961), 1. I am deeply indebted to this luminous work. (Cited hereafter as Marais.)

[2] John Hays Hammond, *The Transvaal Trouble* (1900), 13.

[3] N. G. Garson, 'The Swaziland Question and a Road to the Sea, 1887–1895' n *The Archives Year Book for South African History*, 1957, vol. II.

interests throughout South Africa; beyond this, he looked towards a South African federation as a step in the process of imperial consolidation. Cecil Rhodes's vision of empire was, perhaps, somewhat cruder; but he too regarded the Transvaal state as something to be cleared from the route that he saw stretching to the north. Kruger, well aware of the weakness of his position, did his best to play off rival groups of capitalists against one another, so that the Transvaal should not become economically dependent upon any single combination. He encouraged the Netherlands Railway Company to build a line to the Portuguese port of Lourenço Marques which would give the Transvaal access to a harbour that was not owned by Britain. A 'railway war' of rates and tariffs followed. In 1895 the Cape railways attempted to move goods by ox-wagon from the southern frontier of the Transvaal to the Witwatersrand, to evade the heavy rates charged within the Republic; Kruger countered by closing the drifts across the Vaal River. Threatened with a British ultimatum, Kruger gave way; and the impression was formed in London that the Transvaal was more susceptible to menace than to persuasion.

At the end of 1895 there occurred the Jameson Raid. The details of this escapade were bizarre and often vulgar; the ultimate consequences were tragic. The Raid itself and the protracted and furtive proceedings of the Committee of Inquiry in London, which hushed-up evidence that pointed to the complicity of the Colonial Secretary, left in the minds of Afrikaners throughout South Africa the conviction that the British Government had criminal designs upon the life of the South African Republic. The Transvaal began to arm upon a formidable scale. A telegram of congratulation from the German Emperor to Kruger, referring to the possible 'help of friendly powers' magnified the Raid into an international incident. Within South Africa old enmities between British and Afrikaners became sharper and harder to reconcile. As pressure upon Kruger from the British Government was intensified, so sympathy for the Transvaal grew in the Orange Free State and among Afrikaners in the Cape Colony, and sympathy reinforced the aspirations of Afrikaner nationalism. In turn, Afrikaner nationalism stimulated British chauvinism, each movement drawing strength and heat from its rival. In 1896 *Ons Land*, the organ of the Afrikaner Bond, the political party to which most of the Cape Afrikaners adhered, wrote: 'Afrikanerdom has awakened to a sense of earnestness and consciousness which we have not observed since the heroic war for Liberty in 1881. . . . The partition wall has disappeared . . . a new glow illuminates our hearts; let us now lay the foundation stone of a real United South Africa on the soil of a pure and all-comprehending national sentiment.'[1]

Apart from the long-settled inhabitants of the Western Province, there was little but the accident of British citizenship to distinguish the Cape Afrikaners from the burghers of the Transvaal and the Orange Free State. They spoke the same language, professed the same religion, were linked by the ramifying bonds of marriage and inter-marriage. They had no emotional ties with England; they were often repelled by the 'loyalist' British of Cape Town and Durban, with their exaggerated patriotism of the expatriate, their condescension, and their ignorance of the Dutch language and of Afrikaner ways of thought. The colonial Afrikaners regarded with pride the achievements of the northern republics, and this sentiment was fortified by the dislike of a rural people for the city-dweller and the 'capitalist'. Olive Schreiner who, like her brother the Prime Minister of the Cape, would probably have described herself as South African first and English after that, could write: 'Ultimately we have nothing left to fight the capitalists with but the guns and forts of the Transvaal'.[2] But Olive Schreiner was in a small minority among those of English descent or association within South Africa. For the imperial statesman, from the Jameson Raid onwards, the problem of the 'loyalists' was added to the problem of the Afrikaners: it was argued that if Britain did nothing to protect her subjects in the Transvaal she would risk a diminution of loyalty there and elsewhere. In 1904 Frederick Graham, then an assistant-secretary in the Colonial Office, recalled that 'before the war we used to think with dread of the Transvaal becoming a British Republic.'[3] In 1896 Roger Casement, the British consul in Lourenço Marques, reported on the temper of the Uitlanders in a letter that was read by Lord Salisbury:

What in my opinion an English Minister has to fear in the Transvaal more than anything else is an alienation of the sympathies of the English-speaking people there. The future of the Transvaal, whether England or whether Kruger likes it or not, lies with these people: the Government of

[1] Quoted in *A Century of Wrong* (English ed., 1900), 49–50.
[2] Quoted by E. A. Walker, 'Lord Milner and South Africa', in *Proceedings of the British Academy*, 1942.
[3] C.O. 291/70, minute of 7 June 1904.

the country must some day fall into their hands—and the question is whether they will preserve an entirely friendly feeling towards England— or whether they will by that time have imbibed sufficient Afrikanerism with a sprinkling of various other isms to render them quite as obnoxious to a United South African politician as any Boer in Boerdom.

At present most Englishmen in the Transvaal strike me as being loyal: but there is certainly a widespread feeling of regret at what they call the 'climb-down' since the beginning of the year. They don't reason—they only feel—and their feeling was expressed by one the other day whose summing up of the situation was that England had allowed a miserable little country like the Transvaal to put its fists in her face: 'and if a man did it to me—by Jingo!'[1]

A few weeks later Casement wrote that there was a cooling of patriotism among the Transvaal British, 'not because they love Boer misrule but because they have lost faith in England's earnestness to maintain her supremacy in South Africa'.[2]

The 'jingo spirit' found an outlet in 1896 with the formation of the South African League. As it established itself in the Transvaal, this was in part a patriotic association and in part a political pressure group which looked to Britain rather than to the Republican Government for the redress of grievances.[3] In such an atmosphere any difference of opinion between the Imperial Government and the South African Republic might suddenly become complicated by a supercharged emotion generated in Johannesburg. In 1896 the Volksraad passed a bill by which an alien who was considered to be 'a danger to the public peace and order' might be summarily expelled from the Republic. Chamberlain protested, on the ground that the bill was a breach of the Convention of London. An immigration law, passed in the same session, gave the Republic power to check the inflow of 'undesirable foreigners' within its borders and to secure the registration of those who had already been admitted. In January 1897 Chief Justice Kotzé delivered a judgement in the case of *Brown v. Leyds* in which he claimed to exercise a testing right over the legislation of the Volksraad. Kotzé was grounding himself upon considerations of policy rather than strict legality; he had decided before the Raid, he wrote later, that something should be done to curb hasty legislation in the interests of political minorities.[4] The Transvaal Government reacted to the judgement in *Brown's* case by declaring that no judge who affirmed the testing right would be

---

[1] Salisbury PP., bound volume 'Private, miscellaneous, A–C', f. 194.
[2] Ibid., f. 192.   [3] Marais, 161 seqq.   [4] Ibid., 142.

suffered to remain on the bench; Kruger later expressed his personal opinion that the testing right had been invented by the Devil in the Garden of Eden.[1] The quarrel between Kruger and his judges became a political issue of the greatest seriousness, in which Kotzé was indiscriminately supported by the South African League inside and outside the Transvaal. The intervention of Sir Henry de Villiers, Chief Justice of the Cape, produced a truce between the executive and the courts; but the affair demonstrated once again how easily an incident within the Transvaal could grow, or be magnified, into a South African crisis.

In April 1897 two British dispatches were delivered to the South African Republic, one rehearsing alleged breaches of the Convention of London, the other demanding the immediate repeal of the immigration law. To add force to remonstrance and demand Chamberlain persuaded the Cabinet to increase the British garrison in South Africa to a total of 8,000 men and twenty-four field guns. He did not believe that they would have to fight. 'If they see that we are in earnest', he wrote to Lord Salisbury, 'I believe they will give way, as they have always done.'[2] In that instance he was right: in May the Volksraad repealed the immigration law and in July it indicated that it was having second thoughts about the expulsion law.

While these events were in train the South African Republic and the Orange Free State had concluded a new treaty of alliance to replace that signed eight years earlier. In the revised treaty the clause that bound the two republics to assist each the other 'when the independence of one of the two States may be threatened or attacked, unless the State which should render the assistance can show the injustice of the cause of the other State' was reaffirmed and a new clause provided for consultation between the two governments. This was inserted at the wish of President Steyn of the Orange Free State, who wished to have means of influencing his stubborn ally. In itself the new treaty could hardly be regarded as a threat to British security, but the timing of its negotiation and the insertion of a provision that proclaimed the ideal of a federal union of the two republics, might be interpreted as a pointer towards extravagant Afrikaner pretensions.[3] Chamberlain referred in a public speech to the aspirations of 'eminent persons in South Africa' who looked towards a federation in which Afrikaner interests would

[1] Ibid., 9.   [2] Garvin, iii. 141; Marais, 157.   [3] Marais, 147.

predominate, and issued a general warning that any activity in that direction would be regarded as 'incompatible with the highest British interests . . .'[1]

Chamberlain's words were, by his own standards of rhetoric, cautious and qualified. He had, however, touched upon a fear that was growing among British South Africans (and was certainly fostered by the South African League), that of the 'Pan-Afrikaner conspiracy'. What this conspiracy was thought to be may be seen in a letter from Casement, dated from the Rand Club in Johannesburg on 3 February 1897, which was shown to Salisbury, Arthur Balfour and Chamberlain: 'there seems such a large body of the public in England who will persist in regarding the Boer patriot as a simple peasant only desirous of governing himself and being left alone. He's nothing of the kind. He is scheming, plotting and planning night and day, back door and front door, how to become the undisputed master of South Africa as a whole.'[2]

No firm evidence, then or later, was produced to justify this interpretation of Transvaal policy. The Transvaal was arming fast, but this was regarded in the Colonial Office as a defensive measure, and Chamberlain feared no more than a possible denunciation of the Convention of London, and then only if Britain were engaged in a European war.[3] But, as a polarization took place of British and Afrikaners, the deadly situation was approaching in South Africa in which each side increasingly feared the other. The British had previously looked to Rhodes as their champion, but since the Raid Rhodes had lost the ear of the Colonial Office. In 1897 Chamberlain presented them with a more favoured champion, with the whole backing of the British Government, when he appointed Sir Alfred Milner as High Commissioner and Governor of the Cape.

II

Milner had enjoyed a career of astonishing academic brilliance as an undergraduate at Oxford. Thereafter he had worked for a time under W. T. Stead on the *Pall Mall Gazette*, had been private secretary to Goschen, had served in Egypt as under-secretary of finance, and had for the past five years been chairman of the Board of Inland Revenue in London. His imperial philosophy was forged

[1] Marais, 159.   [2] Salisbury PP., loc. cit., f. 192.   [3] Marais, 210.

in Egypt and tempered in South Africa. He was capable of expressing sentiments that may be described as indicating an embarrassed mysticism, but for the most part he was in the habit of stating his imperial creed in prosaic terms.[1] In 1913, when he believed that his days as a servant of the State were over, he wrote of himself: 'my public activities have been wholly dominated by a single desire —that of working for the integrity and consolidation of the British Empire'.[2] Integrity and consolidation were desirable not merely to ensure Britain's prosperous survival in a world in which the great powers were becoming greater and the small powers smaller, but to enable Britain to fulfil a duty to the human race by exercising an influence for civilization. He tended to equate civilization with good governance, and he regarded it as an axiom that the British were the best fitted for governance of all peoples on this planet.

There was nothing particularly sophisticated or profound in this doctrine, but there was much that those not endowed by birth with effortless superiority might reasonably find distasteful. Milner took with him from Oxford an accumulation of prizes but no large stock of general ideas; later, as his mind clamped down upon the cares of the moment, he ceased to read or even to speculate widely. It was not perhaps, surprising that those of more intricately articulated minds, as they speculated upon the British proconsuls of the silver age of imperialism, should invest these prefects of perfidious Albion with a subtlety and a grasp of the submerged implications of economic theory that Milner (for all his remarkable abilities as a financial administrator) did not possess. J. A. Hobson's theory of imperialism, upon which Lenin was to build, bore only the most distant relationship to what Milner had in mind when he worked for the expansion and consolidation of the territorial possessions of what he called 'the British race'. To Milner, civilization in the backward parts of the earth, such as Egypt and the Transvaal, came with irrigation works, railways, schools, agricultural improvement, veterinary science, police, roads and telegraphs—in short, with regulated order. On this level, the imperial mission was akin to advanced estate management of a paternalistic nature; it was the plain duty of an advanced people to elevate those lower on the rungs of civilization.

[1] Cf. 'My patriotism knows no geographical but only racial limits. I am an Imperialist and not a Little Englander, because I am a British Race Patriot . . .' From 'Credo. Key to my position', found among Milner's papers after his death. *The Times*, 27 July 1925.
[2] Milner, *The Nation and the Empire* (1913), preface.

He wrote in 1897 (in a passage heavy with the influence of the Oxford Greats School):

The qualities which we may have contributed to the Egyptian Administration are not novel or extraordinary qualities. They are the commonplaces of civilization. But it needs only a little experience of the East to realize how vast an improvement may be effected in the condition of a country by the introduction of nothing more than the ordinary methods and principles of civilized government. We have it on the authority of the classical poets, that it is as far from Tartarus to this commonplace Earth as it is from the Earth to the abodes of the Gods. It is the road from Tartarus to Earth along which Egypt has been travelling, and it is no small achievement to have covered the distance in a few years.

As this has been the nature of our influence, it is evident that it could never be out of place . . .[1]

To prefer bad government of one's own to good government handed down from a superior height was, to Milner, evidence of immaturity at best, moral obliquity at worst. Of Nubar Pasha's attempts to rid himself of the tutelary hand of Sir Evelyn Baring, Milner wrote that Nubar could 'not be excused for his failure to recognize that, since English help was necessary for the salvation of Egypt, he was bound to show a large receptiveness for English ideas'.[2] Later, Milner applied the same reasoning to the Boers.

Thus far, it may seem, Milner was speaking the familiar language of the white man with his burden, of God's Englishman performing a thankless duty towards the lesser breeds. But why did this require imperial consolidation? Because Britain was approaching a condition, relative to rival powers, when she could no longer continue her self-imposed task unaided but needed the help of the self-governing colonies of the Empire. They, in turn, needed to merge their strength with Britain's if they were not to find themselves weak, ignored and, it might be, imperilled in a world dominated by the politics of power. This condition was becoming urgent just when the Empire, which already stood in a precarious equipoise of parts, was being influenced by centrifugal forces making for greater independence—or, as Milner regarded it—greater wilfulness at its extremities. These forces were especially strong in South Africa, where Kruger's republic was becoming a rival of the Crown for the sentiments and, it might be, the loyalty of Afrikaners within the British colonies. This duality Milner was determined to remove when

[1] Milner, *England in Egypt* (1897), 290–1. [2] Ibid., 116.

he took up his position as, in his own words, 'a civilian soldier of the empire'.[1] At forty-three he was a middle-aged man in a hurry.

Milner, with all his gifts, lacked one quality indispensable to those who would conquer or govern greatly—the ability to appraise opposition, to understand the resistance that may be evoked from the weaker by the pretensions of the stronger, to guess correctly what was happening on the other side of the hill. Once he had made up his mind he behaved as if he could command fortune by will. The light of his intelligence shone out as from a fixed mounting, illuminating with wonderful clarity the way ahead but leaving the rough ground at either edge in shadow. From his disciples, especially the young men whom he chose as his favoured subordinates, he could evoke the response which is sometimes called out from brilliant students by a tutor who shows them a new world, stretches their capacities and finds their work to be good. It is with this qualification that one may accept the judgement passed on him at Oxford, that he was 'eager to organize rather than to influence, and fearful to give generous impulses full rein'.[2] His arguments were directed to those of the same faith: the heretic was crushed or ignored. In his early years he called himself a Liberal in politics, but his was the liberalism of Aquinas: disputation must be confined to those matters that were indifferent to salvation. The consolidation of the British Empire was not to him a matter for argument; it was a question, he said, on which he could never see the other side of the case. He did not comprehend, if indeed he did not despise, the subtleties of political management. He neither professed nor understood the pliant arts by which supporters are reassured and opponents disarmed. He did not make allowance for the fact that his own actions might send vibrations through the intricate network of personalities, relationships, convictions, prejudices, and interests that connects a parliamentary majority. He felt himself to be enmeshed and held down in the web of the Constitution. 'Representative government', he wrote in 1904, 'has its merits—no doubt—but the influence of representative assemblies, organized upon the party system, upon administration—"government" in the true sense of the word—is almost uniformly bad'.[3] It is a misfortune, he writes in 1903, that

[1] Milner used these words in his farewell speech before leaving London for the Cape.

[2] Quoted by Basil Williams in *The Dictionary of National Biography, 1922–1930*, 589.

[3] Milner MSS. S.A.: Box 12, Milner to Sir L. Michell, 13 May 1904.

Chamberlain 'is necessarily a politician, with his eye fixed on the House of Commons and electorate, and that, therefore, while he is both strong and plucky and ready to risk a good deal for what he knows to be right, he will not risk everything. I always do, so we may fall out yet'.[1] Milner would perhaps have been more successful had he ever sat in the House of Commons, had he won the seat he contested at Harrow in 1885. As it was, he thought that every session of the Imperial Parliament damaged some imperial interest.[2]

In his first diagnosis of the South African situation after his arrival in the country Milner saw a vast complication of his task of upholding British paramountcy in the relationship between Whites and non-Whites, in which there was only a difference of degree between the attitudes of most British and Afrikaners. 'I feel that, if I fail out here, it will be over the Native question', he wrote to Asquith in November 1897, in a long letter in which he examined the 'two great principles' which, he agreed, should guide his work: '(1) we should seek to "restore the good relations between the Dutch [sc. Afrikaners] and English" and (2) we should "secure for the Natives . . . adequate and sufficient protection against oppression and wrong".'[3] Milner continued:

What I am so anxious that you and other English statesmen—especially Liberal statesmen—should understand, is that object No. 2 is the principal obstacle to the attainment of object No. 1—is, and always has been. In spite of Majuba, in spite of Jameson, I remain firmly of the opinion that, if it were not for my having some conscience about the treatment of the blacks, I *personally* could win over the Dutch in the [Cape] Colony and indeed in all of the South African dominions in my term of office, and that I could do so without offending the English. You have only to sacrifice 'the nigger' absolutely and the game is easy . . .

But, he went on, to insist upon better treatment for the non-White peoples in the British colonies or in the Chartered Company's territory in Rhodesia, would be to bind together all fragments of White opinion against the British Government.

You have, therefore, this singular situation, that you might indeed unite Dutch and English by protecting the black man, but you would unite them against yourself, and your policy of protection.

There is the whole *crux* of the South African position. You say and say truly that self-government is the basis of our colonial policy and the keystone of colonial loyalty. That principle, fearlessly and unflinchingly

1 Ibid., xlvi. Milner to Dawkins, 31 January 1903.
2 Ibid., xli, f. 153.   3 Headlam, i. 177.

applied, would make South Africa as loyal as Canada—but what would b the price? The abandonment of the black races, to whom you have promised protection, and the tolerance of a state of things in a self-governed state under the British flag, which we should never tolerate for a moment in India, in Egypt, or in any of the Crown Colonies.[1]

Milner believed at that time that the 'Transvaal question' would answer itself, 'because the Transvaal oligarchy is bound sooner or later to topple over'. Within a few weeks he had changed his mind.

Milner had placed particular hopes upon the growth of an internal opposition to Kruger among discontented burghers. The year 1897 had been one of depression. Kruger had found himself in unusual difficulties with the Volksraad, and Milner hoped that Schalk Burger, who had been chairman of the industrial commission that had inquired into the grievances of the mining industry, would prove a formidable rival in the presidential election of 1898. A serious division within the Boer oligarchy might mean that both parties would find it to their advantage to woo the Uitlanders. Milner placed, too, some reliance upon Chief Justice Kotzé as a source of embarrassment to Kruger: the truce that de Villiers had negotiated was expiring without sign of the legislation Kruger had promised. All these hopes came to nothing. When the result of the presidential election was announced on 10 February it was found that Kruger had polled 12,858 votes, against 3,750 for Burger and 2,001 for Commandant-General P. J. Joubert. Kotzé, who had announced five days earlier his intention once again to exercise the testing right, was dismissed. Kotzé had indeed acted rashly; the expected public support for him did not show itself, and Chamberlain made it clear that the Colonial Office would not take up his case.

Milner's hope that the 'Transvaal question' would answer itself vanished for ever. On 23 February he wrote flatly to Chamberlain: 'There is no way out of the political troubles of S. Africa except reform in the Transvaal or war'. He no longer believed in the possibility of spontaneous reform. He had come to regard Kruger as incorrigible: the old man had returned to power 'more autocratic and more reactionary then ever'. But Milner did not think that Kruger would take the initiative. 'Of one thing I am quite certain. Kruger will never take any step which he thinks will provoke us to fight. But if he is assured that our hands are full in other directions

[1] Asquith PP. Dep. 9. Headlam omitted the greater part of the passages which I have quoted.

he will certainly seize the opportunity to assert his independence in a very pointed way'. However, Milner argued, the situation had become intolerable because the surface of South African politics was continually being agitated by vibrations that had their source in the Transvaal. He thought that it was no longer profitable to protest against isolated grievances or particular breaches of the Convention; the situation should be dealt with as a whole, and the Transvaal brought to a reckoning once and for all. *'Looking at the question from a purely S. African point of view*, I should be inclined to work up to a crisis, not indeed by looking about for causes of complaint or making a fuss about trifles, but by steadily and inflexibly pressing for the redress of substantial wrongs and injustices. It would not be difficult thus to work up an extremely strong *cumulative case'*.[1] The intention was clear: the High Commissioner was asking permission to bring matters to a point at which Kruger must either capitulate or go to war. Milner had exposed his thoughts with even greater candour in a letter to Conyngham Greene, the British agent in the Transvaal, on the day after Kruger's re-election when he referred to the 'farce' of repeated protests to the government of the South African Republic and added that he continued to go through the motions of diplomacy as seriously as he could, 'not with any immediate hope of results—but with a view to the great day of reckoning . . .'[2]

Milner was exhibiting a temper too hasty and too belligerent for the British Government's purpose. On 19 March Chamberlain telegraphed to him: 'The principal object of H.M. Government in S. Africa at present is peace. Nothing but a most flagrant offence would justify the use of force'.[3] Three days earlier, replying to Milner's letter of 23 February, he had restated the conditions that governed British policy towards the Transvaal—to avoid if possible 'all causes of offence', to maintain Britain's rights under the Convention if they were seriously challenged, but otherwise to eschew public pressure on lesser grievances. Nothing essential had changed since Milner's appointment, he pointed out, to justify a new departure. Then, as before, the guiding considerations of British policy were:

(1st) The conviction that a war with the Transvaal would certainly rouse antagonism in the Cape Colony, and leave behind it the most serious

---

[1] Headlam, i. 221, 222.   [2] Ibid. 215.   [3] Ibid., 226.

difficulties in the way of South African union. We felt that if a struggle was to come, it was most important that the Transvaal should be the aggressor, and that the Imperial Government should have the active sympathy of at all events a considerable section of the Dutch in the Colony. (2nd) We felt that the Raid has placed this country in a false position and has alienated the confidence of the Afrikaner Party, and that it would be desirable that the irritation caused by this event should pass away before we resumed any pressure upon the Transvaal in regard to its internal policy. (3rd) We were of opinion that the waiting game was the best for this country as time must be on our side. The misgovernment in the Transvaal will in the long run produce opposition within its borders, and when the present rule of President Kruger comes to an end, as it must do before many years are over, we might confidently look for an improvement in the position. (4th) A war with the Transvaal, unless upon the utmost and clearest provocation, would be extremely unpopular in this country. It would involve the dispatch of a very large force and the expenditure of many millions.[1]

If further reasons for restraint were wanting, they could be found in the delicacy of Britain's relations at that time with Russia, Germany and France, and in the commitment of troops to the reconquest of the Sudan.

Milner had perforce to possess himself in patience, although it had become clear that differences, less in purpose than in timing and method, had begun to show themselves between his inclinations and the policy of the Colonial Office. Unlike Chamberlain and unlike Lord Selborne, the Under-Secretary of State for the Colonies, Milner had ceased to believe that time was on Britain's side. Furthermore, he had begun to interpret the 'Transvaal question' as the product of a juxtaposition of irreconcilable alternatives. 'Two wholly antagonistic systems—a medieval race oligarchy, and a modern industrial state, recognizing no difference of status between various white races—cannot permanently live side by side in what is after all *one country*. The race oligarchy has got to go, and I see no signs of its removing itself'.[2]

Before Milner had received orders to restrain himself he had delivered a speech at Graaff-Reinet on 3 March in which he had rebuked the Afrikaner Bond and referred openly, albeit obliquely, to the possibility of war in South Africa. The local branch of the Bond had presented him with an address in which complaint was made that the propaganda of the South African League implied that

---

[1] Ibid. 227.   [2] Ibid. 234–5. Milner to Selborne, 9 May 1898.

the Bond was disloyal. In his reply Milner said: 'Well, gentlemen, of course you are loyal. It would be monstrous if you were not'.[1] The way to prevent war, he went on, was not for the Bond to warn the British Government of the sympathy its members felt for President Kruger, because Britain had no 'occult design' upon the independence of the Transvaal, but rather to impress upon Kruger the necessity of reform in his Republic and the need to 'assimilate its institutions and . . . the temper and spirit of its administration to those of the free communities of South Africa, such as this colony or the Orange Free State'.

That, for the time being, was as far as Milner could go. For the remainder of 1898 he brooded over the iniquities of the South African Republic and regarded with misgiving the change of government in the Cape Colony, with the fall of Sprigg's ministry and its replacement by a composite administration under W. P. Schreiner (who was nominally an independent), which owed its majority to the support of the Bond. At the beginning of November Milner left Cape Town on leave for England, determined there, if he could, 'to stamp on rose-coloured illusions about S. Africa . . .'.[2]

He found policy in the Colonial Office unchanged and Chamberlain still determined to keep the peace unless Kruger proved 'very outrageous'.[3] Milner had no success in pleading for an accelerated tempo; but as he wrote to Selborne during his voyage back to South Africa: 'If I can advance matters by my own actions, as I still hope I may be able to do, I believe I shall have support when the time comes'.[4] He could comfort himself with the improvement in Britain's international position during the second half of 1898. In September General Sir Herbert Kitchener had beaten the Khalifa at Omdurman; In November the French had decided to withdraw from Fashoda; and, most important of all from Milner's viewpoint, Germany had renounced interest in the Transvaal. The Anglo-German agreement of August, which was principally concerned with a possible division of the Portuguese colonies, contained the implied assurance that Germany would not intervene if Britain acted against the South African Republic. On 23 November Milner wrote from London to G. V. Fiddes, the Imperial Secretary at the Cape, that he was certain that the agreement 'does formally and for ever eliminate Germany as a *political* influence in the Transvaal and the countries

[1] Ibid. 244; Marais, 207.   [2] Headlam, i. 299.   [3] Garvin, iii. 380.
[4] Headlam, i. 302.

immediately surrounding it. Therefore, while its immediate effect is
nil, its importance in view of future contingencies is great'.[1]

III

During Milner's absence in England, the South African League
had provoked or aggravated a new crisis in the Transvaal. In
October 1898 the Republican police, during a series of raids in
search of non-Whites who had offended against the pass laws, acted
with harshness against certain Cape Coloured men. The League at
once took up the matter, although its attitude, considering the
racial prejudices of most of its members, contained more than a
tinge of hypocrisy. The next incident was more serious. On 18
December an Uitlander named Edgar was involved in a drunken
street-brawl in which a second Uitlander was struck down and left
for dead. Edgar retreated to his house; the police broke in; Edgar
resisted arrest and was shot dead. The League used Edgar's case as a
chance to protest vehemently against 'the intolerable state of affairs'
existing in the Transvaal, and attempted to appeal to the Queen by
petition. This move was blocked by the acting High Commissioner,
General Sir William Butler, who had little sympathy for the League.

To Milner's intense chagrin, he refused to accept the Uitlanders'
petition and he gave his opinion of their conduct in a series of emphatic
reports to Joseph Chamberlain. The government of the Cape Colony also
put the blame upon the Uitlanders and their backers. All this made it very
difficult to use the Edgar case for working up to a crisis.

Nevertheless, this trivial and vulgar episode has real historical importance. It was the first 'appeal to Caesar'. Sir William Butler stopped it
from getting through; but Milner would see to it that the next one got
through. Henceforth, he and Conyngham Greene maintained the closest
possible relations with the South African League and used it as an instrument of Imperial policy.[2]

The activities of the League were now intersected by negotiations
which seemed to indicate that the Republican Government was
attempting to come to terms with the Uitlanders. In December 1898
it became evident that the Volksraad was likely to renew the
dynamite monopoly for another twelve years. This monopoly was
one of the chief grievances of the mining industry, since it increased
the price of the explosives used in excavations. In January 1899,

[1] Ibid., 299.
[2] W. K. Hancock, *Smuts: The Sanguine Years, 1870–1919* (1962), 83.

pressed by Milner, Chamberlain agreed to take up the matter as an infringement of the Convention.

This decision had momentous consequences. Chamberlain entered into an understanding with the mining magnates. Henceforth their leading spirits acted in close concert with him and his representatives in South Africa. Milner and Greene were thus able to reconstitute the reform movement of pre-raid days on the Rand with some of the magnates taking a share in public. Chamberlain had, in fact, stepped out along the road that led to vigorous intervention within the Republic.[1]

Kruger was determined to keep the dynamite monopoly, which he regarded as one of the safeguards of independence, but it was clear to him that the time was coming when he would have either to make some concessions or expose himself to the likelihood of British intervention. In February and March 1899 discussions took place between representatives of the mining industry and officials of the Republic. These 'capitalists' negotiations' ended with a statement of terms and counter-terms, offered but not accepted, from which it appeared that Kruger would be prepared in certain circumstances to allow Uitlanders to acquire the franchise after less than the existing term of fourteen years' residence.

The franchise question, once raised, remained at the centre of disputation during the remaining months of peace. On 24 March the organizers of the South African League handed to Greene a second petition to the Queen, containing 21,000 signatures, which set out the grievances which, in their opinion, made their condition 'well-nigh intolerable' and appealed for British intervention. This petition, which Milner received and sent forward to the Colonial Office, placed Chamberlain in a dilemma: to refuse it would be to offend the 'loyalists', to accept it would be to provoke the crisis which he still wished to avoid. In a memorandum to the Cabinet of 28 April Chamberlain wrote: 'If we ignore altogether the prayer of the petitioners it is certain that British influence in South Africa will be severely shaken. If we send an ultimatum to Kruger, it is possible, and in my opinion probable, that we shall get an offensive reply, and we shall then have to go to war, or to accept a humiliating check . . .'[2]

Meanwhile Milner was sending to London a series of dispatches progressively stiffer in language. Their refrain was that the time had come for resolute action and that the best method of bettering the

---

[1] Marais, 244–5.   [2] Garvin, iii. 393.

lot of the Uitlanders was to insist on their enfranchisement and thus to endow them with a share of political power. The most flamboyant of these compositions was sent on 4 May and was known later as the 'helot dispatch'. Its critical words were: 'The case for intervention is overwhelming'.[1] Milner continued: 'The spectacle of thousands of British subjects kept permanently in the position of helots, constantly chafing under undoubted grievances, and calling vainly to Her Majesty's Government for redress, does steadily undermine the influence and reputation of Great Britain and the respect for the British Government within its own dominions'.

He went on to speak of the effect of newspaper propaganda for an Afrikaner republic of South Africa in producing disaffection in the British colonies.[2] 'I can see nothing which will put a stop to this mischievous propaganda but some striking proof of the intention, if it is the intention, of Her Majesty's Government not to be ousted from its position in South Africa. And the best proof alike of its power and its justice would be to obtain for the Uitlanders in the Transvaal a fair share in the Government of the country which owes everything to their exertions . . .'

This was advocacy rather than analysis. Milner's purpose in these dispatches was to convince Chamberlain, to strengthen Chamberlain's hand in the Cabinet, and to arouse the British public. In the first two of these he was successful: on 9 May Chamberlain persuaded the Cabinet that the Uitlanders should be supported, and obtained approval for a dispatch which, he assured Milner, would be 'very strong' although it would not be in the form of an ultimatum.[3] Chamberlain had allowed Milner to do two things—to switch the issue from the redress of particular grievances to the extension of the franchise, which lay altogether outside the terms of the Convention, and to present the case against the Transvaal in such a way that, if Kruger did not concede what was demanded of him, British prestige would be publicly diminished.

For the moment all these dispatches remained in the files of the Colonial Office. It was decided, in consequence of pressure and advances from various quarters, that Milner and Kruger should hold a personal meeting. The Cape Ministry, the Government of the Orange Free State, and members of the Afrikaner Bond in the Cape had all, in different ways and with different motives, been urging Kruger to make some concessions and to undertake some reform in

[1] Headlam, i. 349 seqq.   [2] Ibid. 353   [3] Marais, 270.

the Transvaal. To all these, the thought of war in South Africa was abhorrent; on a lower level, none wished to see imperial intervention in the Transvaal for fear of the effects which this would have on themselves. It had been Chamberlain's original intention that Milner should go to Pretoria; instead, through the mediation of President Steyn, it was arranged that the meeting should be held in Bloemfontein. Kruger accepted Steyn's invitation with no outward show of enthusiasm: he was 'disposed to come', he said, and would discuss any proposals conducive to better relations between Britain and the South African Republic, 'provided that the independence of this Republic is not impugned'.[1] Milner was even less enthusiastic: the conference, he wrote to Selborne on 17 May, 'really *is* a good stroke of business on part of enemy, as it holds up dispatch and spoils, or at least delays, a great stroke on our part.'[2] He was afraid of a 'plausible offer of reform', which would be difficult for him to reject but would postpone the 'day of reckoning'. He insisted that a full account of the proceedings of the conference should subsequently be published; this meant that both he and Kruger would, as it were, be talking over each other's shoulders to their respective publics. He refused to allow Schreiner to be present at Bloemfontein in any official capacity, in spite of Chamberlain's argument that Schreiner's attendance, even on the sidelines, would predispose him towards the British point of view.[3]

Chamberlain and Milner were now in basic agreement upon purpose, although their motives and the use to which they wished to put the expected failure of the conference, differed in certain respects. Milner wished to bring matters to a final crisis, because he was convinced that war was an evil less to be feared than a continuation of the 'nightmare' of continued procrastination.[4] Chamberlain had allowed Milner to advance matters by his own actions, as Milner had intended to do when he returned from England at the beginning of the year;[5] but Chamberlain was willing to bring on a diplomatic crisis because he wished to use the occasion to arouse public opinion at home, demonstrate that Britain was in deadly earnest, and move if necessary to the brink of war in the expectation that Kruger would give way, even at the last moment, as he had given way before. Selborne wrote to Milner on 25 June that he and Chamberlain had moved British public opinion towards

---

[1] Headlam, i, 374.   [2] Ibid., 384.   [3] Marais, 278.
[4] Ibid., 266.   [5] See above, p. 15.

recognizing that some remedy must be found for the Transvaal situation, but not yet to the point of accepting 'either that you can't believe a word Kruger says, or that he never has yielded and never will yield till he feels the muzzle of the pistol on his forehead, or that the surest way to avoid war is to prepare openly for war'.[1]

IV

The Bloemfontein Conference began on 31 May. Milner's strategy was to demand a large and prompt creation of Uitlander voters and, if that were refused, to manœuvre so that Kruger should appear to be in the wrong in whatever he did or said. Kruger had already declared that he would concede nothing that would impair independence, but he showed himself ready to bargain. He brought forward the possible incorporation of Swaziland in the Transvaal, the unpaid indemnity for the Jameson Raid, and a proposal that disputes between Britain and the Transvaal under the Convention should be decided by arbitration within South Africa. Milner, in refusing to discuss these matters, was bound in part by his instructions, but his attitude throughout was that he would have the franchise or nothing. He asked for a voters' qualification of five years' residence, to be applied retroactively, and for the creation of seven new seats for the Witwatersrand in the Volksraad, which would give the Uitlanders nine representatives in a house of thirty-five.[2] Kruger did not reject this proposal out of hand, but wanted to know what would be conceded in return that he could show to his burghers: 'I must tell them that something has been given in to me, if I give in to something'. Milner dismissed this reasoning as an attempt to strike a 'kaffir bargain', to indulge in diplomatic horse-trading on a matter in which he regarded his own demands as wholly justified. On the third day Kruger produced a proposal of his own under which the franchise would be granted on a sliding scale of from two to seven years' residence: Uitlanders who had settled in the Transvaal before 1890 might have the vote after two years, those of two or more years' residence after five, and newcomers after seven, provided that none of them had been convicted of a crime carrying a 'dishonouring sentence' or had been guilty of acts 'against

---

[1] Headlam, i. 445.
[2] For the Bloemfontein Conference, see C.9345, C.9404, C.9415; Headlam, i. ch. 15; Marais, ch. 10.

Government or independence'. There would be five seats for the
Witwatersrand.

Milner considered that this scheme was too complicated and
would be too slow in its effects; what he wanted was the immediate
enfranchisement of a large body of Uitlanders. This was precisely
what Kruger did not wish to concede. Neither protagonist would
accept the other in good faith. Milner told James Rose Innes a few
days later that he could have come to terms with Kruger if he had
trusted him.[1] ('There was', wrote one of Milner's admirers, 'a
gnarled magnificence in the old Transvaal President, but he saw
only a snuffy, mendacious savage'.[2]) To Kruger it seemed that
Milner, with his insistence on the franchise and his scarcely veiled
threats to use force if the franchise were refused, was offering him a
choice between the slow surrender of his independence and its swift
annihilation. ('It is all one', wrote an American commentator at the
time, 'to have your Government captured by a troop of horse, or to
have your privileges taken away by alien voters'.[3]) 'It is our country
that you want', Kruger said at the end of the conference. Milner
made the conventional denial that Britain had any intention of
abrogating the independence of the Transvaal, but Milner's interpretation of 'British paramountcy' was inconsistent with more than a
limited autonomy for the government of the South African Republic.
On 5 June Milner broke off the conference, stating that nothing that
had been said there should be regarded as binding upon either side;
a telegram from Chamberlain, urging him to prolong discussion,
arrived too late.

From the breakdown at Bloemfontein onwards, Milner worked
openly for war. His relations with General Butler became increasingly strained. Butler's attitude was correct but unenthusiastic
towards the policy of the High Commissioner. (South Africa, Butler
had said when he was acting in Milner's absence, needed rest, not
surgery.) He did not want war himself, and he did not believe that
the Boers wanted war either. On 17 June, after a prolonged series
of disagreements, he wrote to Milner discounting the value of
evidence that suggested that the Boers might attack, and pointing
instead to British preparedness and provocation. 'I can find in the

[1] James Rose Innes, *Autobiography* (1949), 179.
[2] John Buchan, *Memory Hold-the-Door* (1940), 470.
[3] James Gustavus Whiteley, 'The Relation of England to the Transvaal in
International Law', *Forum*, October 1899.

balance of things', he concluded, 'no reason to suppose that the Dutch *could* be desirous of a war with us. Can they think the same about us?'[1] Milner sent a copy of this letter to Chamberlain and asked for Butler's recall. Chamberlain was not pleased. 'Milner is really rather trying. Think of our difficulties and how they would be enhanced by recalling Butler at this juncture . . .

'I shall do my best for Milner, and for the policy which is mine as well as his . . . but he is overstrained. I wish he would remember the advice to the lady whose clothes caught fire, "to keep as cool as possible".'[2]

Butler was given a strong hint that he was embarrassing the High Commissioner. When Milner confirmed this in a personal interview, Butler resigned early in August.

Milner had come to believe that war with the Transvaal was both inevitable and desirable. Chamberlain was prepared for war, but thought that it could be avoided if the Transvaal realized that Britain would fight rather than abandon the Uitlanders' cause without having obtained for them some notable advantages. Both attitudes pointed towards increased military preparations. Selborne, in a letter to Chamberlain of 23 June, said that the British Government had placed themselves in a position from which they could not retreat without humiliation, and that they were 'bound to see redress applied to the grievances of the Uitlanders, by peaceful pressure if possible, but if necessary in the last resort by war'. But the great difficulty in the way of frightening Kruger was that

public opinion does not yet realize the supreme importance of the crisis; that it does not understand that Kruger's word cannot be trusted and that he never has yielded and never will yield a point till a pistol is put at his head;[3] and that consequently the Government do not feel strong enough to apply that pressure which alone can fulfil their policy without war.

The danger follows that we are drifting towards war, that we may find ourselves there to the surprise of the country when we might have avoided it.

He referred to Chamberlain's enemies, who were already using the argument that his policy confronted Britain with a choice between national humiliation and an unpopular war, and concluded: 'The success of your policy without war is the only perfect checkmate for

[1] Chamberlain PP. J.C. 10/9.
[2] Ibid. J.C. 10/4. Chamberlain to Selborne, 26 June 1899.
[3] Cf. Selborne's words to Milner, p. 20 above.

them, and this success will only be possible if Kruger understands *now* that the Cabinet *mean business* this time once for all, however patient they may be.'[1]

Chamberlain needed no prompting. In the middle of June he had published a Blue Book devoted to 'the complaints of British subjects in the South African Republic'[2] which contained, among other documents, Milner's 'helot dispatch'—of which Chamberlain had written five weeks earlier: 'This is tremendously stiff, and if it is published it will make either an ultimatum *or* Sir A. Milner's recall necessary . . .'[3] He tried unsuccessfully to persuade Sir Henry Campbell-Bannerman, the leader of the Liberal opposition, to join him in a bipartisan statement of policy towards the Transvaal. On 26 June, in a speech in Birmingham, he said that 'having undertaken this business we will see it through'.[4] But although he was bellicose in public, he was much more cautious in private. 'I am not', he minuted on 2 August, 'prepared to put Her Majesty's Governmen in a position in which the refusal of the South African Republic to comply with their demands would place them under the necessity of going to war or retiring ignominiously'.[5]

Kruger had indeed not made his last offer. At Bloemfontein he had offered to bargain, after the manner of his people—an invitation to trade, a long haggle over the price, an insistence on a *quid pro quo* 'to show to his burghers'. Since then he had been subjected to further pressure by his wellwishers and candid friends in the Cape and the Orange Free State. Steyn, Jan Hofmeyr (the effective leader of the Bond), John X. Merriman (Colonial Treasurer in Schreiner's ministry), Fischer, Schreiner and de Villiers were among those who advised him to concede and reform. In July the Transvaal offered a seven years' franchise to be granted retroactively, and five seats for the Witwatersrand. Chamberlain's immediate opinion was that the crisis was over, and he telegraphed to Milner that the Cabinet wanted a second meeting with Kruger, this time in Cape Town, at which the details of representation could be arranged. Milner replied that experience showed that it would be useless to discuss a 'multitude of complicated details' with Kruger, and proposed instead that there should be a joint inquiry, by British and Republican commissioners, into the proposed law. This proposal was formally put to the South African Republic in a dispatch of 27

---

[1] Chamberlain PP. J.C. 10/4.   [2] C. 9345.   [3] Marais, 267.
[4] Garvin, iii. 416.   [5] Chamberlain PP. J.C. 10/4.

July. On the following day Salisbury and Chamberlain made strong statements in each House of Parliament: Salisbury spoke of the Transvaal British as reduced 'to the condition almost of a conquered, certainly of a subjugated, race', and Chamberlain said that the 'humiliating inferiority' of the British was detrimental to British predominance in South Africa.[1]

Kruger was not prepared to consent to a joint inquiry; it would be a humiliating admission of inferiority, he thought, to permit such an interference in the domestic affairs of the Republic. On 13 August J. C. Smuts, the State Attorney, made a startling offer on behalf of his government; it amounted to acceptance, and more, of the demands which Milner had made in Bloemfontein. Smuts offered a five years' retroactive franchise, with a quarter of the seats in the Volksraad for the Witwatersrand. There were, however, three essential conditions: the intervention of the British Government was not to be accepted as a precedent, the British claim to suzerainty over the Transvaal was to be dropped, and future disputes under the Convention were to be settled by arbitration within South Africa.

Chamberlain's first reactions were favourable. The Boers, he wrote to Salisbury, seemed to have climbed down; and he added that he had instructed Milner that it was important 'that the Boers should not be rudely snubbed at this stage, but rather encouraged to put their concessions on record'.[2] On 19 August the formal offer came in writing; two days later, however, the Transvaal presented an amendment, stating that the provisions for the franchise and the Witwatersrand constituencies were to be regarded as 'expressly conditional' upon a preliminary assurance from the British Government that there would be no further interference in the internal affairs of the Transvaal, that the claim to suzerainty would be dropped and that arbitration would be accepted.

On 26 August Chamberlain made what his biographer described as 'a short, clanging speech'.[3] Kruger, he said, 'procrastinates in his replies. He dribbles out reforms like water from a squeezed sponge . . . The sands are running down in the glass'. Two days

---

[1] 4th *Parl. Deb.* lxxv, 661 seqq. and 697 seqq.

[2] Chamberlain PP. J.C. 11/6. Chamberlain to Salisbury, 16 August. Note the importance which Chamberlain attached to Boer offers being recorded in writing. Professor Marais suggests that it was his intention to use such records as the basis for further demands. Marais, 250–1 and 310.

[3] Garvin, iii. 438.

later he telegraphed to Milner the British reply to the Transvaal's proposals: the British Government would accept arbitration in principle, but in effect rejected the other two conditions. On 2 September the Transvaal withdrew the offer made by Smuts and reverted to the previous offer of a seven years' franchise, with four seats for the Witwatersrand.

On 8 September the British Cabinet decided to send a 'final offer' to the Transvaal. It was made in threatening language. It said in effect that Britain would accept a five years' franchise without conditions, and that if this were not accepted the British Government would 'formulate their own proposals for a final settlement'.[1] In a memorandum which Chamberlain circulated to his colleagues on the eve of the meeting, the issue was stated as that of the danger to British power in South Africa from the pretensions of the Transvaal. In this memorandum Chamberlain accepted (at least for debating purposes) the theory of the 'Pan-Afrikaner conspiracy'. No real progress, he wrote, was being made in negotiations. He continued:

It is impossible that this state of things should be tolerated any longer. I doubt if public opinion in this country would stand it, but what is of much greater importance, I am certain that it cannot be prolonged without the most serious danger in South Africa.

It must be clearly borne in mind that what we have to deal with is not the individual cases of grievance, numerous as they have been, for which friendly remonstrances secured no redress—nor is it even the complete failure of the Transvaal Government to fulfil the promises on which its independence was conceded, and to observe the letter and spirit of the Conventions by which that independence was conditionally secured— but it is the general situation which has been created by the policy uniformly pursued by the South African Republic since 1881 and directed against any assertion of supremacy on the part of Her Majesty's Government and any claim to equality for British subjects.

What is at stake is the position of Great Britain in South Africa— and with it the estimate formed of our power and influence in our Colonies and throughout the world.

The Dutch in South Africa desire, if it be possible, to get rid altogether of the connexion with Great Britain, which to them is not a motherland, and to substitute a United States of South Africa which, they hope, would be mainly under Dutch influence. This idea has always been present in their minds, and has frequently been publicly avowed by indiscreet advocates of their cause . . . But it would probably have died out as a hopeless impossibility but for the evidence of successful resistance to

1 Ibid., 442.

British supremacy by the South African Republic. The existence of a pure Dutch Republic flouting, and flouting successfully, British control and interference, is answerable for all the racial animosities which have become so formidable a factor in the South African situation . . . The ill treatment of the Uitlanders has always been of a kind difficult to formulate as in itself a *casus belli*. It has, however, had for its object and result the reduction of Englishmen in the Transvaal to the position of an inferior race, little better than that of the Kaffirs and Indians whose oppression has formed the subject of many complaints—all ignored with stolid indifference by the Transvaal Government.[1]

This reasoning convinced the Cabinet. At the meeting on 8 September it was decided to send troops to South Africa, to bring the total there up to 22,000 men. This was the critical decision. Reinforcement of the garrison meant war. 'The Transvaal government were determined to give way no further. They knew that they must expect an ultimatum, and here were the troops coming to enforce it. It was obviously sound military strategy to strike as soon as possible. On the other hand, it was sound diplomatic tactics to wait for the British ultimatum provided there was no undue delay. If there was such delay, military considerations might be expected to prevail'.[2]

In the event, the British ultimatum was delayed. It was sanctioned by the Cabinet on 29 September, but it had not been delivered when, on 9 October, the Boer ultimatum was handed to the British Agent in Pretoria.[3] On 11 October the war began.

V

Neither side blundered blindly into war. Kruger sent his ultimatum because he believed that he had no choice between fighting and surrendering the independence of his country. Milner had at last convinced Chamberlain, and Chamberlain had convinced the British Government, that British supremacy in South Africa would be jeopardized unless the power of the Transvaal were broken. Each of the protagonists adopted the logic of the ultimate consequence, the argument of the irreconcilable alternative.

An historian of the present day has concluded that whatever

[1] Salisbury PP. S.A.: Box 3. This document has been published in part in R. Robinson, J. Gallagher and A. Denny, *Africa and the Victorians* (1961), 454–5.
[2] Marais, 320.
[3] For the British ultimatum, see E. Drus, 'Select Documents from the Chamberlain Papers concerning Anglo-Transvaal Relations, 1896–1899' in *The Bulletin of the Institute of Historical Research*, xxvii (1954).

might be 'the verdict of the specialist historian on the particular actions of Rhodes or Chamberlain, Milner or Kruger, it can hardly be denied that the Boer War of 1899–1902 shares with the Russo–Japanese War of 1904–5 the unenviable distinction of coming closest to the simple Marxist pattern of imperialist war.'[1]

The facts do not support this contention. Nevertheless there were men at the time who interpreted the event with equal simplicity. J. A. Hobson, who was feeling his way towards the conclusion that wars of expansion were necessary consequences of capitalism, put the blame upon 'a small confederacy of international financiers working through a kept press' who were seeking to obtain for their mines on the Witwatersrand 'a full, cheap, regular submissive supply of Kaffir and White labour'; this need led them to widen the sources of supply and thus 'our international capitalists are expanders of the British Empire'.[2] W. T. Stead saw the war as the seizure of Naboth's vineyard and added: 'The Candidates of Cain are those who defend, condone, justify or excuse the war with the South African Republics'.[3] There were many Afrikaners and still more Western Europeans who agreed that the war was a product of imperialist or capitalist conspiracy. The manifesto of the Transvaal, *A Century of Wrong*, which was issued in the name of F. W. Reitz, the State Secretary, but written by Smuts, linked capitalists and the British Government as co-conspirators and declared: 'If it is ordained that we, insignificant as we are, should be the first among all peoples to begin the struggle against the new-world tyranny of Capitalism, then we are ready to do so, even if that tyranny is reinforced by the power of Jingoism . . .'[4]

Others, however, were not so sure. 'The remarkable thing', said John X. Merriman, 'is that if you get nine men together, they all give you a different reason for the war'.[5] For the most part these reasons were expressed in simple terms which imputed total guilt to one side or the other. The overwhelming majority of British South Africans endorsed the judgement of Sir Edward Grey: 'We are in the right in this war. It is a just war. It is a war which has been

[1] Hugh Seton-Watson, *Neither War Nor Peace* (1960), 310–1.
[2] J. A. Hobson, 'What We Are Fighting For', *The Speaker*, i (n.s.), 366, 367 (January 1900).
[3] W. T. Stead, *The Candidates of Cain* (1900), 1.
[4] *A Century of Wrong* (English ed., 1900), 98. For Smuts's authorship of this manifesto, see Hancock, op. cit., 108
[5] Cape House of Assembly debates, 24 September 1900.

forced upon this country'.[1] Technically, the Boers were the aggressors; the fact that Kruger got his ultimatum in first alienated from the Transvaal much sympathy that it might otherwise have received in Britain, temporarily silenced many of Chamberlain's critics, and provided the occasion for what the *Annual Register* called 'music-hall militarism' about avenging Majuba. L ord Salisbury expressed the mood of the moment in Britain when he said that the Boers had 'issued a defiance so audacious' that he could hardly speak decorously, and in doing so had 'liberated us from the necessity of explaining to the people of England why we are at war'.[2] There were, however, important dissenting opinions. James Bryce, whose influence outside England was extensive, did not suggest (as others were to do) that the Boers, in consequence of being mistreated by the British Government, had suddenly acquired virtue and wisdom. 'An exclusive government may be pardoned if it is efficient, an inefficient government if it rests upon the people. But a government which is both inefficient and exclusive incurs a weight of odium under which it must ultimately sink; and this was the kind of government which the Transvaal attempted to maintain'.[3]

But all this, he concluded, though doubtless reprehensible, was beside the point. Britain, in her relations with the Transvaal, might properly remonstrate, advise or warn; she had no right to threaten and demand. The responsibility for the war, in Bryce's judgement, rested with the Boers only in the most formal sense. 'The real cause . . . was the menacing language of Britain, coupled with her preparations for war'.[4] Britain had allowed herself to appear before the world as an aggressor without a *casus belli*. When Bryce produced the substance of this argument in the House of Commons, he was rebuked for want of patriotism by Goschen, the First Lord of the Admiralty, who told him that he had been 'good enough to give a brief to every foreigner to expose the injustice and immorality of the war'.[5] Another eminent scholar, Professor Westlake of Cambridge, agreed in essence with Bryce, but thought that the issue transcended legalities. There was no cause for war, he reasoned, either in the allegations that the Transvaal Government had broken the Convention of London or in the claims put forward by the Uitlanders; he recognized indeed that the 'franchise

---

[1] 4th *Parl. Deb.*, lxxviii, 378.   [2] Ibid., lxxvii, 71.
[3] J. Bryce, *Impressions of South Africa* (3rd ed., 1899), xviii.
[4] Ibid., xxxiv.   [5] 4th *Parl. Deb.*, lxxviii, 378.

and representation asked for by Sir Alfred Milner could not be otherwise than a death-blow to the Boer ideal'. But, he continued, the insistence that British ideals should predominate in South Africa, though not founded on any legal right,

> may have been justified, probably was justified, by one of those situations that occur in the mutual relations of nations, soluble by no canons of legal right but for which a higher justice must be appealed to, that larger justice which in this country is exercised not by courts of justice applying the law as it is but by parliament altering the law, and which is sometimes necessary between nations, bringing into operation demands not founded merely upon a legal position but upon the intolerable character which a certain situation has assumed.[1]

In other words, the war was justified by *raison d'état*. A variation of the doctrine that necessity knows no jurisprudence was adopted by two notables of the Fabian Society. Sidney Webb coined the slogan: 'The war is *wholly* unjust but wholly necessary',[2] and George Bernard Shaw wrote that 'the fact remains that a Great Power, consciously or unconsciously, must govern in the interests of civilization as a whole; and it is not to those interests that such mighty forces as gold-fields, and the formidable armaments that can be built upon them, should be wielded irresponsibly by small communities of frontiersmen'.[3]

The explanation of the war as a capitalists' conspiracy must be discarded; it is too smooth and rounded to fit easily into the jagged background of events and personalities, although it appealed at the time to some who were sophisticated and some who were simple-minded. Two of the dominating facts of the South African situation were that the Witwatersrand gold mines were the richest in the world and that their geographical location meant that the balance of power was shifting from the 'cradle of white civilization' in the Cape to the turbulent frontier society of the Transvaal. One cannot ignore the direct and indirect effect of the possession

[1] J. Westlake, *The Transvaal War* (1899).

[2] Courtney PP., xxix, Mrs. Courtney's diary, 19 January 1900.

[3] *Fabianism and the Empire* (1900), 23. It was, by Shaw's own account, Ibsen who made up his mind for him. 'During the war a curious thing happened in Norway. There, as in Germany, everyone took it for granted that the right side was the anti-English side. Suddenly Ibsen asked in his grim manner, "Are we really on the side of Kruger and his Old Testament?" . . . I saw that Kruger meant the seventeenth century and the Scottish seventeenth century at that; and so to my great embarrassment I found myself on the side of the mob.' Hesketh Pearson, *Bernard Shaw* (1942), 246.

of South African stock among the investing public in London; but to say that is to say no more than that the mines were of international interest. It is true that John Hays Hammond, one of the magnates of the Witwatersrand, publicly estimated after the war had begun that the additional profit which the mines could make once they were emancipated from Kruger's government would be £2½ millions a year, and admitted that it would be made by reducing wages; such a reduction was not possible earlier, he said, because of the need to present to the Boers a united front of labour and management. But, whatever the ambitions of some of the magnates may have been, they were not a homogeneous group, nor were they united in purpose. What they wanted, in the main, was not war, which would certainly disrupt their operations and might lead to the destruction of their shafts and equipment, but the coercion of Kruger in their interests. Cecil Rhodes was so certain that Kruger would give way that he left Cape Town by train for Rhodesia on the eve of the ultimatum and was stranded in Kimberley in consequence. Whatever the magnates may have wanted, it was not they who took the decisions. Chamberlain and Milner, when they pushed Kruger to war, were thinking not of goldfields but of the political supremacy of Britain in South Africa; and that supremacy, they had decided, was incompatible with the independence of Kruger's republic.

Lord Salisbury, speaking *ex cathedra* at the Lord Mayor of London's banquet on 9 November 1899, stated that Britain's sole interest in the Witwatersrand mines was that they should be worked under good government. 'But that is the limit of our interest. We seek no gold fields. We seek no territory. What we desire is equal rights for men of all races, and security for our fellow subjects and for the Empire'.

What this meant was almost the opposite of what Salisbury said, a point which was instantly clear to *The Times*. It was, that newspaper said on the following day, 'the rigid truth' that Britain sought no territory, yet 'since it is abundantly clear that no paper guarantees will bind the Boers, it is impossible to carry out the task we have set before us—the attainment of equal rights for all—without taking away the territorial power and the military privileges that have been abused to the injury of peaceable and law-abiding fellow-subjects and to the danger of the Empire'.

The Uitlanders, one may conclude, had demonstrable grievances, but these could hardly be regarded as intolerable; furthermore the complainants, as W. E. H. Lecky pointed out, had become aliens for the sake of making money, like the Armenians under Turkish rule, at the price of living under a detestable government.[1] Kruger moreover was moving, however sluggishly, in the direction of reform. Indeed the exaggerations in Milner's 'helot dispatch' were scarcely removed in temper from the sentiments expressed in Alfred Austin's *Jameson's Ride:*

> There are girls in the gold-reef city,
> There are mothers and children too!
> And they cry, 'Hurry up! For pity!'
> So what can a brave man do?

In Hobson's phrase, 'The helot wore his golden chains with insolent composure of demeanour'.[2]

VI

What of the danger to the Empire? In September 1899 Chamberlain used language which implied that he believed in the existence of the 'pan-Afrikaner conspiracy'. ('Afrikaner alliance' was the expression used by Milner: 'I never', he wrote on 28 November 1900, 'called it conspiracy'.[3]) Did this conspiracy exist, and if so how dangerous was it?

An extreme statement of the case that the Boers were a danger to the Empire was made in the House of Commons in the early days of the war by Sir H. Meysey-Thompson: 'The Cape is the very keystone of the British Empire. If we acknowledge, as I think we must, that the Boers had it in their power to engage in war at the moment which suited them, then the British Empire would exist only at the grace of President Kruger'.[4]

A tradition of dislike of the British among Afrikaners could be traced back to the first occupation of the Cape in 1759. By the end of the nineteenth century, such events as the annexation of the Transvaal, the war of Majuba and, above all, the Jameson Raid and the British Government's apparent condonation of the raiders and those behind them, had transformed dislike, in the hearts of some Afrikaners, into hatred. A fat anthology of anti-British propaganda could have been compiled from the Dutch press of the

[1] W. E. H. Lecky, *Moral Aspects of the South African War* (1900).
[2] J. A. Hobson, *The War in South Africa* (2nd ed., 1900), 61.
[3] Milner MSS, xxv, f. 155.   [4] 4th *Parl. Deb.*, lxxviii, 496.

Cape. Extracts from newspapers were solemnly and indiscriminately quoted, principally by the South African League but once at least by the High Commissioner,[1] as evidence of Afrikaner aggression in the making. One believer in the conspiracy quoted an article written in the school magazine by a student of the Dutch Reformed Church seminary at Burghersdorp, in the Cape, in May 1899:

When I meet an Englishman as a private individual I must regard him as my fellow-creature; if, however, I meet him as an Englishman, then I, as an Afrikaner must regard him as the enemy of my nation and my religion—as a wolf that is endeavouring to creep into the fold . . . I think I can with truth add that race-hatred was encouraged amongst the children of Israel, if not indeed commanded. Afrikaners, let us take heed that we are not deceived; the English will be our oppressors, but never our friends.[2]

But it is a long way from the writing of nonsense by adolescents to the deliberate planning of aggression by men in power. It may at once be admitted that there were many Afrikaners who heartily wished that the British had never established themselves in South Africa. In the heated atmosphere of the 1890s, expressions of that sentiment might be construed as a deliberate movement towards what L. S. Amery, on 30 September 1899, called the 'mischievous ideal of a purely Dutch republican South Africa'.[1] But those who agreed with Amery could point to nothing more substantial than a general tendency of demeanour among the Afrikaners. Lord Salisbury, replying to a letter from Leonard Courtney which asked why he had endorsed the theory of conspiracy, wrote on 5 October 1899:

Of course I cannot produce evidence which would convict Kruger of conspiracy in a Court of Law. In political life you have to guess facts by the help of such indications as you can get. At first I accepted the favourable theory of the Dutch proceedings. But watching the course of negotiations I became convinced that Kruger was using the oppression of the Outlanders as a lever to extract from England a renunciation of suzerainty; and the conduct of President Steyn and Mr. Schreiner, of the Afrikaners generally and of their sympathizers in Europe, has brought home to me the belief that there is an understanding among the leaders of Dutch opinion

[1] Headlam i. 323.

[2] Quoted by T. L. Schreiner, *The Afrikander Bond and Other Causes of the War* (1901). Theophilus Lyndall Schreiner took a different view of Afrikaner culpability from that of his sister, Olive Schreiner, and his brother, the Prime Minister of the Cape.

[3] Courtney PP., vii, f. 76.

and that their aspiration is the restoration of South Africa to the Dutch race . . .[1]

But, as Courtney pertinently wrote back, once the hypothesis were accepted that there was an Afrikaner plan to 'regain' South Africa, 'a thousand innocent things will seem to fit in with this conspiracy. The most harmless suggestion becomes part of a plot'.[2]

The facts were that prominent Afrikaners outside the Transvaal did their best, for a long time and almost until the last minute, to encourage Kruger to make concessions.[3] Some continued their efforts up until the outbreak of war; others, like President Steyn, changed their attitude to Kruger only when they had lost faith in the British Government's sincerity in wishing to come to a peaceful accommodation with the Transvaal. Chamberlain later admitted as much. He wrote to Milner on 23 July 1900:

I have just been reading the letters found at Bloemfontein from Merriman, De Water [sic] and others. They are very interesting but appear to show two things:—(1) that in their hearts these representatives of the Bond felt strongly the weakness of Kruger's position and did urge him according to their lights to make concessions. There are, however, some remarkable qualifications, as, for instance, where they indicate that the concessions need not be final, and that if there is a reaction in England and the Liberal Party come into power, the Boers might retrieve their old position; (2) the papers seem to show that so far as the political leaders were concerned they hoped to avoid war up to the last.[4]

The Transvaal fought when it had decided that, in self-respect, it had no alternative; its ally, the Orange Free State, joined it on a point of honour. Both regarded themselves as acting on the defensive. In a statement dated 11 October 1899 Kruger said: 'The Republics are determined, if they must belong to England, that a price will have to be paid which will stagger humanity'; and to his brother President, Steyn, he telegraphed on 20 January 1900: 'This war can only be ended in one of two manners: either by our practical extinction or by our getting what we want. With us, the only question is one of freedom or of death. It must be so. If we lived to be sub-dued, our children would be slaves. If we die for our freedom, then our children can draw the greatest advantage from our example. This we know, that if a self-governing people places itself under the yoke of another, its moral fall is assured'.[5]

[1] G. P. Gooch, *Life of Lord Courtney* (1920), 377–8.
[2] Courtney PP., vii, f. 90. [3] Marais, c. xi.
[4] Milner MSS., xxv, f. 31. [5] C.O. 417/289, f. 123.

On 1 February 1900 Balfour was asked in the House of Commons whether the British Government had any evidence which 'justified them in believing that the policy of the Transvaal Republic . . . is the establishment of Boer supremacy over the colonies of Natal and Cape Colony'. He replied:

The conclusion which we have formed upon this very important question of course is the result of the consideration of a vast number of particular circumstances which, at all events in my opinion, all lead up to the conclusion I have more than once expressed in public, and which the hon. Gentleman has embodied in this question. But if he asks me if there is any statement by President Kruger and President Steyn to this effect, whether they have ever announced in public that they were parties to this conspiracy and communicated the fact to any British official whose word might be embodied in a Blue Book, of course that is not the case.[1]

There one may leave the 'Pan-Afrikaner conspiracy'.

VII

Lord Salisbury, early in the war, had declared that Britain sought no territory. Later, in a more comprehensive statement of war aims, he said: 'With regard to the future, there must be no doubt that the sovereign power of England is paramount. There must be no doubt that the white races will be put upon an equality, and that due precaution will be taken for the philanthropic and kindly and improving treatment of those countless indigenous races of whose destiny I fear we have been too forgetful'.[2]

There were contradictions in these aims. British supremacy and equal rights for white men need not necessarily mean the same thing: throughout South Africa, Afrikaners were in the majority.[3] Previous experience did not suggest that 'equal rights' would be any guarantee that the non-White peoples would enjoy kindly and improving treatment. Milner saw his way with myopic clarity. The 'native question' receded to the background of his mind. The immediate task was to break the power of the Afrikaner; the other could wait. L. S. Amery who, as correspondent of *The Times* and as

[1] 4th *Parl. Deb.*, lxxviii, 257.   [2] Ibid.
[3] The inconsistency in war aims was noted at the time. Cf. Alfred E. Pease, M.P., *Imperial Justice* (1900), 9: 'When war broke out it was declared to be an unavoidable and necessary war, for the establishment of British supremacy in South Africa. That it was a just war, because it was to place all white people on an equality. These two things are a contradiction in terms.'

a Balliol man, was close to Milner's confidence, wrote in 1899 that 'what we are committed to is the stamping out of a national movement which we have allowed to grow up in the last twenty years'.[1] As Milner wrote later to Lord Roberts (in the words quoted at the head of this chapter), he prided himself on having precipitated the crisis.[2] He did not underestimate the immediate military difficulties which Britain would face. His papers, published and unpublished, verify the accuracy of the impression which Amery formed of his state of mind in September 1899. Milner, Amery wrote:

was fully prepared for the Boer commandos sweeping over most of Cape Colony, and doubling their numbers by the spread of rebellion among the Dutch population, before our reinforcements could stem the tide. It was this very sense of the greatness of the danger . . . that made him prepared to face all that he knew war might involve, sooner than agree to some face-saving compromise which might have satisfied the House of Commons at home, only to leave the British position still more desperately weak when the next crisis came.[3]

Milner believed that the power of the Boers could be broken, once for all, in a war that would be fierce but short. Thereafter, he intended to ground British supremacy upon a conquered Transvaal which would be transformed into a British colony. In Milner's reasoning, the future of South Africa would be settled in the Transvaal. The colony of Natal was a secure outpost of England, loyal in the fashion of Ulster. The Orange Free State was, and would remain, preponderantly Afrikaner. The Cape Colony had an Afrikaner majority which would grow with the years. The Orange Free State and Natal each offset the other. The Cape, then, must be outweighted by a British Transvaal. The Transvaal was the agate point on which the balance of power in South Africa would turn. Once the Boers had been beaten, the Transvaal would be reconstructed on an heroic scale, with the object of transforming the nature and distribution of the white population. Once Kruger's republic had been overthrown, Milner estimated that British immigrants would flock in their thousands to the Witwatersrand; but a local and unregulated influx would not be enough. A British influence must flow into the country districts, where the dull mass

---

[1] Courtney PP., vii, f. 121.   [2] 101 Milner MSS., xlv, f. 60.
[3] L. S. Amery, *My Political Life*, i (1953), 100–1.

of the *backveld* Boers must be stirred, diversified and uplifted by judicious plantations of British settlers. This, in turn, would mean that the outer regions of the Transvaal must be developed and made fit for profitable cultivation. The making of railways, roads and irrigation works, the improvement of stock breeding, and the application of science to agriculture, would help to achieve and maintain British supremacy. In July 1900 Amery wrote: 'In the Transvaal certainly the Boers will be a rapidly dwindling minority. Johannesburg, Pretoria, Heidelberg, Standerton, Potchefstroom, Krugersdorp, Barberton, Klerksdorp, Pietersburg either are already or will in a year or two be English towns, and under an English government English farmers will settle everywhere within accessible reach by road or rail of the Johannesburg market.'[1]

This, then, was Milner's 'grand design', in which military victory would be the prelude to a gigantic exercise in physical and social engineering. This was an attempt to use warfare as an extension of policy by other means. It was essential to Milner's plans that the war should be quick, decisive and limited. It should do the minimum of damage to the country's resources, it should do the maximum of damage to Boer morale. The first aim, quick and decisive victory in a limited war, required (in Napoleon's phrase) a 'thunderclap of victory'—an Austerlitz in the *veld*. The second aim, the breaking of morale, justified the demand which Milner approved and Lord Roberts promulgated, for 'unconditional surrender'.[2]

The manner in which Milner's grand design was frustrated is the theme of this book. The war was neither decisive nor limited. It lasted for more than thirty-one months, and in the course of it the British Empire put into the field 448,000 men against two republics in which the white population, in Lloyd George's comparison, 'did not exceed that of Flintshire and Denbighshire'. These vast forces were handled by their commanders with a disregard for the political consequences of their operations. Things were done, some by accident and some by design, which were neither forgiven nor forgotten by the Boers and their descendants. In the end, a peace was made which abandoned not only the Natives, but also the Indians and Coloureds, to the prejudices of the white inhabitants of the former republics. How did all this happen? There are two short answers. First, although Milner had not underestimated the strength of the Boers, he in company with almost

[1] Courtney PP., vii, f. 208.   [2] See below, p. 85.

everybody else had overestimated the competence of the British Army. Second, once the war had begun, its control passed in matters of 'military necessity' from the hands of civilians into those of professional soldiers.

CHAPTER TWO

THE FIRST CAPE REBELLION

> A war in South Africa would be one of the most serious
> wars that could possibly be waged. It would be in the
> nature of civil war. It would leave behind the embers of
> a strife which, I believe, generations would hardly be
> long enough to extinguish.
>
> *Joseph Chamberlain, May 1896.*

> . . . England is going to lose South Africa, and some-
> thing much worse is going to happen—South Africa is
> going to lose England. England can afford to lose South
> Africa, but South Africa cannot afford to lose England.
>
> *John X. Merriman, September 1900.*

THE Boer ultimatum was generally regarded in England as an
exorbitant demonstration of Afrikaner *hubris*. The propaganda of
the time emphasized the seriousness of Boer designs upon Natal
and the Cape Colony: the pan-Afrikaner conspiracy was given, as
it were, a justification *ex post facto*. There was an outburst of
patriotic rodomontade. There was also a rise in the prices of
Witwatersrand gold shares on the London stock exchange. Some
representative figures for the period were:

	3 October 1899	20 October 1899
Rand Mines	$27\frac{1}{2}$	$38\frac{1}{4}$
Goldfields	$5\frac{1}{4}$	$7\frac{1}{2}$
Modders	$7\frac{1}{2}$	$10\frac{1}{2}$
East Rands	$4\frac{7}{8}$	$7\frac{1}{4}$
Chartereds	$2\frac{5}{16}$	$3\frac{1}{8}$

Parliament assembled in special session on 17 October. The
Marquess of Granby expressed the prevailing sentiment when, in
moving the Address in the House of Lords, he said: 'It is difficult
to say whether the ultimatum is characterized more by audacity
or by insanity'.[1] The Government obtained without difficulty a

[1] 4th *Parl. Deb.*, vol. lxxvii, c. 6.

supplementary vote of £10,000,000 for the war, although there were protests from their own side of the House by Leonard Courtney and Sir Edward Clarke, rasping speeches from Lloyd George and John Burns, and angry clamour from the Irish. The official Opposition was widely and deeply divided. The war brought into the open the divergent philosophies and smothered hostilities which had long existed beneath the surface, and the Liberal Party drifted apart in three fragments which seldom united in action, with Sir Henry Campbell-Bannerman as suzerain rather than leader. The Liberal Imperialist wing, led by Asquith, Grey and Haldane in the Commons and blessed enigmatically by Rosebery from the Lords, regarded the war as just and necessary. At the other extreme were those like Morley and C. P. Scott, who thought that the war was immoral. In the centre with Campbell-Bannerman were those who promised a qualified support to ministers while the Boers were invaders of British territory, but asserted their right to criticize the diplomacy which led to war. Almost all that these groups had in common on the South African issue was a distaste for Chamberlain; but it was difficult to attack the Colonial Secretary without attacking the High Commissioner and, as Campbell-Bannerman noted with regret, the 'Oxford group' led by Asquith had friendly confidence in Milner. When Campbell-Bannerman, referring to words imputed to Milner about breaking 'the dominion of Afrikanerdom', said: 'If we are to coin barbarous words, I would say that if South Africa is to be saved to the Empire it will be saved by Afrikanerdom and never by Downingstreetery',[1] Asquith rebuked him.

Campbell-Bannerman consistently expounded the doctrine that his party took no responsibility for what was being done by the Government in South Africa and that, as soon as it came to power, it would apply liberal principles to the Transvaal and the Orange Free State. In his philosophy, that meant home rule for the Boers within the Empire; in this he differed from the extreme 'pro-Boers' in England, who wanted the war to end with the independence of the Republics intact. Throughout the war, Campbell-Bannerman returned again and again to the theme that the Empire could not be retained by force. 'If we are to maintain the political supremacy of the British power in South Africa . . . it can only be by conciliation and friendship; it will never be by domination and ascendancy, because the British power cannot, there or elsewhere, rest securely

1 Speech at Manchester, 15 November 1899.

unless it rests upon the willing consent of a sympathetic and contented people'.[1]

On this reasoning, the chances of a lasting settlement depended upon whether military defeat of the Boers would settle the underlying problems in South Africa which, in Milner's opinion, had been insoluble by peaceful means in 1899. In the first weeks of the war, the Boers showed no signs of being defeated and, at the same time, racial enmity became fiercer. Olive Schreiner said that she felt as if her mother had stabbed her step-brother and quoted, as her sentiments towards England, Browning's lament for the lost leader:

> Life's night begins; let him never come back to us;
> There would be doubt, hesitation and pain;
> Forced joy at meeting, the glimmer of twilight,
> Never glad, confident morning again.

But men and women of this persuasion, on either side of the racial line, were few and scattered. The 'jingo spirit' blossomed in full flower in the Cape ports and in the colony of Natal. As early as 1 September 1899, Natal Ministers had submitted a minute to the Governor asking for prompt and vigorous action in coming to a final reckoning with Kruger; delay, they added, was vexing the loyalists on whom British supremacy depended, 'and if prolonged will tend to disgust, will weaken the support which Natal has hitherto given to Her Majesty's Government and will produce an unfavourable effect on the native population'.[2] The British in Natal, one of their notables wrote, were looking for a settlement which would 'include the final overthrow of the power for evil of the Krugerian faction . . . The franchise matter is dead. The issue now is British supremacy or Boer supremacy'.[3]

The Government of Natal, in short, was as resolute and uncompromising as Milner could have desired. Matters were otherwise in the Cape. There the Progressive, or British, party was in a minority in the House of Assembly. The cabinet of W. P. Schreiner (who was nominally an independent) consisted of three Englishmen and three Afrikaners and depended for its majority upon the Afrikaner Bond, a party which took its instructions from Hofmeyr rather than from the Prime Minister. Schreiner had used his influence for peace, had urged moderation upon Kruger, and had tried to put Milner's case

[1] Speech to Eighty Club, Oxford, 2 March 1901.
[2] C.O. 179/206, f. 204.
[3] Ibid., f. 287, F.S. Tatham to Hely-Hutchinson, 13 September 1899.

to the Transvaal and the Transvaal's case to Milner. In the event, he had pleased nobody. 'Poor Schreiner's position is very difficult', Amery wrote at the end of 1899, 'and after this business is over neither side will have anything but abuse for him till the time comes for people to judge more dispassionately'.[1] Schreiner's situation was complicated by Milner's dual capacity as Governor of the Cape and High Commissioner in South Africa. As governor, Milner was bound in his dealings with Schreiner by the usual constitutional conventions which limited the representative of the Crown in relation to the prime minister of a self-governing colony. But those limitations applied only to matters which were not imperial interests; in these, Milner was confined only by his reponsibility to the Colonial Secretary; and it was Milner who, within wide bounds, decided what and what was not of imperial significance.

To Schreiner, the war was none of the Cape's doing. Before the ultimatum, he had refused to do anything which either of the Republics might have regarded as an unfriendly act, such as prohibiting the transport of war materials consigned to the Transvaal, or fortifying the frontier towns of the Cape. When war came, he hoped that operations might be carried out exclusively by imperial troops and that the Cape might maintain a *de facto* neutrality. On 12 October 1899 he said in the Cape House of Assembly that 'it is the general duty of Her Majesty's Ministers in this colony . . . to save our country as much as possible from being involved in the vortex of war into which it is now apparently a certainty that South Africa has been drawn'.[2]

The invasion of the Cape by commandos from the Orange Free State came to him as a personal disappointment; he had imagined that he had concluded a gentleman's agreement of non-aggression with President Steyn. On 17 November he protested to Steyn, expressing his 'surprise and regret' at the invasion and at the purported proclamations of annexation of Cape territory. 'The people of this Colony have not deserved such treatment. Some may thereby be misled into conduct for which they may in future suffer very heavily, and the consequences of such wrong action will be justly laid to your Honour's charge, if it be not put a stop to without delay wherever it has taken place'.[3]

1 Courtney PP., vol. vii, f. 121.
2 Cape Hansard, House of Assembly, 1899, p. 648.
3 C.O. 48/543, f. 602.

Schreiner was referring to the enthusiasm with which young Cape Afrikaners welcomed the commandos. There was little sympathy for Britain in the country districts: the feeling of most Cape Afrikaners was summarized by a minister of the Dutch Reformed Church in Stellenbosch who said to a British acquaintance: 'I tell you what it is, Mrs. Moodie, I can't be honest and loyal at the same time'.[1] Merriman, the Colonial Treasurer, wrote to James Bryce on 1 November 1899:

The position in the Colony is terrible. We are doing our best to keep the peace but the natural feeling of sympathy on one side and the insulting exultation on the other makes the task very difficult. What hatred and what distrust will remain when the war is finished! The women are fierce. One charming and pretty woman, wife of a late British official in the Transvaal, said to some soldier who was praising the valour of the Boers and expressing the hope that they would all shake hands when the war was over: 'Shake hands! I have three children and I shall bring them up to hate the English.'[2]

There was a tendency in Britain to assume that the war would be a solvent of racial hatred and that, like characters in juvenile fiction, British and Afrikaners would be better friends after a good clean fight. This illusion was shared by some in South Africa who might have been expected to know better. J. G. Kotzé, the former chief justice of the Transvaal, wrote to Milner on 7 March 1900: 'Upon the whole I am rather inclined to look upon the present hostilities as a thunderstorm that will clear the political atmosphere to a certain extent'.[3] Campbell-Bannerman, with clearer insight, ridiculed the view that 'you should make the Boers love you by soundly thrashing them . . . after all, war is not either a humane or a good-natured proceeding'.[4]

II

Those in Britain who had believed that the war would be 'over by Christmas' were disillusioned by the military events of the first two months. When the ultimatum was sent, British forces were numerically inferior to those of the Boers; there was a critical gap of about six weeks, between the first shots and the expected

[1] C.O. 48/546, f. 658.   [2] Bryce PP.   [3] C.O. 417/287, f. 402.
[4] Speech at Birmingham, 24 November, 1899.

arrival of the army corps from Britain at the end of November, during which the British would necessarily be on the defensive. The Boers invaded Natal and the Cape Colony, and were joined there, in all, by rather more than 10,000 Afrikaner rebels. The first phase of the war was fought entirely on British soil. The Boers did not press their advantage; instead, they immobilized the greater part of their forces in besieging the towns of Kimberley, Mafeking and Ladysmith. The British feared that the fall of any of these towns might be the occasion for a general rising of Cape Afrikaners. It seemed to Sir Redvers Buller, when he arrived as commander-in-chief of the British forces in South Africa at the end of November, that his most pressing duty was to raise the sieges. The general strategy formulated in outline in London had been that the army corps should advance by three railway lines, from Cape Town, Port Elizabeth and East London, towards the Orange River and should then converge on Bloemfontein, in the hope of bringing to battle and decisively defeating the main army of the Orange Free State. The process would then be repeated with an advance along the railway from Bloemfontein to Johannesburg and Pretoria. Buller scrapped this plan. Without consultation, he decided to split the army corps. Part was sent under Lord Methuen to relieve Kimberley, a division was sent under General Gatacre to discourage the central Cape from rebellion, and the remainder went by sea to Natal, with the object of relieving Ladysmith. Buller himself accompanied the Natal divisions, leaving Cape Town in such secrecy that Milner did not know that he had gone and refused to believe the news when he first heard it. With Buller enmeshed in tactics in the Natal midlands, there was no effective central direction of the British operations until the arrival of Lord Roberts to supersede Buller at the end of January 1900.

In the first weeks of the war, certain facts became evident. One was the superiority of Boer equipment—the Boer Krupp and Creusot guns over the British artillery, the Mauser rifle over the Lee-Metford. Another was the superiority of Boer marksmanship, and the advantage which smokeless powder and accurate shooting gave to Boers firing from prepared positions on British troops advancing in drill order over open country. Yet another was the failure, in the main, of British generals to devise any tactical manœuvres more sophisticated than frontal attacks upon an enemy whom they could not see, whose whereabouts they had imagined and whose strength they did not know. One of the earliest books of the war by a war correspondent began:

'It seems to me,' said a well-known colonel of the Guards, 'that our leaders find out the strongest position of the enemy, and then attack him in front.'

'It appears to me,' put in a brother-officer, 'that they attack him first, and find out his position afterwards.'[1]

The year ended with the triple Boer victories of 'Black Week', over Gatacre at the Stormberg, Methuen at Magersfontein, and Buller at Colenso. At Colenso, Buller lost 1,200 men and ten guns. He also lost his nerve: he proposed to abandon his attempt to relieve Ladysmith, and sent a heliographic message to Sir George White, the garrison commander, ordering him to fire off his ammunition and surrender. White did not obey; but the order, when it was received in London, impelled the Cabinet to intervene. Balfour and Lansdowne, the only ministers in London that week-end, sent a peremptory signal to Buller requiring him to continue with the operations to relieve Ladysmith or else to lay down his command and return to England. The defence committee of the Cabinet then decided to supersede Buller as commander-in-chief in South Africa and to replace him with Lord Roberts (who had repeatedly offered his services), with Lord Kitchener as chief of staff. This decision produced friction between the Cabinet and Lord Wolseley, the commander-in-chief of the British Army, who was not consulted, and between the Cabinet and the Palace. (Two sets of personal animosities and affinities should be noted: the hostility between Wolseley and Roberts, and the friendship between Sir Arthur Bigge, the Queen's private secretary, and Buller.) On 19 December 1899 Balfour wrote to Lord Salisbury:

When I arrived at Windsor yesterday, I found Bigge full of grievances as to the recent treatment of the Queen by her Ministers. According to him, she complained (i) that no account of the Defence Committee's proceedings had been sent to her on Saturday, (ii) that she had not been consulted before the telegram ordering Butler to relieve Ladysmith was sent, (iii) that Roberts had been appointed without giving her an opportunity of expressing an opinion; and (iv) that the Commander-in-Chief had not been consulted with regard to this important military decision.

I told Bigge as regards (i) that Roberts was really asked to command in South Africa not on Saturday but on Sunday afternoon, when Kitchener's

[1] E. Kinnear, *To Modder River with Methuen* (1900), p. 1.

favourable reply had been received, this being in your opinion an indispensable part of the whole arrangement.

As regards (ii) I said that this represented a theory of constitutional
government which I could not accept. The Queen's advisers *must* be
permitted to issue important military orders without her previous sanction.

As regards (iii) I had absolutely no excuses to offer.

As regards (iv) I told him that it was impossible to consult the Commander-in-Chief upon such an appointment, as his well-known jealousy
of Roberts made his advice on such a subject perfectly worthless.[1]

Friction between the Palace, the War Office and the Horse Guards
recurred throughout the war. Buller's indecision and absence of
determination were not generally known in England (although one
of his accounts of the blunderings of his army was expressed in
language so opaque as to draw from Asquith the reflection that
'Our generals seem neither able to win victories nor to give con-
vincing reasons for their defeats'.[2]) The popular disposition was to
ascribe military failure to the misguided advice of irresponsible
civilians. This was encouraged by the parliamentary tactics of
Campbell-Bannerman, who avoided himself and discouraged in his
followers any direct criticism of the Army; and it fitted the military
mystique that warfare could be understood only by those whose
business it was to fight.

There had also been a certain coolness between Milner and
Buller. Milner did not think that the commander-in-chief in South
Africa was sufficiently conscious of the political dangers of a general
rebellion in the Cape; and reports from the country districts indicated that a rising was possible wherever a commando was unopposed. Buller's abrupt departure from Cape Town had left
a vacuum at military headquarters, which Milner attempted to fill
with advice and exhortation. In particular, he wanted mobile
forces to be stationed in disaffected areas, arguing that experience
showed that the Boers avoided garrisoned towns. Buller and, later,
Roberts disagreed; both preferred to concentrate their forces, and
both resented Milner's interference. Chamberlain warned Milner
not to embroil himself with the soldiery. On 27 December Milner
replied:

As a matter of fact there is nothing that I think more dangerous than a
civilian mixing himself up in matters military, and with what is purely
military I have never interfered. But what is purely military in this country?
Every military movement is so dependent upon political conditions and

1 Salisbury PP.   2 Asquith PP., Dep. 9.

forecasts, that there can be no sound strategy without taking these into account. And also I am compelled to warn, suggest, remind—to worry, in fact, the soldiers in a hundred ways, much to their annoyance (though they are very courteous) and to the absolute wearing to shreds of myself, without as much result as might be hoped.[1]

Three weeks later Milner wrote that: 'With the brief interval of Buller's stay in Cape Town, during which there was some direction, though it was perhaps not always wise, there has been no head here in matters military.'[2] On 20 January 1900 Chamberlain instructed Milner to leave the soldiers to their own devices: the splitting of the British forces, he said, and the calamities which had followed, apparently as a direct consequence, were being blamed in England upon 'political advisers'. 'I have protested against this, and have explained that in my view it is the duty of the Governors of the Cape and Natal to inform the military authorities of the political situation, but that the entire responsibility for military operations rests with the latter, and they must disregard the political question if the exigencies of the military situation demand it'.[3]

This decision meant that the unrestricted control of military activity in South Africa, upon which many critical political consequences depended, was delivered into the hands of the commander-in-chief in South Africa. Roberts and, after him, Kitchener took a wide view of what was implied by 'the exigencies of the military situation', and many of their actions displayed a carelessness towards or a disregard of political objectives.

III

Milner's problems, for the moment, lay in the Cape; the political situation in Natal was relatively simple. The Ministry and the Governor were at one in regarding the war as a struggle between right and wrong. The Natal ministers encouraged the Governor, Sir Walter Hely-Hutchinson, to proclaim martial law throughout the colony, and they proposed the sternest measures against any persons who should aid or comfort the enemy. On 29 September, ten days before the delivery of the ultimatum, a general warning was given by way of proclamation of the penalties for treason, which were stated to include the confiscation of property. The attorney-general of Natal pointed out to the Prime Minister on 14 November that this

---

[1] Headlam ii. 32.   [2] Ibid., ii. 55.
[3] Milner MSS., vol. 25, f. 2. Chamberlain to Milner, 20 January 1900.

was an excess of zeal, in that treason was not punishable by confiscation under Roman-Dutch law; he added that he was opposed to retroactive legislation which would make confiscation a statutory penalty. Hely-Hutchinson, after the law officers in London had concurred with this opinion, reluctantly withdrew the proclamation; he would have liked, he said, to hit in their pockets those who had been guilty of trying 'to upset British supremacy'. He sent to the Colonial Office evidence which, he considered, went 'to bear out the theory of the existence of a widespread and deep-rooted Dutch conspiracy throughout South Africa for the subversion of British rule'[1] Officials in Downing Street were sceptical: there was nothing especially sinister, they felt, in such statements as that made in a letter from a spinster at Mooi River, that 'The plan of the Boers here is to join the Transvaal, should the latter win'. Much of Hely-Hutchinson's evidence was of the same type, extracted from the letters of insignificant persons.

However, apart from the limitations imposed by legality, the Government of Natal was unhampered by political considerations from chastising such rebels as could be caught. The position in the Cape was far more complex. In the first place, opinion was divided throughout the colony on the merits of the war, and this division was sharply apparent in the relations between Milner and his ministers. There was a gap between them in temper and outlook, especially on the questions of how rebellion should be discouraged and how those who had rebelled should be treated.

Early in the war commandos from the Orange Free State moved into the northern Cape, occupied a number of villages and issued proclamations to the effect that these areas were subject to 'the martial law of the Orange Free State'. Some commandants went further and issued proclamations annexing the districts which they had occupied and declaring that the inhabitants could legitimately be commandeered, or called into the service of the invading forces. For the most part, British colonists were not molested, although those living around Aliwal North, on the Free State border, were given a fortnight within which they must either accept republican rule or remove themselves and as much of their property as they could take with them. There was a certain amount of looting of stock and equipment belonging to the British, but the evidence is that most of the looters came not from the commandos but from the

[1] C.O. 179/206.

colonial Afrikaners; it is likely that the chance was taken to gratify individual vindictiveness or to pay off old scores. Many of the younger Afrikaners joined the commandos; large numbers of others welcomed them, and gave or sold them provisions. The magistrate at Kliptown reported: 'Sunday [22 October] was like a fair, with carts containing Dutch farmers, women and children visiting the commando'.[1] Technically, those who had taken part in any of these activities had given aid or comfort to the Queen's enemies and had therefore committed an act of treason.

However, those who joined the commandos and those who merely welcomed them, did relatively little damage to British property, still less to British persons. This was a rebellion of the heart rather than the hand. On their side, the commandos exhibited no markedly offensive spirits; many of their members (as an elderly burgher pointed out to Winston Churchill after his capture in Natal) had taken up arms to kill, if necessary, but not be killed.[2] There were only half-hearted assaults on the besieged towns; the roving commandos kept away from areas where armed resistance could be expected. The progress of the rebellion was dictated by the movements of the invaders; unless a commando were on the spot, there was little chance of concerted disaffection from the Cape Afrikaners. although adventurous or angry young men might leave home to offer themselves as recruits; the Dutch Reformed Church seminary at Burghersdorp was closed because so many of its students had joined the Boers. At the same time, it was clear that some of these youths had become rebels under duress, and others with the reluctance of the schoolboy who gingerly ventures out of bounds rather than face the jeers of his fellows. The crux of the matter was that neither the British Army nor the Cape Government had, at the beginning of the war, sufficient forces to defend the frontiers or to protect the interior of the colony. Measures were taken to disarm those from whom disaffection might be expected; the fact that those whose rifles were impounded were mostly Afrikaners increased racial resentment. At the same time, the Cape ministers resisted pressure from the military authorities that martial law should be proclaimed except in areas where invasion and rebellion were accomplished facts, for fear that such an action might produce the very consequences which it was intended to prevent. The nature of martial law was misunderstood by Cape Afrikaners (some said wilfully), as a means

[1] C.O. 48/543. f. 208.   [2] *From London to Ladysmith via Pretoria* (1900).

of forcing them to fight. It was tolerably certain that, faced with a choice, many would choose rebellion rather than conscription. Milner, prompted by his ministers, thought it necessary to issue a proclamation on 8 November 1899, denying that there was any intention of calling out the militia and stating that 'all that the ordinary citizen is expected to do is to remain loyal to the Queen's Government and to give no countenance or assistance to an invader.'[1] Meanwhile, the Cape Police and the Cape Mounted Rifles were placed under the direct control of the commander-in-chief in South Africa, on the understanding that they would not be employed outside the colony and that the detachments stationed in the Native Territories would not be transferred without the consent of the Prime Minister of the Cape. The ministry assured resident magistrates that there was no intention of suspending constitutional rights, and that martial law was a temporary expedient which would not involve the calling-out of citizens 'to take part in these deplorable hostilities'.[2]

The magistrates' reports to the attorney-general are the main sources for an appraisal of the feeling in the country districts of the Cape. These supported the ministry's contention that either conscription or a general proclamation of martial law would probably precipitate resistance. The consensus was that the Afrikaners would probably remain passively hostile unless a commando came to their locality, or the British suffered a serious military defeat or (a significant proviso) the tribesmen of Basutoland attacked the Boers. There was no doubt whatsoever about their sentiments. Milner wrote in January 1900 that 'the expression of sympathy with the enemy, *as a matter of course*, has become a common form here among most Afrikaners. They generally begin conversation with it, as a sort of "Good Morning".'[3] Some took biblical comfort; a Boer victory was said to be prophesied in Revelations xvii and xviii. At De Doorns there were resignations from the mounted rifle club by members who feared that they would be called out for service. The magistrate of Griquatown, in the north-western Cape, said that if he took any steps to resist a commando he would inflame the spirits of the citizenry; he asked for permission, therefore, to make what terms he could, under protest, with any Boers who approached. On the whole, the field cornets protested their own loyalty and declared that they were doing their best to quieten their wards; one described

[1] C.O. 48/542, f. 269.   [2] Ibid., f. 245.   [3] C.O. 48/545, f. 139.

his people as being 'loyal and neutral'. The field cornets of the Stellenbosch division resolved at a meeting on 27 October that, although 'a large majority of the inhabitants of this division . . . naturally sympathize with their relatives across the Vaal, at the same time they should not forget that we in this Colony are subjects of Her Majesty the Queen, and should endeavour throughout this very trying time to prove the sincerity of our loyalty'.[1]

These instances demonstrate honest perplexity in the face of competing affections. There was, however, evidence of conspiracy. The magistrate of Barkly East reported as follows after the occupation of his district:

. . . At the beginning of the war, many influential farmers spoke to me saying it was a matter between England and the Transvaal, and that this Colony had nothing to do with it. For some time everything was on a satisfactory footing. They admitted having their sympathies, but often said that is no reason why we should be disloyal. As soon as the Free State commandos commenced invading the colonial towns, there was a decided change in their general demeanour and, as the danger came nearer Barkly East, it was not difficult to see that the majority of Dutch were going to assist the Free State in the event of a commando coming. Secret meetings were being held in various parts of the district, but what transpired the police could not ascertain. After Aliwal North was taken possession of, the Divisional Council of Barkly East passed a resolution asking for protection, as some of the Dutch pretended they were afraid of trouble with the Basutos, but no sooner was this done than Mr. Carl van Pletzen called a secret meeting of the Bond, and wired or wrote to the Prime Minister saying protection was not necessary . . . I am of opinion that these Bondsmen knew that if the district was protected no commando would invade . . . I am quite satisfied that the commando came to Barkly East by invitation, Mr. Carl van Pletzen and Jan de Wet proceeding to Aliwal North to let the commandant know when to come, and whether there would be any resistance . . .[2]

Meanwhile, Milner warned Chamberlain that, should the invasion south of the Orange River be pressed hard and be supported by local risings, it would be necessary to proclaim a general state of martial law, and that this would probably involve the dismissal of Schreiner's ministry. He had retained the ministry hitherto, Milner explained, because of its influence with Afrikaners and its value in preventing or retarding rebellion during the dangerous period before the arrival of the army corps. In this task, the ministry had succeeded

[1] C.O. 48/543, f. 278 seqq.
[2] Cape Archives. I am indebted for this reference to Dr. T. R. H. Davenport.

'to some extent but not enough'. But if there were a general rising, 'the policy of trying to appease and temporize is of no longer any use and our only chance is to have a Government which will co-operate promptly and heartily with the Imperial Government in any measures necessary to restore order'.[1]

This meant that Milner doubted the loyalty of his ministers. The words 'loyalty' and 'loyalist', as Milner used them, required some explanation. They involved something more than attention, how-ever scrupulous, to the legal obligations of citizenship; they involved also a positive demonstration of attachment to the Crown, to be shown not merely by obedience but also by enthusiastic acceptance of whatever measures the British Government should choose to adopt. Milner did not go as far as some of the Cape British, and accuse Schreiner of treasonable inclinations, but he was far from regarding either Schreiner or Merriman as 'loyal'. Milner was disposed to appraise a man's loyalty not so much by considering how he had acted in the past, but rather by how, in Milner's opinion, he was likely to act in hypothetical circumstances in the future. It is doubtful whether Milner considered that any Afrikaner, from the chief justice downwards, was capable of loyalty in this extended sense. As the war continued, he was inclined more and more to oppose suggestions that any concessions should be made as a reward to those Afrikaners who had remained passive during the rebellion; anything which was done to gratify these people, he thought, would be no more than an empty gesture to potential enemies, and a gesture moreover which would exasperate proven friends. On the other side of the racial line, representative Afrikaners regarded what Milner saw as profitless appeasement as no more than plain justice to subjects who had committed no hostile actions. Minds were operating, as it were, on different wavelengths; the lack of com-munication became progressively more evident.

Schreiner was not to be budged from his determination that he would agree to martial law only as an extremity; he was unmoved by a request from the general manager of the Standard Bank (which carried the Cape Government's account) that a general proclamation was necessary to protect the bank's business in the frontier dis-tricts.[2] Schreiner's position in relation to the High Commissioner was strengthened (although he could not know this) by Chamberlain's unwillingness to allow the disagreement between Milner and the

[1] C.O. 48/543, f. 405.   [2] Ibid., f. 415.

ministry to develop to the point of open conflict; Chamberlain did not wish the strain of a ministerial crisis to be added to a colony which was already suffering invasion and scattered rebellion. If martial law were considered to be necessary, he telegraphed to Milner on 17 November, he hoped that the ministry could be persuaded to co-operate. 'I am disposed to think that the resignation or dismissal of Schreiner would increase the political difficulties of the situation'.[1]

Throughout November and the early part of December, there was no means, in the interior of the colony, of defence against resolute attack or even of inhibiting the movements of a wandering commando. The magistrates of Cradock and Middelburg reported in mid-November that they could not muster any local forces to defend their districts, and appealed for Imperial troops. But all Imperial troops were already fully committed; there were none to spare. From magistrate after magistrate came reports indicating that rebellion lay just below the surface. There were tales of secret meetings by night in the homes of prominent Afrikaners; the Transvaal colours were flaunted, especially by young women; there was open exultation at the Paarl, near Cape Town, at the news of each British failure. The pervasive influence of the Dutch Reformed Church was exercised in each congregation according to the private convictions of the *predikant*; for the most part, these men preached quietism from the pulpit, but there is evidence that some of them, not without relish, spread exaggerated reports of British defeats and discomfitures. All in all, the report of the magistrate at Steynsburg may be taken as a typical summing-up of the situation: 'It is to be borne in mind that almost every Dutch family in this town and district has near relatives serving among the Republican forces, and while the general feeling is at the moment in favour of quiet, I would not venture to predict the consequences that would attend any untoward development'.[2]

IV

On 3 November 1899 the London *Daily Chronicle* published a report of a conversation between Milner and J. T. Molteno, a member of the Cape House of Assembly and a supporter of the ministry, which had taken place shortly before the outbreak of war.

[1] Ibid., f. 406.   [2] Ibid., f. 496 seqq.

According to Molteno's account, Milner closed the conversation with the words: 'Well, Mr. Molteno, it is of no use; I am determined to break the dominion of Afrikanerdom'.[1] Molteno sent his account to his brother in England, who gave it to the press. It was republished in the *South African News*, a Cape Town newspaper which opposed the war, on 21 November and caused the liveliest excitement at the Cape. Milner, through his private secretary, denied that he had used the words attributed to him, and alleged that Molteno's account of the whole conversation was twisted and distorted. The controversy grew to the point at which Milner, at Chamberlain's request, made a formal disclaimer in a dispatch which was immediately published. He had never, Milner said, uttered such words as 'the breaking of Afrikanerdom' but: 'I stated what I did consider to be the root difference between our policy and that of the South African Republic and its sympathizers, *viz.* that the latter aimed at maintaining throughout South Africa the predominance of a single race, while we were contending for equality'.[2]

This disclaimer, made in a form which publicly endorsed the theory of the pan-Afrikaner conspiracy, gave almost as much offence to many Afrikaners as the statement which it purposed to refute. Sir Henry de Villiers wrote to Chamberlain on 5 December that there would have been fewer rebels if the British had not worked upon the assumption that all Afrikaner colonists were naturally disloyal. 'So long as this cry was confined to party politicians it could not do very much harm, but its apparent adoption by the Governor was greatly resented by the Dutch-speaking population'. The accusation rankled, he continued, and it was 'apt to prove true in the result, although it may have been baseless at the time when it was made'.[3]

There was a disposition among passive Afrikaners, if not openly to justify the rebellion of their fellows, at least to put forward so many pleas in mitigation of their conduct that it appeared as if treason could be regarded as a venial offence. A representative selection of these arguments was put before Schreiner by A. S. du Plessis, a member of the Bond in Parliament, in a letter of 2 April 1900. The 'so-called rebels', du Plessis said, had been the victims of exceptional circumstances and had suffered great provocation. They had been left defenceless against invasion. ('Whose fault was

[1] J. T. Molteno, *The Dominion of Afrikanderdom* (1923), p. 184 seqq.
[2] Cd. 243.   [3] Chamberlain PP. J.C. 11/2.

it', Chamberlain asked, 'that the districts in a self-governing colony were left unprotected?'[1]) 'The people' saw no reason for war with the Republics and believed that its object was to deprive the Boers of their freedom; the 'jingos' and the English press in South Africa fomented hatred of the Afrikaner; white men had been disarmed while rifles were given to 'kaffirs'; martial law had driven loyal men to desperation, because of the unjust arrests made under it. Above all, he said, Afrikaners were incensed at Milner's policy which, they believed, was aimed at 'the entire suppression of the Dutch Afrikaners' and therefore, so ran the implication, was directed equally at Afrikaners who were British subjects and at the burghers of the Republics.[2] Milner, in short, was accused of having been the prime mover in a racial war.

In November Free State commandants proclaimed that the districts of Aliwal, Albert and Barkly West had been annexed to the Republic. Accusations were made by the Progressive Party that certain Bond members of Parliament had presided over republican meetings. Some Afrikaners made despairing apologies that they had joined the Boers because they could not help themselves. Others, it was said, were joining out of ignorance in the belief that the proclamations of annexation meant that they were henceforth citizens of the Orange Free State. Milner thought that the actions of the commandants had been inspired by the local inhabitants. 'There is no doubt', he wrote to Chamberlain, 'that the annexation and commandeering were devices resorted to by the invaders at the suggestion of the Colonists who wished to join them, but, for fear of possible consequences, did not like to do so without some sort of excuse'.[3] The arguments which du Plessis had used to Schreiner were repeated, with variations, throughout the colony. The absence of imperial protection was a favourite theme; so was the disarming of Afrikaners and the arming of Natives. (This was especially vexatious, it was said, because apart from the indignity Afrikaners were no longer able to shoot for the pot.)[4] The lack of imperial troops began to be a matter of resentment to candid friends as well as to doubters. On 23 November the resident magistrate at Dordrecht reported to the secretary of the Law Department in Cape Town that the occupation of his village was only a question of time, and added:

[1] C.O. 48/546, f. 147.   [2] Cd. 264, p. 9.   [3] Ibid., p. 2.
[4] C.O. 48/543. Letter from P. J. du Toit, M.L.A., to Schreiner. 20 November 1899.

'Would it be asking too much to request that the Imperial authorities should be desired by the Colonial Government to state for general information and definitely whether they have yet grasped the fact that incalculable harm is being done by the present state of affairs, and whether they intend at any time to take any action at all to deal with the matter, and when such action is likely to occur?'[1]

On 30 November Milner told Chamberlain that it was evident that the Boers would gain adherents wherever they appeared, that there were 'no adequate means' of preventing an invasion of the Cape midlands, and that there would be panic in Cape Town if the gravity of the position were generally known.[2] A few days later the Cradock branch of the Bond resolved that it 'deplores to the utmost' the state of war and that 'as British subjects we will take no part in the same', and sent a copy of the resolution to the Boer commandant operating in that district.[3]

Towards the end of 1899 the volume of complaint grew at the manner in which martial law was being applied; this evidence was used by the Cape ministers as part of their argument that martial law was doing more harm than good. The British were prepared to endure the inconveniences and even the oppressions of the system. The Afrikaners were not; this was not their war. The officers chosen to administer martial law were seldom the pick of the service: most were unimaginative, some were stupid, and many openly regarded Afrikaners as enemies. The most common grievances related to the detention of Afrikaners on suspicion; the acceptance of evidence, sometimes without corroboration, from Coloureds and Natives, and the rewarding of informers; the commandeering of wagons and stock without adequate compensation (Julius Weil made a fortune by taking up wagons, under imperial authority, at a fixed price and supplying them to the military at a handsome profit); the hiring of farm labourers by the military at wages well above those customarily paid by farmers, so that labourers left the farms for the army. Indeed, the attitude of the British Army to the Native remained a grievance throughout the war, a cloud full of menace to the 'traditional South African way of life'. Not only Afrikaners were affronted. At the end of the war, Merriman wrote that Natives 'have been armed and set on to fight and harry white men . . . They have been employed as drivers and so forth at very high wages, while white soldiers have loaded and emptied the wagons. This is quite

[1] Ibid., f. 765.   [2] Ibid., f. 813.   [3] Ibid., f. 907.

contrary to our customs and has had the effect of making them insolent and difficult to manage'.[1]

On 11 December a ministers' minute to the Governor recorded the opinion that 'the proclamation of martial law in certain districts has not been productive of any such good results as to compensate for the disquieting and irritating effect of its operation upon the people of the Colony'.[2] Milner agreed that, on the whole, martial law was applied sometimes stupidly and sometimes vindictively, and nearly always without imagination or sensitivity to the effect which an accumulation of petty injuries and insults would have upon a troubled and unhappy people. He described the actions of some martial law officers as 'foolish and mischievous',[3] and on 12 January he told Lord Roberts that, in the opinion of some who were un-questionably loyal, the vexatious administration of martial law was tending to drive into rebellion Afrikaners who might otherwise have remained quietly at home. The chief and justifiable complaint, he said, was 'that people are detained for long periods without knowing why'.[4] At the end of January the Cape Town branch of the Bond made the first of many demands for a thorough inquiry into the whole operation of the system. Milner encouraged his ministers to resist this proposal; but he suggested that greater use should be made of civil magistrates, that there should be brisker investigation into charges against men who had been locked up on suspicion, and that in general there should be more reasonableness and uniformity. In February the Cape Government placed Mr. Justice Solomon at the disposal of the military to preside over important treason trials held under martial law; on 8 March Chamberlain issued a firm instruction that no rebel should be executed without the consent of the British Government.[5]

But Milner's recognition that there was some substance in the complaints against the administration of martial law did not alter his conviction that the Cape ministry was over-sympathetic to rebels and republicans. Sooner or later, he thought, the Imperial Government would have to suspend constitutional rights in the Cape as a necessary means of establishing British predominance throughout South Africa. Chamberlain was of a different temper; on this matter he remained in disagreement with Milner for the duration of the war. Chamberlain would overrule the Cape ministry only if

[1] Bryce PP. Merriman to Bryce, 21 July 1902.   [2] C.O. 48/545, f. 97.
[3] Ibid., f. 139.   [4] Ibid., f. 258.   [5] Ibid., f. 336.

clear and pressing imperial considerations gave him no alternative; it followed from this reasoning that he would suspend the Cape constitution only as an ultimate resort, in the face of manifest and immediate peril or defiance. To each of Milner's repeated requests for action he returned what was substantially the same answer; one letter may stand for many:

. . . nothing can alter the permanent facts of the situation which dominate the politics of the Colony, namely, the existence of a Dutch majority largely consisting of persons disloyal to our rule. We have to lie on the bed which our predecessors made for us. The more I think of it, the more I doubt whether the present or any House of Commons would ever consent to take away a Colonial constitution once given without at least the absolute proof of a widespread and dangerous conspiracy. Although this may be said to exist, in effect, at the Cape we have no such evidence as would justify us in putting the conspirators on their trial; and as we should be opposed by many, if not all, of the Progressives, as well as by the Bond, and should have against us the general feeling of every self-governing Colony, I can hardly conceive the possibility of carrying a measure in the face of such opposition.[1]

Milner fell back on the tactics which he had used when he had failed to convince Chamberlain that action should be taken against the Transvaal in 1898: he would wait for events to prove him right, he would try to influence events, and he would press his point of view. On 26 March, after yet another of his requests for imperial intervention had been turned down, he wrote to Chamberlain: 'If public opinion at home is not yet prepared for interference with the domestic affairs of the Colony, I can only wait patiently till we arrive at that deadlock which I clearly foresee when the necessity for such interference will become apparent to the most obtuse.'[2]

V

In the months of February and March, the military situation changed with Roberts's victories—the relief of Kimberley, the surrender of Cronje at Paardeberg and the occupation of Bloemfontein. The Free State commandos retired across the frontier and the Cape rebellion withered away. These events did nothing to mitigate the hostility between British and Afrikaners. British traders found themselves boycotted in the country towns. There was violence in Graaff-Reinet when the local British celebrated Cronje's defeat with a display of fireworks: a rumour spread that

[1] Milner MSS., vol. 25, f. 5.   [2] Ibid., f. 80.

Kruger and Steyn were to be burned in effigy; a number of Afrikaners, armed with cudgels and axe-handles, gathered to prevent this outrage to the dignity of heroes of the *volk;* somebody began throwing stones in the darkness, and there was a *fracas* which might have developed into an ugly riot.[1] Afrikaners were not alone in thinking that British civilians were insufferable in victory. 'I am bound to say', Milner wrote to Chamberlain on 8 March, 'that the unrestrained and positively frenzied jubilation of the Coloured people over British successes has been rather hard upon the Dutchmen. And the English too have rather overdone "Rule Britannia".'[2] The Afrikaners of George protested to the Cape ministry that they had been insulted at a drunken orgy which the local British had held to celebrate Paardeberg; the British of George sent a counterprotest to Milner, that this was an imputation upon their sobriety. Schreiner did not think that Milner should have received the protest: such matters, he said, should be dealt with in the ordinary routine of police investigation, and not made the occasion of an incident in which British colonists appealed over the heads of their own government to the High Commissioner. 'This has an important constitutional aspect', he added delicately, 'which I know your Excellency will appreciate.'[3] Milner had indeed exceeded the limits of constitutional decorum by corresponding directly with subordinate Cape officials, and it was suggested in the Colonial Office that he was laying himself open to a personal attack. Selborne thought not: 'You should never', he commented, 'jog a capable man's elbow more than you can possibly help.'

The British victories brought into the foreground of events two problems—the fate of the Republics and the treatment of captured rebels. Cape Afrikaners began to put their energies into the Conciliation Movement, which urged that the Transvaal and the Orange Free State should be allowed to retain their independence. Meetings began to be held throughout the Cape, in March 1900, at which arguments were used that there would be no peace between British and Afrikaners if the Republics were annexed. Counterpetitions from vigilance committees, voluntary organizations of all kinds and religious bodies (other than the Dutch Reformed churches) were received by Milner in copious quantity. A deputation of the Nonconformist clergy of Cape Town presented an address of

[1] C.O. 58/545. Report of the Civil Commissioner, Richmond, 6 March, 1900.
[2] Milner MSS., vol. 25, f. 75.   [3] C.O. 48/545. Minute of 17 March 1900.

confidence and support to the High Commissioner on 13 April. On 21 April the Anglican Archbishop of Cape Town wrote 'to express to your Excellency my firm conviction, that no enduring peace can be secured to this country, so long as the Northern Republics are allowed to retain their independence, and to remain outside the limits of the Queen's Sovereignty. I believe that the cause of freedom, righteousness, and progress, as well as of justice to the Native Races, depends upon the establishment of British rule throughout South Africa'.[1]

The future of the Republics would be decided in London and not in South Africa; the treatment of the Cape rebels was a domestic issue. With the withdrawal of the commandos, several thousand rebels had surrendered or had been captured. Some were in prison, and others had been allowed to go back to their farms on the understanding that they would come up for trial when summoned. Milner wanted differential treatment for the leaders and the rank and file. He had no wish to try rebels by the hundred, partly because of the administrative inconvenience and partly because he wished to impress on those colonists who were still with the commandos that those who surrendered quickly and voluntarily would be more leniently dealt with than those who held out. Chamberlain concurred.[2] But this did not touch the larger question of what the differing penalties were to be.

The ministry was in general disagreement with the Governor, although its members were divided among themselves. Milner hoped that the ministry would split: that, he told Chamberlain on 31 March, would 'be the best thing that could possibly happen, as if the downright traitors could be expelled I believe majority might be found for the rest reinforced by some Progressives'.[3] A month later he argued against a general amnesty, among other grounds, because to refuse it would be politically profitable in that it would split the ministry and its supporters.[4] He asked once more for imperial interference with the constitution; this, he said, would be the safest course, because if the existing ministry tried and failed to carry a treason bill there would be no alternative, if the constitution were still in operation, but to dissolve Parliament, and a dissolution without the prior disfranchisement of rebels would almost certainly produce a fresh, and more stubborn, majority for the Bond. 'There

[1] C.O. 417/287, f. 7.　　　[2] C.O. 417/286, ff. 492, 500.
[3] C.O. 48/546, f. 147.　　　[4] Ibid., f. 290.

is something preposterous to my mind in allowing people who have just been in rebellion to exercise predominant influence in questions arising out of rebellion, including their own fate.'[1]

Chamberlain had no clear-cut opinion; he confessed that he was perplexed by conflicting purposes. He wanted no persecution, but he did not want rebels, in any circumstances, to be placed in a more favourable situation than that of the persons whose farms had been occupied and whose property had been looted.[2] The issue became distorted by divergent pressures: the 'loyalists' were insistent that the rebels should be punished severely, the Bond was equally insistent that the rank and file should not be punished at all, and the ringleaders as little as possible. The Colonial Office was not impressed by Schreiner's contention that a wide amnesty would conciliate Afrikaners. Graham minuted: 'The mass of the Dutch will only be reconciled by a firm and consistent policy (such has not yet been pursued in South Africa) which they can respect. They do not understand the moral strength of magnanimity. But like all half-educated people they will respect a power, the exercise of which they can feel in their persons or property.'[3]

On general principles, Milner agreed with Graham but, looking beyond the immediate issue, he was principally concerned with turning the rebellion to political advantage by disfranchising a large number of Afrikaners or, if that were impossible, by using the occasion to persuade Chamberlain to suspend the Cape constitution. Again and again he urged that the sentiments of the loyalists must not be affronted by misplaced clemency to rebels. He forwarded to London numerous letters demanding retribution; these, he said, were specimens of an extensive correspondence 'which though perhaps individually of little value, represent collectively an important body of opinion'.[4] Some of these letters said that the time had come to redress the electoral system, which favoured the countryside against the towns. This opinion was expressed by some who were not professional politicians: the daughter of the archdeacon of Cradock wanted the franchise to be manipulated against the Afrikaners in such a way that 'no amount of patient scheming on their part will rob us in the future of the right to rule'. It would, she thought, 'be fair in the extreme', to reduce Afrikaner representation in Parliament by two-thirds, 'considering that we know the

1 Ibid., f. 263.   2 C.O. 417/287, f. 11.
3 C.O. 48/546, f. 258.   4 C.O. 417/287, f. 135.

great bulk of them to be a sadly ignorant people.'[1] A serving soldier put the point of view of the loyalists:

Imagine that you and I hold neighbouring farms; the enemy arrives, we are both commandeered; you refuse to turn rebel; you are turned out of house then and there; your stock is commandeered, your house wrecked, your furniture smashed up or carried away, you are ruined, I, on the contrary, join the enemy . . . When the British arms gain the upper hand, I shall begin to whine; I shall lay down my arms and say that I am loyal, that I never wished to be a rebel, that I had no wish to fight . . . I shall return to my farm to find every thing as I left it; and when you return to find yourself a ruined man I shall laugh at you and tell you that you were a fool to be loyal to such a Government, and I shall tell you that a Dutch Government would treat far differently the man who had stood by it.[2]

There was no problem in Natal. The rebels there were few in number, and public opinion was strongly against them. They should, Hely-Hutchinson wrote to Milner, 'get it as hot and strong as we can give it to them.' Disfranchisement in Natal, with its large British majority, would not alter the distribution of power, and the concern of the British Government was rather to restrain the Natal ministry from retroactive legislation, involving the confiscation of property, than to stimulate it to activity. In the Cape, however, Milner summed up his difficulties, in a letter to Chamberlain of 19 March, as those of having to 'steer between the clamour of the loyalists, demanding the prompt and severe punishment of rebels "without benefit of clergy", and the attempts of the Bond party, more or less supported by the Ministry, to get the rebels off as easily as possible, and to divert attention from their misdeeds by a laborious raking-up of all the little blunders and needlessly arbitrary acts of the military under martial law by getting up a fictitious indignation about them'.[3]

After a tour of the northern Cape, Milner was less sure that the indignation was fictitious—he was scathing about the 'administrative chaos' that he found—but even more certain that disaffection was wide and deep. He had, he wrote to Chamberlain on 25 March, been pressing his ministers for weeks to advise him on how rebels should be treated.[4]

[1] Ibid., f. 141.
[2] Chamberlain PP. J.C. 11/1. Letter from Major Francis Davies, Grenadier Guards.
[3] C.O. 417/287, f. 476.
[4] Chamberlain PP. J.C. 13/1. Headlam (ii. 106) quotes from the copy of this letter in the Milner Papers, which differs from that sent to Chamberlain.

I believe that the attempt to answer this question will split the Ministry, and may even split the whole Afrikaner party, of whom all want to screen the rebels, being, as they are, simply the unlucky members of the party, but not more than four-fifths are prepared to advocate the wholesale condonation of treason.

The fact is, the 'show-up' is going to be more startling than anyone expected. The state of affairs which is being revealed in the North-Eastern districts is staggering. 'Who spoke of Dutch disaffection?' Here are four constituencies (with two members each) all in a block, in which practically the whole Dutch population was under arms, while scores of officials and leading farmers, *prominent Bondsmen and political supporters of the Government*, are in it up to the neck. And there is no longer any doubt that, in the rebel west, when once we recover it, we shall find practically the same state of things. And the guilt of the leaders is aggravated by most odious treachery and humbug. It is a truly revolting business.

I have no doubt that Schreiner has been grossly deceived. He is an obstinate dreamer, who has set up before himself an imaginary idol labelled 'Afrikaner' and endowed it with all the primitive virtues, while the real animal, with all his good qualities, is without an equal among white races, for duplicity and cunning.

VI

By the end of March Chamberlain had decided that every rebel should suffer something, *'pour encourager les autres'*. He thought that a small fine would suffice for the rank and file, with more serious punishment for ringleaders.[1] For the moment, the controversy turned upon the nature of the courts before which rebels would be arraigned. Trial by jury, it was generally admitted, would be unjust: no rebel would be acquitted by a British jury or convicted by one of Afrikaners.[2] This pointed towards a special commission, created by statute. But what should its powers be, and should these originate from the Parliament of Westminster or of Cape Town? Milner posed the questions in a long telegram of 6 April.[3] There were, he said, three possible courses: trial by court-martial, trial under the ordinary law of the colony, and trial by a statutory commission. There were two objections to trial by court-martial: first, that the sentences, if they were not to expire automatically when war was no longer raging, would need to be confirmed by statute, and no Cape Parliament would pass such a statute unless rebels were disfranchised first; second, that there was a chance that the High Court of the Cape would refuse to recognize the judgement of courts-martial, if these came before it on appeal, and that there

[1] C.O. 417/287, f. 177.   [2] C.O. 417/289, f. 491.   [3] C.O. 417/288, f. 228.

might then be a dangerous conflict of authority. There were four objections to trial by the ordinary courts: proceedings would have to start *de novo*, so that they would be protracted and tedious; it would not be easy to find impartial juries; sentences passed in different parts of the country would probably be unequal; and only ringleaders could be dealt with, because it would be administratively impossible to hold thousands of trials and legally impossible to herd together a mass of accused persons under a single indictment.

There remained trial by special commission. This, in Milner's opinion, was 'for the best' and was 'approved by all educated and well-disposed persons whom I have been able to consult'. It would split the ministry, perhaps, but Milner had already indicated that this would be a circumstance to be welcomed. Merriman, Sauer and te Water, he thought, would resign; the first two of these, he said, 'hold their seats by votes of admitted rebels and are sure to put every obstacle in the way of their punishment'. But Schreiner, Solomon and Herholdt might be persuaded to agree to a special commission, and a reconstructed ministry under Schreiner would probably have a small majority in a new House of Assembly, elected under a purged franchise.

What Milner was advising was an exercise of the 'imperial factor' in stages. First, the ministry would be reconstructed. Next, it would invite the Imperial Government to pass its own statute, with the understanding that it would be consulted on its provisions and on the composition of the statutory commission. Finally, there would be a general election, on a revised register from which the names of convicted rebels had been removed. This should produce a small but sufficient 'loyal' majority. There were, Milner admitted, constitutional difficulties in the way of this complicated procedure, but he thought that exceptional conditions justified exceptional measures. Sooner or later, he argued, the Imperial Government would have to intervene in the affairs of the Cape, and the method which he had suggested would keep that interference to a minimum. The critical step would be the invitation from the Cape Government. 'But I cannot urge friendly Ministers to commit themselves by inviting Her Majesty's Government to intervene unless the latter would respond favourably.' What would be the reply of the British Government if such a request were made?

On this point, Chamberlain received conflicting advice from his staff. Lambert thought that if the Bond refused to support the ministry, Schreiner and Rose Innes might be able to form a new administration which, in the absence from the House of four or five Bond members under arrest for treason, could squeeze through a local bill for a judicial commission. But, he admitted, if this attempt failed the Imperial Government would have to legislate at once.

Graham thought that this view was short-sighted: the Imperial Government could not act over the heads of Cape ministers, if the latter tried and failed to carry a bill, without inviting the accusation that they had indirectly suspended the constitution. If the Cape Parliament were unwilling to pass a treason bill, it would be equally unwilling to pass legislation confirming the sentences of courts-martial. An imperial commission seemed to be the only way out of the difficulty.

Selborne, then as always, was for strong measures. There was, he thought, too much timidity in the Colonial Office. 'I say that the Boer revolt and our victory give us an absolutely free hand, free from conventions, free from constitutions, free from boundaries, both as regards the South African Republic and Orange Free State, and rebel districts of the Cape Colony.'[1] He quoted the temporary suspension of the constitution of Lower Canada as a more emphatic, but equally justifiable, exercise of imperial authority.

Chamberlain was cautious. On 8 March he had asked Milner what the probable result of an immediate general election at the Cape would be, and whether the Progressives' estimate that they had a majority of votes was accurate. If there were a chance of even a temporary majority for Sprigg, the Progressive leader, he said, 'we might use it for a redistribution scheme lessening the power of the Dutch and pro-Boer districts, and also get the legislation passed which we require against rebels, disfranchising them among other things'.[2] He would not act over the heads of the Cape ministers unless there were no other way. He minuted: 'I wonder if anyone has thought out the question, what the passing of an Imperial Act to create a special commission to try rebels in a self-governing Colony would mean.

'It can be done no doubt, but it is not a slight task to throw upon a British Government in these days . . .'[3]

Before he decided, therefore, he wanted to know what Natal was

---

[1] Chamberlain PP., J.C. 13/4.   [2] Milner MSS., vol. 25.
[3] C.O. 417/288, f. 224.

going to do, and whether if that colony appointed a special commission the Cape would follow its lead; he wanted to know whether an alternative ministry could be found in the Cape; and he wanted to know whether the existing Cape ministry could not be stimulated to action by the threat that, otherwise, the Imperial Government would govern the Cape indirectly under martial law. A dispatch on these lines was sent to Milner on 10 April.[1] Imperial legislation, he was told, would be the extreme course; to enact it in the 'absence of overwhelming necessity might tend to alienate colonial sympathy as interfering with the constitutional powers of a colonial legislature'. Milner was advised to use political methods, on the borderline between persuasion and coercion. 'Can you not put it to Schreiner that the alternatives are either the indefinite prolongation of martial law, with its unsatisfactory procedure, or the appointment of a statutory commission under a Cape Act?' Could it not be suggested privately to members of the Bond that the sentences on rebels passed by a court-martial (which would then be confirmed by an imperial statute) would be more severe than those passed by a local commission? To that end, Milner was asked for his opinion on the immediate trial of a few ringleaders: if they were convicted and heavily sentenced, their friends might welcome an alternative tribunal for future cases.

The action of Natal was as exemplary as the Colonial Office could have wished; a statutory commission was created promptly by local legislation. On 14 April Milner sent a minute to his ministers, delicately warning them that the alternative to a statutory commission of their own might be trial by courts-martial, with the additional sanction that, in that event, martial law might be prolonged for a period corresponding to the longest unexpired sentence.[2] On 27 April, after protracted and angry discussions, the ministry replied, giving way. It expressed its 'strongest objection' to trial by courts-martial, agreed reluctantly that there would have to be a commission, and stated that it hoped to introduce the necessary legislation in the coming session of Parliament.[3] It seemed that the British Government had won their point.

This impression was false. On the following day the ministry sent a second minute, setting out the terms upon which it was prepared to act against 'those misguided inhabitants of this Colony

---

[1] Ibid., f. 230.   [2] C.O. 417/289, f. 488.
[3] Ibid., f. 491. See also Merriman's diary, Merriman PP.

who have recently risen in rebellion'. The attorney-general would prosecute a limited number of principal offenders, 'whose trials would mark the magnitude of their offence, and whose punishment, if found guilty, would act as a deterrent'; there would be complete amnesty for the rest, provided that they gave sureties for their good behaviour. Ministers urged this course on two grounds 'of sound policy and public morality': first, they said, a general proscription of rebels would leave behind it bitter memories, because it could be regarded as 'the semblance of a measure of political vengeance'; second, anything short of expansive clemency would drive a lasting barrier between the white races and thus produce a dangerous situation in the face of 'a large and increasing barbarian population'. This would be 'doubly unfortunate [considering] the great struggle between civilization and barbarism that is the lasting inheritance of the European in South Africa'. Finally, they pointed out that the rebels formed a small minority of the Afrikaner population of the Cape, and quoted the treatment of Lower Canada as a precedent for mercy.

In telegraphing the substance of this minute, Milner commented that he thought that his ministers expected an unfavourable reply. To Graham in the Colonial Office, this was evidence that the minute had a purely tactical significance: it bore, he said, 'a disagreeable resemblance to the lengthy argumentative effusions we used to receive from the S.A.R. Government in which the issues were put so indefinitely that it was almost impossible to reply to them'. He found the appeal to Canadian precedents unconvincing, and confected debating points in reply. The Cape ministers had confined themselves to the first Canadian rebellion and ignored the second, after which six Canadians had been hanged and sixty-eight transported. About the same number of rebels was involved in both colonies, but the Canadian rebellion had been put down in a week and that at the Cape had already lasted for three months since the offer of terms of surrender in February. Therefore, 'on the Canadian precedent we should hang seventy-two and transport 800'.[1]

Meanwhile, the divergent pressures at the Cape were as strong as ever. Afrikaners said that heavy punishment for their kinsmen would produce irreconcilability towards Britain; the Cape British said that their own attachment to Britain would be weakened if the

[1] C.O. 417/279, f. 491. Minute by F. Graham.

rebels were treated softly. Bryce wrote to Ripon on 26 March: 'Did you notice in today's *Times* the threats of the Cape "Loyalists" that they would turn disloyal if clemency was extended to the disloyal Dutch? There will be more of this before we are through: and very likely it may be as much through these jingo English as through the wronged Dutch that England will lose South Africa'.[1]

The least that the British were disposed to accept was the disfranchisement of the rebels, which would involve the political defeat of the Bond and the accession to power of a 'loyalist' ministry.

On 4 May Chamberlain sent his reply to the Cape ministry's proposals. The British Government did not wish to be vindictive, he said, and hoped for future harmony between the white races.

But in pursuing this object the sentiments of both sides must be taken into consideration, and while on the one hand the worst results may be anticipated from any display of a revengeful policy on the part of loyalists, not less serious consequences would ensue from the rankling sense of injustice which would follow upon a policy which would actually place rebels in a better position after the struggle was over than those who have risked life and property in the determination to remain loyal to their Queen and their flag.

Clemency to rebels is a policy which has the hearty support of Her Majesty's Government, but justice to loyalists is an obligation of duty and honour.[2]

He proposed that rebels should be classified under six headings: (1) ringleaders, (2) looters and committers of outrages, (3) those who had been responsible for 'acts contrary to the usages of civilized warfare', (4) those who had 'openly and willingly waged war', (5) those who had only given information or provisions to the enemy, and (6) those who could prove that they had acted under compulsion. Those in the first three categories should be tried and suffer such punishment as the commission should inflict. Those under (4) and (5) should be allowed to plead guilty, should be disfranchised and either fined or released upon their own recognizances, to come up for judgement if called upon to do so. Those who had acted under compulsion should merely be disfranchised. The Canadian precedent was dismissed as irrelevant: in Canada there had been a rebellion in time of peace in consequence of constitutional arrangements which were afterwards acknowledged to

[1] Add. MSS. 43,542, f. 15
[2] Cd. 294.

have been unsatisfactory; in the Cape there had been adherence to the Queen's enemies by those 'who have for a generation enjoyed full constitutional liberty'.

This might appear as magnanimity to the British, but to the Cape Afrikaners it appeared as political vengeance upon them as a people, in which guilty and innocent alike would be punished— the guilty individually, the innocent by the deprivation of political power which the disfranchisement of their fellow Afrikaners would necessarily involve. The ministry split on the issue of wholesale disfranchisement. Schreiner was prepared to accept Chamberlain's proposals, and he carried with him Solomon and Herholdt; Merriman, Sauer and te Water rejected them. Merriman, in a letter to Schreiner on 20 May, refuted Chamberlain's claim that justice must be done to loyalists. 'I confess that I do not understand the meaning of the word "loyal" in this connexion. If Mr. Chamberlain means the party who have approved the policy of this war, and who have, both before its outbreak and since, by writing and speaking rendered the task of keeping the peace almost impossible, then I think that he fatally misapprehends the political situation in this Colony.'[1]

Merriman was contending that the Afrikaners, rather than the Cape British, were the 'loyal' South Africans; the Cape would have been lost if the Afrikaners had risen *en masse* in 1899. 'There was a time, not many months ago, when it is not too much to say that the British hold upon South Africa lay in the hands of the Dutch-speaking colonists.'

Rebellion had never been considered as a crime of turpitude, and wise policy, therefore, should be to 'compose society to a decent forgetfulness'. Then, in a passage which turned Milner's 'helot' argument inside out, he concluded that the indiscriminate disfranchisement of all rebels would 'deprive their friends and kinsfolk, who have rendered the Colony yeoman service at the most critical time, of that legitimate influence which belongs to a majority. We are asked, in fact, to create a class of political "helots" in South Africa, where we are now waging a bloody and costly war ostensibly for the purpose of putting an end to a similar state of affairs'.

The split in the Cabinet was as complete as Milner could have desired—te Water, in his letter of rejection to Schreiner, referred to

[1] Cd. 264, p. 40.

the war as 'unjust and infamous'[1]—but it did not produce a split in the Bond, which refused to follow Schreiner. Chamberlain was still reluctant to override the ministry, and in the Colonial Office only Selborne fully identified himself with the 'loyalists'. No definite period of disfranchisement had yet been proposed: Selborne wanted a term of twenty years, 'not only as a stigma and punishment but in order to influence the result of the polls. I should deprecate, therefore, any pretence to the contrary'.[2] Chamberlain thought that twenty years were too long, and suggested that disfranchisement might be justified as the 'political disarmament of persons who have shown that they would use the vote as they have used the rifle to destroy the Empire'. H. W. Just destroyed his political chief's argument: if disfranchisement were justified not as punishment but as prevention, he minuted, it would invite the accusation that the constitution was being tampered with by indirect means. That argument, pushed to its conclusion, would lead to a reversion to Crown Colony government. What, he asked, was the difference in principle between subjecting Cape Afrikaners to 'political disarmament' and disfranchising the members of any party in Canada or Australia which advocated separation from Britain?

The right policy, it seems to me, is to have faith in the Dutch . . . and to give public expression to the view that once annexation [of the Republics] has taken place and things have settled down, all the rank and file will become . . . loyal subjects of the Queen without any hankering after a separate South African nation except as a federation forming an integral part of the Empire. I would not give them the satisfaction of thinking that they were feared . . . Ostensibly the war arose out of the demand for the franchise and for an honest distribution in proportion to population.[3]

No more was heard of 'political disarmament'.

The ministry had split down the centre and the prime minister had lost his parliamentary following. Chamberlain still did not wish Schreiner to resign but instead to rid himself of the Merriman faction and take in some Progressives. He instructed Milner to tell Schreiner privately that he alone stood between a continuance of parliamentary government and the suspension of the constitution.[4] But Schreiner had had enough. On 8 June he called a meeting of Bond members of Parliament and asked them to support him in passing legislation for the creation of a commission to try leading

---

[1] C.O. 48/546, f. 780. [2] Ibid., f. 620.
[3] Ibid., f. 750 seqq. [4] C.O. 48/546, f. 809.

rebels and for the disfranchisement for five years of the rest. The vote went against him by twenty-nine to eight; the feeling of the majority was that they would not 'take away the franchise from their own people'.[1] On 12 June Milner wrote to Schreiner that he must have a ministry which would give him unanimous advice, and once more suggested that the cabinet should be reconstructed.[2] Schreiner refused: there was no one fit for ministerial office, he said, among such personal followers as he possessed, and if he coalesced with the opposition he would lose all his influence over Afrikaners. On 13 June he resigned. In his parting letter to Milner he said: 'I had hoped to steer the ship of the Colony into the port of peace: but as I must hand her over to another pilot, I wish him a good voyage. She has not been hulled, though her tackle has been damaged here and there'.[3]

Milner viewed the departure of Schreiner with equanimity; he was, he telegraphed to Chamberlain on 15 June, no longer of service. He had got out of Schreiner all that there was to be got, and Schreiner had only taken 'his present so-called loyalist line' because he feared that otherwise the constitution would be suspended. 'Had his loyalty been genuine he could of course have kept office, in which case he was certain to have been able to pass the necessary measures.'[4] Milner developed this point of view in a dispatch of 19 June, in which he argued that the difference between the two wings of Schreiner's cabinet extended beyond the controversy over the rebels.

It was, to put it briefly, the difference between a desire to minimize and, if possible to get over, difficulties arising with Her Majesty's Government, and a desire to magnify, or at least not to try to find a way out of, those difficulties. Mr. Schreiner's idea was to accept in principle (while possibly regretting) the policy of Her Majesty's Government, and to seek to influence it in detail by friendly representations. The idea of the other section of the Cabinet was to resist that policy tooth and nail, to make it as invidious as possible in the eyes of their followers, and to stir up an agitation in England in the hope of reversing it.[5]

Milner sent for Sprigg. Schreiner had advised Rose Innes as his successor; but the titular leader of the opposition could hardly be passed over, and Sprigg accepted office with alacrity. The nominal state of the parties in the House of Assembly was: 'Afrikaners,' 51;

---

[1] Merriman PP., diary 9 June.   [2] C.O. 48/546, f. 809.
[3] Ibid., f. 811.   [4] Ibid., f. 815.   [5] Ibid., f. 836.

Progressives, 43; and the Speaker. Two Progressives (Rhodes and Edmund Garrett) were likely to be away for the entire session. There were five absentees from the ranks of the Afrikaners—two in prison, two who had fled the country and one who was 'mysteriously absent' in the Transvaal. Of those present there were 41 Progressives and 46 'Afrikaners'. The support of Schreiner and Solomon, with a handful of others who followed their example, gave Sprigg a precarious and friable majority. But it was enough for him to pass a bill of indemnity for acts done under martial law, to set up a special commission and to carry the disfranchisement proposals. (Schreiner's support for these measures caused Merriman to nickname him 'Treason Bill'.) Thereafter, Parliament was prorogued; it did not meet again until the war was over.

With the fall of Schreiner, the last restraints were lifted from the Afrikaner Bond. Unshackled by the responsibility of sustaining a ministry, its members could now denounce the war with a vehemence which exceeded anything that had gone before. The annual congress of the party, which met at the Paarl on 15 June, passed a resolution which referred to the war as 'bloody and unrighteous'. There was an organized boycott of English traders in some country towns. A speaker at Graaff-Reinet told an enthusiastic audience that England had only one friend in Europe—the unspeakable Turk. Rumours were spread of scandalous conduct by British troops on and off the field of battle. Once the passage of the Treason Bill became a foregone conclusion, the Bond turned its energies to a demand for a negotiated peace which should preserve republican independence. On 19 July Milner reported that feeling was worse than at any time since Black Week, and that only martial law in some districts and the confiscation of arms and ammunition in others prevented a new outbreak of rebellion. Racial hostility reached a crescendo at the end of the year, with the meeting of an Afrikaner Congress of the People at Worcester, at which inflammatory speeches were made and the usual resolutions passed demanding peace with independence for the Republics.

All this strengthened Milner's already formed opinion that the Cape Colony was unfit for responsible government. On 14 November he had written to Chamberlain that 'one is sometimes tempted to wonder, whether another rising would not really be the best thing in the long run. I believe it would, if it finally disabused the public mind at home of what I can only call the superstition that you can govern a country, in which the majority of citizens are your enemies, by a system of autonomy more complete than any Separatist ever proposed even for Ireland'.[1]

Before the end of the year, Milner's wish was gratified. On 16 December—Dingaan's Day—commandos under General Kritzinger and General Hertzog invaded the Cape, and the second rebellion began. To understand these developments, it will be necessary to consider events north of the Orange River during 1900.

[1] Milner MSS., vol. 25, f. 113.

CHAPTER THREE

THE LINGERING WAR

> My terms with the Transvaal Government are unconditional surrender.
>
> *Lord Roberts, June 1900.*
>
> Here you have a clean slate. Write 'English' on it.
>
> *Hely-Hutchinson to Milner, October 1900.*

FROM the moment when Kruger's ultimatum was received, it was clear that the British Government would be satisfied with nothing less than the annexation of the Transvaal. For a time, Britain's intentions towards the Orange Free State were less definite; but the invasion of the Cape, the purported annexations by Free State commandants, and the encouragement given to rebellion rapidly produced the conviction that annexation should extend to both republics. The very successes of the Boers worked against them in England. The speed of events, Campbell-Bannerman wrote to Bryce on 10 November 1899, had made previous points of controversy out of date. There was still room for speculation about the deeper origins of the war, but 'now the ordinary man, even if a Liberal, is saying: "All this may be very true and very interesting, but the disclosure since the war began of the vast war power of the Boers, far beyond anything that could be necessary against a raid or a revolt shows that they meant mischief against *us*, that they thought they could do for us; this explains their insolence and their ultimatum; and it shows that they must be put down".'[1]

L. S. Amery was speaking not only for the South African 'loyalists' and for *The Times* but was voicing the predominant opinion in Britain, when he wrote that 'I am very earnestly convinced that between annexation and complete evacuation of South Africa there can be no tolerable middle course.'[2] Lord Salisbury was quick to explain that his statement in November 1899 that Britain desired no territory referred only to her intentions before

[1] Add. MSS. 41,211, f. 61.
[2] Courtney PP., vol., vii, f. 121. Amery to Courtney, 29 December 1899

the war began. On 5 March after the first major Boer defeats, the two presidents offered to make peace in return for the recognition of 'the incontestable independence of the two republics as sovereign international States' and the assurance that the colonial rebels who had come to their help should suffer no harm. This offer was formally refused by Salisbury on 11 March; the British, he said, had been 'compelled to confront an invasion which has entailed upon the empire a costly war and the loss of thousands of precious lives. This great calamity has been the penalty which Great Britain has suffered for having in recent years acquiesced in the existence of the two republics'.

British supremacy and equal rights for white men in South Africa: these were the stated aims for which Britain was at war. More vaguely, there was a general feeling that something should be done to improve the position of the non-White peoples. At the beginning of January 1900 Chamberlain drew up a memorandum on the future settlement, which he sent to Milner for the private comments of himself and Hely-Hutchinson. The memorandum was for their eyes only; Milner was instructed to keep its existence secret, but to canvass the suggestions which it contained as though they were his own.[1]

Chamberlain at this stage was thinking aloud. His preoccupation, then as always, was with the problem of maintaining or establishing self-government, while retaining British supremacy, in a country in which the British were in a minority among the white population. It was his intention that the period of military rule in the Transvaal and Orange Free State, following the conquest of the republics, should be as brief as possible and should then be succeeded by representative government with or without an interlude of civil administration directly under the Crown. He looked to federation as the ultimate goal, and he was concerned therefore that there should be a British preponderance both in the individual colonies and throughout South Africa at large. A general British majority could be achieved only by immigration or by a marked alteration in breeding habits; but artifice might aid nature in the component parts of South Africa. He did not favour the union of the Transvaal and the Orange Free State in a single colony, as some had suggested; it would contain too many Afrikaners. For the same reason he was cautious when considering the territorial ambitions of Natal, for

1 Milner MSS., vol. 25, f. 11.

fear that too large an accretion of land would bring into that colony a disturbing weight of Afrikaners, concentrated in homogeneous areas. He suggested that the northern Cape might be joined to the Free State to form, as it were, a national home for the Boers. If that were done, and assuming that there was massive immigration into the Transvaal and that Rhodesia would enter a federation, four South African provinces out of five would have British majorities in their domestic legislatures, which would be reflected in the federal parliament. For the rest, he suggested the extension of the Cape franchise, which was based upon a property qualification which took no account of colour, to the rest of the country, the creation of self-governing municipalities in the former republics, the raising of loans for development and to provide for a contribution to the imperial exchequer for the cost of the war, and he asked for opinions on the status to be accorded to the Dutch language.[1]

In private to Milner, Chamberlain expressed himself more candidly and less sanguinely.[2] He dwelt on the difficulties of working institutions of self-government under conditions of Afrikaner predominance—hostility towards the Governor as the representative of Downing Street, the possibility that supplies might be refused, and the resentment which would be bred by imperial charges for the support of a garrison, for a sinking fund, for interest on loans and for a war contribution. But these difficulties were hardly avoidable. ' . . . I believe it is hopeless to attempt permanently to govern a white population with the tenacity and stubbornness of the Dutch by a Crown Colony system.' It might be possible, by manipulating boundaries, to divide South Africa into colonies that were either preponderantly British or preponderantly Afrikaner. He had already suggested that the Free State should be enlarged by the Afrikaner districts of the northern Cape; it might also be possible to partition the Transvaal—Pretoria and the Witwatersrand for the British, the rest for the Boers. But such arrangements, even if political opposition could be overcome, would still leave untouched the question of what form of government should be established in the Afrikaner areas. He asked for Milner's views on the appropriation of railways and public lands, to raise revenue and to settle new colonists.

[1] The memorandum is summarized in Headlam, ii. 41–1.
[2] Milner MSS., vol. 25., f. 11 seqq. 28 February 1900.

The possession of the Railways would also enable us without difficulty to raise money from the Boers by indirect taxation upon imports or exports levied at Imperial Customs Houses on the frontier. These Customs Houses, or something equivalent, would be necessary in any case to prevent the future introduction of artillery and munitions of war.

Having obtained security for the indemnity and the necessary taxation, we might give free institutions to the Dutch population and allow them to mould these according to their own desires subject, however, to some arrangement by which we could interfere if they ever abused the powers so conferred.

One essential condition would be the payment of taxes, strict equality between white races, and protection of the blacks. If there were any serious breach of these conditions, we might give the Governor power, with the consent of the Home Government, and by an Order-in-Council, to suspend the Constitution for fixed periods and temporarily to take the whole Government into the hands of the Imperial authorities.

Amid all these complexities, he proposed to hasten slowly. He did not think that there should be an immediate settlement at the end of the war—which was then quickly expected—but that a commission should be appointed from London, 'like the Mission of Lord Durham in Canada', to report and recommend. He mentioned as possible members Sir Henry Norman, Sir George Goldie and Lord Kitchener, with the addition of someone like Sir Edward Grey, 'as representing the best characteristics of the Opposition in this country', and perhaps one or two 'loyal Colonists'.

The suggestion of an imperial commission brought an instantaneous and almost violent reaction from Milner.[1] 'Resolutions are pouring in from all parts of the Colony and Natal, all of them containing a fervent expression of hope that the settlement may be inspired by the present High Commissioner. The Separatists have publicly proclaimed their hopes for the future, and their platform has two planks—the Independence of the Republics and the removal of Sir A. Milner. They recognize that the second is indispensable to any success in the first.'

Therefore, Milner pleaded, the appointment of a commission would be regarded as a sign of the withdrawal of confidence from himself. No such step had been demanded by public opinion either in Britain or in South Africa, he said. A commission would disagree, it would produce a compromise plan which would satisfy nobody but would encourage the Afrikaners to renew their pre-

[1] Ibid., f. 16, 5 March 1900.

tensions, no suitable colonists could be found to serve on it, and it would be regarded as yet another example of the government of South Africa by strangers. The loyalists, by whom he was 'absolutely trusted', 'will receive the appointment with dismay and—unless I am mistaken—with something like fury. They will find a parallel, not in the Durham Commission which indeed presents but few points of analogy (we already have our Lord Durham here, with the additional advantage of intimate local knowledge), but in the Royal Commission of 1881 from which they date all their troubles; and they will believe that another—as they always term it—betrayal is being prepared for them'.

For the rest, Milner favoured autocratic government directly under the Crown until the Afrikaners had accepted British supremacy. He agreed that no arrangement that could be advised would ever guarantee a permanent British majority in the Cape Colony; the answer, therefore, was to anglicize the Transvaal. To this end, he would keep the Transvaal free from any customs entanglements: otherwise, there would probably be demands for agricultural protection—'a farmers' weapon unsuited to industry'— and for the same reason he deprecated any partition of the Transvaal. That colony was to be transformed through industry, especially mining, and it was impossible to forecast where mineral deposits would be found; it would be a repetition of an old story if new goldfields were discovered in regions where the Afrikaners were in even local command. To partition the Cape would produce a grievance both among Afrikaners and among loyalists who would be placed under Afrikaners. In any event, to multiply entities would be to put more barriers in the way of an eventual federation.

He did not approve of an extension of the Cape franchise. 'It would be very unfortunate to raise the question of native voters. There would be practically none in the Transvaal, and for the sake of a theory it would be unwise to start with a conflict with the Whites. The Cape experience is not encouraging. If necessary the thing could possibly be brought about *sub silentio*'.

The territorial claims of Natal, he thought, were preposterous. The Natal ministers were, indeed, showing signs that they regarded the war as having been waged exclusively for their benefit. This temper was shared to some extent by Sir Walter Hely-Hutchinson, the Governor, who pointed out to Milner that Natal expected to be consulted on the settlement, 'and to have a voice in it bigger than in proportion to her size'.[1] His own views at this time were as embracing as the most fervent of Natal loyalists could have desired. 'I am not sure that the best solution would not be a big Natal, including Transvaal and Free State, with the representation adequately gerrymandered so as to be sure of British majority in the Assembly, and local assemblies with restricted and delegated powers, so that if the Free State Assembly were inclined to be disloyal it could do no real harm'. A less extreme version of this solution had already been suggested by H. Escombe, a Natal notable: to take land from the Transvaal, he thought, would be to establish an Alsace-Lorraine within Natal's borders; therefore, the Transvaal and Natal should be amalgamated into one colony, and the Orange Free State should be 'given to the Cape'.[2]

For the rest, Hely-Hutchinson's comments upon Chamberlain's memorandum produced little that was novel. He was against the use of Dutch in the conquered republics, on the grounds that if it were permitted the opportunities there for Natalians would be limited, because they could not speak the language. He thought that federation should neither be rushed nor postponed for so long that local opinion would harden against it; and he did not want the extension of the Cape franchise. 'People in Natal are very strongly against what they call the "blanket vote" in the Cape Colony: and their prejudices in this matter are believed to be shared by the bulk of the Uitlanders. No measure would annoy the Dutch more. I will only say at present that the subject should be approached tentatively and cautiously.'[3]

In short, no imagination was forthcoming from Natal, except in the formulation of territorial claims which no one else took seriously, and Milner was seeking to have his own hands tied as loosely as possible. To him, the end would be achieved through resolute administration, preferably under his own direction. The fewer promises that were made to the defeated, the better. He had the lowest opinion of the ordinary Afrikaner's idealism or attachment to abstract principles. On 31 January he had written to Chamberlain:

Of course, one thing the Bond will tell us is that, if we insist on putting an end to Republican Government the burghers of both states will fight to the last man. Nonsense! The idea that the individual Free Stater or Transvaaler cares so enormously as all that about his state, is a fiction of the political Afrikaners at headquarters. What the actual Boer on the veld cares about

---

[1] Ibid., vol. 18 (a), f. 7 seqq.   [2] Ibid., f. 31.   [3] Ibid., vol. 44.

intensely is his personal independence within the wide limits of his own domains. In his desperate appeal to the Boers to stick to the war last week, President Kruger felt it necessary to assure the burghers that we were *coming to take their farms from them.* That, and the companion lie, that we want to *put them under the Natives* is what keeps them fighting. It is a complete delusion that the men who are doing the bulk of the fighting care much about 'the great Afrikaner nation', or will shed the last drop of their blood for the political ambitions of Hofmeyr, Fischer and Steyn. They hate and dread the English, and they don't want to be bothered with them, if they can help it. But there are limits to what they will suffer for *a form of government* . . . [1]

II

In the early months of 1900 it seemed that military events might outrun even the tentative plans for reconstruction. Lord Roberts and his staff reached Cape Town on 10 January. Their arrival produced a fresh and imaginative direction of the war. Under the restless energy of Kitchener, a wagon train was assembled large enough to free an army corps from dependence upon railways, and thus to allow of marching and manœuvring instead of a head-on advance against prepared positions. Thus equipped, Roberts crossed the Modder River into the Orange Free State on 13 February and made a wide sweep to the east, outflanking the positions at Magersfontein in which General Cronje had held off the forces with which Lord Methuen had been trying to raise the siege of Kimberley. Roberts's cavalry, under General French, rode round the Boers and entered Kimberley on 15 February. Cronje abandoned his fortifications and retired with his entire wagon train towards Bloemfontein. He was intercepted at the Modder River near Paardeberg, entrenched himself in the river bed, and severely repulsed the frontal attacks which Kitchener, using his authority as chief-of-staff to overrule divisional commanders who were his seniors, pushed forward over open country. Thereafter, Cronje's position was heavily shelled. After holding out for eight days, Cronje surrendered with 4,000 burghers on 27 February, the nineteenth anniversary of the Boer victory at Majuba. On the following day, Buller at last relieved Ladysmith. On 13 March Roberts entered Bloemfontein unopposed. Six weeks later, after a halt forced upon him by the extent of typhoid fever among his troops, he resumed his advance along the

[1] Ibid., vol. 25, f. 61.

railway line to the Transvaal. He occupied Johannesburg on 31 May, Pretoria on 5 June. Thereafter he shepherded the Transvaal forces eastwards along the railway line to Lourenço Marques. President Kruger left his country and took refuge in Holland, turning over his authority to Schalk Burger as acting-president. By 1 September annexation proclamations had been issued both for the Orange Free State and for the Transvaal. It semed that the war was in its last stages and that it remained only to mop up isolated bands of burghers.

For the time being, Roberts was given plenary powers for the military administration of the annexed republics, with the proviso that he should consult the High Commissioner on all matters of political significance. After canvassing a variety of names, it was decided that the new colonies should be called the Transvaal and the Orange River Colony. (John Morley, in a speech in Oxford, commented: 'I am sure it is the first time in the history of this country that it has begun its acquisition of the territory of a white community by blotting out, as the Russian censor blots out an obnoxious newspaper article, the sacred word "free".[1])

Military administration, it had been decided, should last only so long as the necessities of war demanded. Milner was told in May that he was to be the administrator of the new colonies. He proposed to transfer himself as soon as he could to the Transvaal, taking the high commissionership with him. Throughout 1900 he sent dispatch after dispatch to Chamberlain, amplified by long private letters, setting out his plans for administration and reconstruction. He was alarmed lest he find himself committed in advance by premature arrangements made by the military, and especially lest he find that critical posts had been given to men of inferior ability whom he would find it difficult to remove. As soon as the situation permitted, he wished to send the imperial secretary, George Fiddes, as civilian adviser to Roberts. For the rest, he wanted to recruit his own administrators. He thought it best to keep the administration of the Transvaal and the Orange River Colony separate from the beginning; their problems were of a different order. The pastoral economy of the Orange River Colony presented no great complexities, apart from the technical problems of railway administration, police and taxation. This simplicity was very different from 'the various vast conflicting interests of the Transvaal, with the great

---

[1] *Manchester Guardian*, 11 June 1900.

mining groups jealously watching one another, the commercial community more or less pulling against the mining community, and the Boer farmers hostile to and suspicious of them both'.[1]

Therefore he wanted an administration which was neither aloof nor inflexible, and which should associate with itself the ablest of the local inhabitants. He looked to the creation of municipal institutions and district councils, the development of an educational authority, and the granting of semi-official status to the Chamber of Mines, the mine-owners' organization, to give breadth to his regime. At first, he advised caution in the imposition of new taxation, because to tax heavily before reconstruction was well advanced would 'be likely to give rise to an agitation for representative government, perhaps before we are ready for it.'

It was important, then, that military government should not have time to consolidate itself: the heads of departments whom he would rely upon in the future should be chosen quickly. Milner proposed to seek outside South Africa for men of first-rate ability: only 'the *fairly good man* is always obtainable here'. But it would not be easy to lure bright young men from England, unless they were available 'owing to some accident, which has thrown them out of the regular course of professional advancement; the accident, for instance, of having delicate lungs, to which South Africa owes much of its best talent'. They would have to be paid high salaries: 'South Africa is the most expensive place that I have ever lived in, and the Transvaal is the most expensive part of South Africa, and this it will continue to be for years to come—for civilized Europeans'. In particular, he made a suggestion which he admitted was 'startling' as to the head of the finance department of the Transvaal. 'The man I propose, if he were willing to come, is Mr. Patrick Duncan, one of the principal clerks of the Inland Revenue Department, who was at one time my private secretary in that office. He is very young—still, I think, under 30—but if he possesses the other necessary qualifications, youth, especially in South Africa, is rather an advantage than otherwise.'

This suggestion did, indeed, meet opposition in the Colonial Office, largely on the grounds of Duncan's youth: it was also argued that a Treasury man might be unlikely 'to fall in with Sir A. Milner's liberal ideas of expansion'.[2] Chamberlain cut short

[1] C.O. 417/290, f. 432. Milner to Chamberlain, 30 May 1900.
[2] Ibid., f. 247.

the developing discussion: 'I should let Sir A. Milner have Mr. P. Duncan if he desires it.'[1]

Duncan was the forerunner of a group of talented young men from Oxford whom Milner attracted to his service. They came later to be known as 'the kindergarten', a term of disparagement which they adopted with a certain pride. They brought with them vigour, dedication to their vocations, trained minds, incorruptibility, a common background, and enthusiastic respect and admiration for Milner. Their influence, direct and indirect, on the government of South Africa and thereafter on the development of the British Empire, was pervasive and extended. Besides Duncan, their number included Lionel Curtis, Robert Hichens, Philip Kerr, Robert Brand, Geoffrey Dawson and Richard Feetham. John Buchan joined them later; L. S. Amery was with them in spirit. With them, Milner relaxed as perhaps he relaxed nowhere else.

III

For the most part, Chamberlain allowed Milner a free hand in preparations for reconstruction of the Transvaal; in two matters, however, he asserted his authority. The first concerned the future status of the Dutch language. Milner would have excluded it from the routine business of administration, allowed it in the courts only when a litigant knew no English, dropped it gradually from school curricula and, in general, relegated it to the position of a local dialect which, he hoped, would wither for lack of nourishment. Chamberlain was doubtful whether a policy of official discouragement would be likely to succeed. He quoted the unbroken development of Dutch in the Cape, although English had been the sole language of education and administration between 1827 and 1882. The experience of the Cape, he wrote, 'seems to indicate that there would be little chance of ousting Dutch by a policy of proscription, and I think that it is, on political grounds, highly desirable to avoid the appearance of attempting such a policy, more particularly in view of the importance which has been attached to the complaints made by the Uitlanders in the late South African Republic with regard to the proscription of English.'[2]

His inclination was that English should be the official language,

1 Ibid., f. 249.
2 Milner MSS., vol. 44. Chamberlain to Milner, 22 January 1901.

but that Dutch should be allowed in the legislature and courts, and taught in school at the discretion of parents.

The second matter concerned the future capital of the Transvaal: the question dragged on until 1902, but it will be convenient to summarize the controversy here. On 18 June 1900, Chamberlain asked Milner for his opinion on whether Pretoria, because of its torrid climate, should remain as the capital. There were, he said, disadvantages in superseding Pretoria by Johannesburg; since the Raid and more particularly since the recent attacks made upon him for his business interests by Lloyd George, Chamberlain was especially sensitive to any accusation that he was favouring capitalist interests. Was Johannesburg not too directly under the influence of the mining industry? At about the same time, an agitation in favour of Johannesburg began among the former Uitlanders. At this time, Milner claimed that he had an open mind on the matter though, he said, 'I certainly lean rather against Johannesburg.'[1] He was determined that he was not going to pander to the Johannesburgers or allow them to force the hand of the British Government. Roberts was strongly against any change. 'Johannesburg may collapse altogether some day should the mines cease to produce gold', he wrote to Milner on 4 July 1900. 'It is what may be termed an accidental town.'[2]

When Milner moved from Cape Town to the Transvaal, he settled himself in Johannesburg and established part of his administration there and part in the old republican offices in Pretoria. He did not disguise his dislike of Pretoria, and on 7 September 1901 the leading British residents of Pretoria felt their interests sufficiently threatened to cause them to draw up a petition protesting against a removal of the capital. Milner replied that he would not prejudge the issue; ultimately the matter would have to be decided by the Transvaal legislature, when it was established. In the meantime, he had no intention of moving his own staff and household.[3] Chamberlain did not approve, and Milner argued the case with tenacity. He would not accept the contention that the administration would be unduly under capitalist influence in Johannesburg; on the contrary, it was the duty of the Governor to keep in touch with the predominant industry and he could only do this if he shared part of its environment. As to the alternative: 'The more I see of Pretoria the

[1] Headlam ii. 147.   [2] Ibid., ii. 82. Milner to Roberts, 28 June 1900.
[3] Milner MSS., vol. 45, f. 26.

more I am impressed by its unfitness to the be capital of anything . . .
It will certainly never be the capital of British South Africa, if that
country is going to remain a part of the Empire.' He asked that his
own convenience should be considered, said that he was over-
worked and pointed out that he could not endure to live in Pretoria,
'the most enervating place I know'.[1] Chamberlain ended the matter
on 17 April 1902.[2] He would not require Milner to move, but the
capital must remain in Pretoria. The division of departments between
the two towns, he said, would 'result not merely in inconvenience
but in grave danger to the efficiency of the Government' and he
would not, therefore, allow Johannesburg to be used indefinitely as a
second seat of the administration. As matters stood, he said, members
of Milner's purely personal staff were usurping the functions of those
who held official positions but were isolated in Pretoria. 'Such a
system would be open to obvious objection even if members of the
Administrator's personal staff had the same training and experience
as the chief officials of the Colony.' On more general grounds, he
thought that the influence of Johannesburg was corrosive:

It is not possible for any man, however strong his personality, to escape
being influenced by the social atmosphere in which he lives from day to
day, and the influence of that of Johannesburg seems to me to be one to
which it is not desirable to expose the members of the Administration.
I do not wish to be understood as holding that the moral tone of Johannesburg society is lower than that of similar society elsewhere; my objection
is that it necessarily lacks that diversity which in other great cities renders
public opinion healthy and impartial. No doubt Johannesburg society
contains the same elements as other great cities; but in Johannesburg all
these must of necessity take their tone from the one overshadowing
industry on which they are dependent, and without which Johannesburg
would not exist.

IV

Desultory planning continued throughout 1900; but schemes
on paper became increasingly unrealistic as it became clear that
the fall of Bloemfontein and Pretoria had not produced the conquest
of the republics. The Boer forces had been scattered, not broken.
Milner recognized this before the soldiers. 'The Boers die hard',
he wrote in July, 'and what is worse, they have never been properly
beaten.'[3] That judgement represented a change in his opinion. In
the earlier period of the war, he had regarded the Cape Afrikaners as

[1] Ibid. vol. 44, 21 December 1901.   [2] Ibid.   [3] Ibid., vol. 25.

the most insidious enemies of the British Empire; the burghers of the Orange Free State and the Transvaal, he thought, would soon become discouraged by military failure once the British took the offensive. He had wanted no terms to be offered: the formula of 'unconditional surrender', borrowed from General Grant, was suggested by Milner, approved by Chamberlain, endorsed by Lord Salisbury, and communicated to the Boers by Lord Roberts in June.[1]

The expectation that republican resistance would soon collapse was reflected in the British attitude towards the burghers on commando. In the first proclamation after his invasion of the Orange Free State, Roberts declared that those burghers who returned to live peacefully at home would not be penalized, in their persons or property, for having fought. He expanded this in his third proclamation, of 15 March, into an implied promise of British protection to those who gave up their arms and signed a pledge to take no further part in the war. This 'oath of neutrality' (as it was somewhat confusingly called) was as follows: 'I will not take up arms against the British Government during the present war, nor will I at any time furnish any member of the Republican forces with assistance of any kind, or with information as to the numbers, movements, or other details of the British forces that may come to my knowledge. I do further promise and swear to remain quietly at my home until the war is over.'

Many of the burghers who surrendered and took this oath— the 'hands-uppers', as they came to be called—were confronted by a cruel dilemma. The Boer Governments refused to recognize the annexations or to concede to those whom they still regarded as republican subjects the right to contract out of the war. The commandos rounded up those burghers whom they encountered during their operations and swept them back, sometimes by force, into military service. Many an individual was faced with the grim alternative of being treated by the British as an oath-breaker or by his own people as a renegade; and usually it was his own people who presented the immediate alternative more compellingly. The British were unable to protect many of those who had returned to their farms, especially in remote districts, from the wrath of their country-men. At the same time, commandos began to raid British communications. Roberts attempted to counter this by exacting retribution from civilians, as a means of deterrence. On 16 June 1900 he pro-

[1] Milner MSS., vol. 44.

claimed that damage to railways, bridges and telegraph wires could
not be done 'without the knowledge and connivance of the neighbouring inhabitants and the principal civil residents in the districts concerned'; therefore, whenever such incidents occurred, he would hold
these civilians responsible 'for aiding and abetting the offenders',
would burn houses in the vicinity and would confine the principal
inhabitants as prisoners of war.[1] Three days later he proclaimed a
doctrine of collective responsibility. A levy would be made on the
property of civilians, and: 'The houses and farms in the vicinity of
the place where the damage is done will be destroyed, and the
residents in the neighbourhood dealt with under Martial Law.'
Further, he ordered that civilians should be compelled to travel
on military trains over those sections of the railway which might be
blown up. This practice, regarded in the Colonial Office as equivalent
to the taking of hostages, was forbidden after Chamberlain had
remonstrated with the War Office at the end of July. Its underlying
fallacy was demonstrated by John Morley:

... I would like to ask you ... to consider whether because somebody
else is a bandit and brigand and ruffian it is a very just thing to put me,
who am not a bandit, brigand or ruffian, upon the engine of a train and
jeopardize my life. That is one consideration. But there is a second.
Suppose the train-wrecker to be a brigand and a bandit, I do not suppose
he will much care if a quiet, respectable man like myself is put upon an
engine and driven into these dangerous traps. But, third, who are the
men who are put on the trains? They are the men who would not fight on
commando. Therefore, the fighting Boers will not care a straw for such
men coming to grief by the wrecking of the trains.[2]

By the middle of 1900 the war had changed its nature. The
'gentleman's war' was over—if warfare may ever be regarded
thus, except in sentimental retrospection. It was in this second
phase that the British Army did much, because of the manner in
which it was directed, to assist in creating an Afrikaner nationalism
more cohesive, more vengeful and more ambitious than the
'Afrikanerdom' which Britain had set out to break. More and
more, the activities of the British Army assumed the characteristics
of a punitive expedition. It was more than coincidence, perhaps,
that both Roberts and Kitchener had made their early military
reputations against semi-savage opponents.[3] In the first period

[1] Proc. No. 5 of 1900.   [2] Speech at Arbroath, 31 October 1901.
[3] See the observations in A. M. S. Methuen, *Peace or War in South Africa* (1st
ed., 1901), *passim*.

of the war, said Winston Churchill, blood flowed freely, but from a healthy wound; in the second period, the wound was sluggish and festering.[1] Much of what was done had its root in the reluctance of British commanders to recognize the fact that the war had not been ended by the annexation of the republics. The Boer armies were still in being; the republican governments, constantly on the move though they were, still exercised authority and commanded obedience; there was no effective occupation either of the greater part of the Orange Free State or the Transvaal. Nevertheless, the fiction was maintained that the continued resistance was the work of bands of irregular troops.

In August Roberts proclaimed that those who had broken the oath of neutrality would in future be punished by death, imprisonment or fine, and that all burghers in occupied territory who had not taken the oath would be treated as prisoners of war and 'transported or otherwise dealt with as I may determine'.[2] On 1 September, he issued a further proclamation to the effect that all burghers of the Orange Free State, except those who had been continuously in arms since the annexation, had become British subjects and that any resistance from them would be regarded as rebellion. On 14 September, after announcing the resignation and departure of Kruger, he declared that no prisoners of war would be released until those Boers who were still in arms had surrendered unconditionally. Except where Botha was in command of the main army of the Transvaal, he continued:

the war is degenerating, and has degenerated, into operations carried on in an irregular and irresponsible manner by small, and in very many cases, insignificant bodies of men.

I should be failing in my duty to Her Majesty's Government and to Her Majesty's Army in South Africa if I neglected to use every means in my power to bring such irregular warfare to an early conclusion.

The means which I am compelled to adopt are those which the customs of war prescribe as being applicable to such cases. They are ruinous to the country and entail endless suffering on the burghers and their families, and the longer this guerilla warfare continues, the more vigorously must they be enforced.

This amounted to a confession of military failure. By the middle of 1900 there were a quarter of a million British soldiers in South Africa, but they were strung out along many hundreds of miles of

---

[1] Quoted by Morley at Arbroath.   [2] Proc. No. 12 of 1900.

communications. It was demonstrated in South Africa, as it was demonstrated in Cuba and the Philippines at about the same time, that a large and elaborate army may be effective only when it is opposed by another large and elaborate army. The British were neither equipped nor trained to counter the operations of the small, swiftly moving commandos. March Phillipps, a captain in Rimington's Guides (which was one of the most efficient of the British mounted formations) wrote of the prevalent tactics: 'As for our wandering columns, they have about as much chance of catching Boers on the veldt as a Lord Mayor's procession would have of catching a highwayman on Hounslow Heath . . . [the Boers] are all round and about us like water round a ship, parting before our bows and reuniting round our stern. Our passage makes no impression and leaves no visible trace.'[1]

V

The hand of the British soldier fell lightly upon the enemy, but heavily upon the countryside. The methods which Roberts had threatened to use in September had already been used for some months: they amounted to the burning of farms. The first protest from the two Boer presidents to Roberts, against the destruction of farms, was sent on 3 February; Roberts replied three days later denying that such actions were in accordance with his orders.[2] The presidents reiterated their protest on 19 February. *The Times* correspondent in Bloemfontein, in a report dated 27 April, said that a column had been sent out to 'render untenable' the farms of burghers who had broken the oath of neutrality.[3] The burnings spread into the Transvaal as the British Army moved northwards; Botha protested to Roberts on 4 July, mentioning that his own home, near Standerton, had been destroyed. General de Wet, commandant-general of the Free State, protested on 10 July and threatened that, if burnings continued, he would order reprisals both in the Free State and in the British colonies. (De Wet's own farm had been one of the first to suffer under the doctrine of collective responsibility announced by Roberts in June.) The evidence suggests that the fate of Boer farms depended in great measure upon the attitude of the individual British commanders, exercising the wide discretion allowed them by the commander-in-chief. It was argued that,

---

[1] *With Rimington* (1901), p. 123.
[2] Emily Hobhouse, *The Brunt of the War* (1901), p. 4.   [3] Ibid., p. 10.

since the Boers wore no uniforms, it was impossible to distinguish between combatants and civilians; that farms had become bases of supply for the enemies; that British forces were sniped at from behind farm walls; and, in short, that military necessity justified destruction. In September there were reports that British columns were 'sweeping the country'; by then, farm-burning had acquired a momentum of its own. It was done with a casual and undiscriminating ruthlessness. March Phillipps (who strongly disapproved) wrote of the operations of his own column:

Farm-burning goes merrily on, and our course through the country is marked as in prehistoric ages by pillars of smoke by day and fire by night. We usually burn from six to a dozen farms a day; these being about all that in this sparsely-inhabited country we encounter. I do not gather that any special reason or cause is alleged or proved against the farms burnt. If Boers have used the farm; if the owner is on commando; if the line within a certain distance has been blown up; or even if there are Boers in the neighbourhood who persist in fighting—these are some of the reasons. Of course the people living in the farms have no say in these matters, and are quite powerless to interfere with the plans of the fighting Boers. Anyway, we find that one reason or another generally covers pretty nearly every farm we come to, and so to save trouble we burn the lot without enquiry; unless indeed, which sometimes happens, some names are given in before marching in the morning of farms to be spared.[1]

Phillipps commented that those who thought that the Boers could thus be terrorized into surrender were tragically mistaken. 'There will be a Dutch South African conspiracy, but it will be one of our own making. We shall have our treatment of these people to thank for it. Be sure of this, that for every house up here that is destroyed, three or four in the south are slowly rousing to arms.' Many soldiers and civilians thought that the burnings were sickening and unwise. 'What fool in his folly', Lionel Curtis, who was then on Milner's staff, wrote home, 'taught us we could prevent men from brigandage by making them homeless?'[2] Colonel Seely, who returned to England from service in South Africa after he had been elected to the House of Commons in his absence, remonstrated personally with Chamberlain and drew the reply: 'All you soldiers are what we call pro-Boers.'[3] This retort was far from expressing Chamberlain's inner feelings on the matter. Both he and Milner disapproved of a policy

[1] *With Rimington*: Letter from Frankfort, O.F.S., of 23 November 1900.
[2] *With Milner in South Africa* (1951), p. 142.
[3] J. E. B. Seely, *Adventure* (1930), p. 90.

which was transforming into a desert the territory which Britain would have to restore and administer, and was increasing bitterness in the hearts of those whom it was intended to transform into loyal British subjects. Both Chamberlain and Milner, however, were in general powerless to intervene when confronted by the commander-in-chief's insistence that the destruction was demanded by military necessity. In October Milner protested strongly but ineffectually. Punitive measures against individuals who had offended against the usages of war, he said, could be justified; but this was a very different thing from the 'indiscriminate burning of all the houses in a particular neighbourhood, simply to make it untenable by the enemy . . . To that, I object, thinking it (1) barbarous, and (2) ineffectual'.[1]

It is worth noting that Milner used the adjective 'barbarous' to describe British military methods eight months before Campbell-Bannerman's phrase, 'methods of barbarism', rang round Europe. Orders were, indeed, sent from London in November that farms were to be burnt only when a criminal action could be proved against their owners. However, St. John Brodrick, who had succeeded Lansdowne as Secretary of State for War after the election of 1900, added in a telegram to Roberts: 'Severe methods are inevitable, and in their ultimate result humane as tending to bring the war to a close.'[2] In November, a British Blue Book gave details of the burning of more than 600 farms in the Orange Free State; but these records dated only from June, and burning had begun several weeks earlier.[3]

Roberts replied to Brodrick, assuring him that measures taken against what he described as treachery were 'severe and permanent'; their effect was shown by the fact that 'women and children are flocking into the towns for food, which they cannot get in the country'.[4] On 23 November Brodrick pointed out to Roberts that it was not justifiable in terms of the usages of war to destroy property in reprisal for the actions of raiders coming from a distance, without the connivance of the local inhabitants; but he weakened this admonition by conceding the overriding force of military considerations.[5] Kitchener, when he took over the chief command at the end of November, telegraphed to the Secretary of State:

1 Milner MSS., vol. 25. Milner to Chamberlain, 28 October 1900.
2 War Office Confidential Telegram No. 365, 7 November 1900.
3 Cd. 605.   4 War Office Confidential Telegram No. 368.   5 Ibid., No. 381.

'I have let it be generally known that I am not in favour of burning farms.'[1]

Roberts's report of the influx of homeless and famished families into the towns indicated a new problem—the treatment of refugees. At first it had been Roberts's intention to throw the care of these people upon the commandos. On 2 September he had notified Botha that the dependants of the belligerents would no longer be allowed to live in the towns. 'This is no longer a matter of commissariat, but rather of policy,' he said, 'and in order to protect ourselves against the transmission of news to our enemies.'[2] He proposed therefore to hand them over to the Boers. But this was a practical impossibility; and the British therefore set up 'camps of refuge'. These, as they were first projected, would serve a number of purposes: they could be used as protected areas where un-relapsed oath-takers could exist without molestation from the 'bitter-enders'; they could provide subsistence for the destitute; and, after Roberts's proclamation of September, they could be used as detention centres for those whom it had been decided to treat as prisoners of war. From the first, they were under the direct control of the army. Milner approved of them in principle, but regarded their establishment as a transition to what he called 'reconstruction under arms'—the settlement of Afrikaners who were weary of the war in protected areas where they could gradually return to their normal occupations. On 23 August he wrote to Roberts that the duration of the war would depend largely upon what policy Britain adopted towards those who surrendered volun-tarily. He had changed his mind in the past few months, he said, and he now thought that it was not profitable to allow surrendered Boers to return haphazardly to their farms, from which they might be commandeered for further service against the British. Nor did he want to transport Boers overseas, because their horror of the sea might deter them from giving themselves up. Therefore, he wanted large prisoners' camps.[3] A month later he crystallized his proposals, and emphasized the political consequences of military operations. The alternative to 'months of desultory chasing of guerillas', he said, was to set up protected areas under settled government. This would admittedly be a slow process, but it would

---

[1] Ibid., No. 393.   [2] Milner MSS., vol. 45, f. 77.
[3] Ibid., f. 85. Milner to Roberts, 21 September. In the event, Milner did not send this letter.

drive a wedge into the core of Afrikanerdom, dividing those who were ready to collaborate with their conquerors from those who were resolved to continue to the bitter end; this division, by judicious management, might be prolonged into the days of peace. What he was suggesting would not bring quick results but, he implied, the army was producing no significant results at all. He particularly disapproved, he said, of 'scouring . . . a possibly much larger area without leaving anything behind us except the destruction we may have caused'.[1] A few days later he sent a letter remonstrating against Roberts's proposal to treat members of the commandos as rebels:

. . . in common fairness I do not see how we can so treat them as long as we do not merely annex, but *effectively occupy*. When we have driven the enemy out of a District, and *hold on to it*, establishing civil government and doing our best to maintain it, I think we are justified in proclaiming that any inhabitant of such district found in arms against us, or harbouring the enemy, shall be treated with the utmost severity, even with death.

But when we merely march through a District, even several times, without attempting to govern or hold it, I hardly feel that we can deal equally severely with its inhabitants, if, being left to their fate, they take up arms—possibly, indeed probably, under compulsion.

Hence, he wanted the army to 'kraal all we catch'. Later, men could be sorted out in the prison camps, and those who had given up the struggle in spirit was well as in person could be set at liberty under protection. Every settled district would be an object-lesson, encouraging others to surrender.

This policy was tried, but only in certain areas and there without continuity. In particular, the commander-in-chief repeatedly allowed garrisons to be withdrawn from districts in which 're-construction under arms' had begun, to take part in operations elsewhere, leaving the resettled Boers to make a choice between becoming refugees or risking the descent of a commando upon them. In particular, Milner complained that British officers showed no discrimination between Boers who were still enemies at heart and Boers who were trying to collaborate. On 14 January 1901 he wrote to Kitchener that 'there is no doubt that we are imprisoning some people who ought never to have been imprisoned at all, but who, after surrendering, remaining loyal, and being, in some instances, bullied by their own people for doing so, were subsequently arrested by us in error . . . I am sure that . . . the separation of the sheep from

1 Ibid., f. 85.

the goats and the release—under control—of a few particularly white sheep, would have a most salutary effect'.[1] Milner's suggestions had little effect. In 1901, after Kitchener succeeded Roberts, military control became tighter and less responsive to civilian argument.

[1] Ibid., vol. 45 (*b*), f. 22.

CHAPTER FOUR

'METHODS OF BARBARISM'

> When is a war not a war? When it is conducted by
> methods of barbarism in South Africa.
>
> *Sir Henry Campbell-Bannerman, June 1901.*

AT THE end of November 1900, Lord Roberts handed over the
command to Lord Kitchener, and returned to England to be re-
warded with an earldom, the Garter, a parliamentary grant of
£100,000 and the office of commander-in-chief of the British
Army. It was some time before it was generally realized that the
war was not over, and that the Boer forces, broken up into
self-contained and self-supporting commandos, purged of the
weaker brethren, unencumbered by wagon-trains or artillery,
were more elusive, if not more formidable, than before. At the
end of November, at the same time as the transfer of command,
the Boers took the decision once more to invade the Cape Colony.
In part, this was an act of reprisal against the devastations in the
Orange Free State; in part, it was a decision forced upon them
by those devastations, since it was increasingly difficult to obtain
supplies; in part, it was a last effort to obtain reinforcements by
encouraging a British colony to rebellion. The war had become
a double contest of attrition, the British seeking to wear away
the Boer forces, the Boers to wear away the British patience and
resolution.

Patience was a virtue which Lord Kitchener possessed in no great
abundance. His mastering obsession was to end the war as soon as
possible by any means which might seem to be immediately
effective; he paid little attention to the political consequences
his actions might produce. There was an overpowering anxiety
in his mind: that the office of commander-in-chief in India, which
he regarded as the proper and desirable reward of his services, might
be disposed elsewhere if he were tied down by protracted operations
in South Africa. Later, when a certain reaction against Lord Roberts

set in, Kitchener was determined not to leave South Africa until he had finished the war; there would be no premature jubilation on his account. Kitchener had many friends in high places in Britain; he well knew that there were two sharply contrasting opinions as to his suitability for the Indian Command. Lord Curzon, the Viceroy, wanted him, and he had supporters within the Ministry. The opposition came from the Palace. On 5 October 1900, the Queen let Lord Salisbury know that she felt strongly that Kitchener was, by experience and disposition, 'eminently unsuited' to the position, that she could not agree to his appointment, and that she thought that his talents could be better exercised at the War Office.[1] A week earlier Bigge had written privately, for Salisbury's information, that the Queen 'will not hear of Lord Kitchener's going to India—though she admires him immensely she does not think his general manner would go down with the natives'. The opposition begun by the Queen was continued after her death by Edward VII. As late as February 1902, when the matter was becoming urgent, he wrote to Brodrick that he had 'grave doubts' whether Kitchener was the right man for India, 'as he has absolutely no knowledge of the country and people'. Two days later, the King reiterated his objections but said that he would no longer press them, in the face of the Viceroy's repeated requests for Kitchener.[2] In April 1902, the appointment of Sir Power Palmer who, on the death of Sir William Lockhart in March 1900, had been appointed acting commander-in-chief in India, first for one and then for a second year, was extended for a final six months, to expire in October 1902. By February, therefore, Kitchener's immediate future was as good as settled; but in the meantime he had endured nearly eighteen months of tortured ambition, during which it seemed that the longer the war lasted the slighter became his chances of achieving what he then regarded as the prize of his life. These considerations were to have an important effect upon his actions. Kitchener had inherited from Roberts almost plenary powers to act as military necessity seemed to require. He exercised these powers sometimes without Milner's knowledge or approval, sometimes in bland contradiction to Milner's wishes or policy. He alternated between calculated conciliation and calculated ferocity.

His first actions seemed to show an awareness of Milner's policy of dividing Afrikanerdom from within. Milner had, in furtherance

[1] Salisbury PP.   [2] Ibid.

of 'reconstruction under arms', been trying to separate 'tame' from 'wild' Boers in the prison camps, and to encourage, with promises of immediate protection and later preferment, the tame Boers to accept British rule and to use such influence as they had with their companions still in the field. In December 1900, Kitchener encouraged the formation in Pretoria of 'Burgher Peace Committees', composed of Boer notables who believed that further resistance was useless and who were prepared to send emissaries to plead with the commandos to surrender. The moment for such advances was not well chosen: de Wet in the Free State, and Botha and de la Rey in the Transvaal, had won local victories, and Generals Kritzinger and Hertzog had begun the invasion of the Cape. The emissaries of peace were regarded and treated as traitors. One of them, Morgendal by name, was flogged and shot by de Wet's burghers; the Blue Book which publicized the event hinted strongly that de Wet would be tried for murder if the British laid hands upon him.[1] The chairman of the Peace Committee, Meyer de Kock, who had visited the Transvaalers, was sentenced to death by a council of war and executed by a firing squad.[2] In short, the activities of the Peace Committee failed to influence the commandos.

Nevertheless, these men put forward, and Kitchener accepted, a suggestion which was to have profound consequences. The 'camps of refuge' should be used also as camps of concentration for the families of men still on commando, where they should be subjected to a certain amount of hardship. On 27 December 1900, when informing the Secretary of State for War of the formation of the burgher peace committees, Kitchener added that Boers who surrendered as a result of these efforts would 'be allowed to live with their families, property, and livestock in laagers, under our protection near [the] railway in their district'.[3] After the failure of the committees, the camps became repositories for all Boers who were swept up by Kitchener's columns. Elaborating on this policy, in June 1901, Kitchener admitted that an additional reason for the camps was as a means of inducing Boers to surrender so as to rejoin their families.[4] To this end, there were at first differential diets for those who had surrendered and those who had been interned. The weekly rations in the Natal

1 Cd. 903   2 Ben Viljoen, *My Impressions of the Anglo-Boer War* (1902), c. 32.
3 War Office Confidential Telegram No. 424.   4 Ibid., No. 559A.

camps for voluntary inmates (with those for the interned in brackets) were:

	meal	salt	coffee	sugar	meat
Adults	7(7)lb.	4(4)oz.	6(4)oz.	12(8)oz.	2(nil)lb.
Children under 12	$3\frac{1}{2}(3\frac{1}{2})$lb.	2(2)oz.	6(4)oz.	8(8)oz.	nil(nil)lb.

In the opinion of a prison doctor, the diet for the voluntary inmates was deficient in fats and phosphates, and that for those interned was 'not consistent with the maintenance of health for any lengthened period'.[1] This differentiation was discontinued on orders from London early in 1901.

II

'Unconditional surrender' still remained the official British policy. Nevertheless, in February 1901, Kitchener opened peace negotiations with General Botha on his own responsibility, using Botha's wife as an intermediary. At the end of February, Kitchener and Botha met for lengthy negotiations at Middelburg, in the Eastern Transvaal. Milner was not consulted on Kitchener's intentions, and played no part in the discussions, although he expressed his opinions emphatically on the draft terms of peace which were formulated for consideration. Kitchener had made it clear that he was not prepared to consider any proposals which left independence to the Republics. However, the draft proposals presented to the Boers, with the approval of the British Government, could have been considered as moderate. The new colonies were to be governed from the first by a Governor and an executive council consisting of the principal officials, with a nominated legislative council containing unofficial members to which a representative element should be added 'as soon as possible' as an intermediary step to responsible government. Natives would not be enfranchised until a representative element had been added to the legislature, and the franchise which might then be conceded would be under such conditions that did not 'endanger the just supremacy' of the white races. The Boers would be given guarantees that private property,

1 Milner MSS., vol. 19, f. 43.

the property of churches and the funds of public trusts would not be expropriated, and that they would be given assistance to restock and rebuild their farms. Kitchener would have gone much farther. He wished for representative government almost at once; he wished a full amnesty for all rebels, with disfranchisement as the sole punishment, he would have the British Government assume the legal debts of the Republics up to the sum of £1,000,000, and he proposed that the Boers should be assisted to rehabilitate themselves by an outright gift of money. Chamberlain was not prepared to go so far, and he was supported by Milner on three matters—the postponement of representative government, the refusal of amnesty, and the refusal to assume the debts of the Republics. (Chamberlain was prepared, however, to set apart £1,000,000 to repay the inhabitants of the new colonies for goods legally requisitioned.) Milner agreed with Kitchener that a gift would be administratively preferable to a loan.

The Transvaalers, it was clear, were showing themselves more disposed to consider peace terms than their comrades-in-arms of the Orange Free State; but it is doubtful whether the terms offered at Middelburg had any chance, at that stage, of being accepted. The Free State had not been consulted, and President Steyn was incensed when he learnt of the negotiations. Botha had told Kitchener, at the beginning of the negotiations, that the Boers would accept nothing less than their own independence and an amnesty for rebels. When the terms were later discussed with the Free Staters, de Wet said firmly that it was profitless to examine the proposals in detail 'as the only object for which we are fighting is the independence of our Republics and our national existence.'[1] However, it was some time before the Boers communicated a formal refusal. Thereafter, after communicating with President Kruger and the delegation in Europe, the two republican governments met at Waterval in June, and formally resolved that: 'No peace conditions will be accepted by which our independence and national existence or the interests of our Colonial brothers shall be the price paid.' Kitchener did not hide his disappointment, and he came to the conclusion that the stumbling block was not independence but the refusal of an amnesty for rebels; for this, he blamed Milner. He wrote to Brodrick on 22 March 1901: 'Milner's views may be strictly just, but they are to my mind vindictive . . . We are now carrying the war on to put two or

---

1 Chamberlain PP. J.C. 14/4. Captured Boer Documents.

three hundred Dutchmen in prison at the end of it.'[1] In his account of the negotiations, Kitchener mentioned, and the British Government published, Botha's objections to Milner as the Governor of the new colonies. The differences between Milner and Kitchener lent currency to the view that it was the intransigence of the civilian, which sharply contrasted with the magnanimity of the soldier, which stood in the way of peace.

III

Kitchener had, in his own mind, offered generous terms and had been rebuffed and thwarted. He turned next to a policy of furious energy. He began the great drives by columns of mounted men, coupled with what was known as 'clearing the country'—blowing up or burning the farm buildings, destroying the crops and herding in the livestock. The inhabitants—mostly women and children—who were captured in these operations were sent to camps, which now began to multiply at selected points close to the railway line. Kitchener began to build a vast network of blockhouses connected by barbed wire barricades: these simple fortifications were at first used to protect the railways, and they were later extended across great areas of country as barricades. In work of this nature— improvisation backed up by energy and will—Kitchener had few equals in the British Army. By the end of the war, there were 8,000 blockhouses, and the barbed wire barricades stretched in all for 3,700 miles. The theory behind this activity was, in brief, that the country would be divided into an innumerable number of squares. In one after another, the country would be cleared until it could scarcely support life; such Boers as could be found would be rounded up; the process would then be continued to the next square. Militarily, the area of combat would be progressively diminished, so that eventually the commandos would be compressed into an area small enough for superior force to be brought against them. Provided that this policy were carried on long enough, and ruthlessly enough, it could scarcely fail: the Boer strength was slowly rubbed away, while the British had the resources of the Empire behind them. But it was slow, and above all it was ruinous to the country. It also spread bitterness and hatred among the enemy. Furthermore, it involved the abandonment in many areas of 'reconstruction under arms': settled districts suddenly found troops withdrawn, and in

[1] Quoted in Arthur, *Kitchener*, vol. 2, p. 26.

many instances these districts were occupied by the commandos, and the 'hands-uppers' or collaborators treated with some malevolence. Tactically, the results were not spectacular. The British mounted columns were slow and cumbrous. Not a single commando under a leader of the first rank was captured. Nor could it be claimed that the theatre of war was substantially reduced, for the commandos scattered still more widely and, most damaging of all, carried the war back to colonial soil. The second invasion of the Cape Colony was a more formidable episode than the half-hearted excursions of 1899. In April 1901, practically the whole of the Cape, except the ports and the native territories, was under martial law. In these areas, Kitchener had almost complete jurisdiction.

The jurisdiction of the special commissions within the Cape, set up to try rebels under the Treason Act of 1900, had expired on 12 April 1901, six months after the Act came into force. (There was no such time limit upon the activities of the special courts for rebels in Natal.) Sprigg's ministry agreed that, in consequence of the second rebellion, they were prepared to hand over jurisdiction to the military in areas in which martial law had been proclaimed. On 22 April 1901, Kitchener, with the concurrence of the ministry, issued a notice proclaiming that 'all subjects of His Majesty and all persons residing in the Cape Colony who shall, in districts thereof in which martial law prevails, be actively in arms against His Majesty, or who shall directly incite others to take up arms against him, or who shall actively aid or assist the enemy or commit any overt act by which the safety of His Majesty's forces or subjects is endangered, shall immediately on arrest be tried by court-martial, convened by my authority, and shall on conviction be liable to the severest penalties of the law.'

Kitchener used these wide powers with a severity which brought him into conflict with a ministry which had been regarded as thoroughly 'loyal'. In particular, Kitchener began to inflict the death penalty on rebels captured in the field. Some of these executions were carried out in revolting circumstances, in the compulsory presence of the condemned man's fellow-townsmen: this practice was forbidden on orders from London, but its use did nothing to endear British rule to the Cape Afrikaners. On 17 June, Kitchener was told by the War Office that the fact of rebellion alone, considering other sentences passed in the Cape, did not justify the death penalty, which should be confined to those who had 'committed outrages or attacked trains, or can be convicted of sniping or similar murderous proceedings . . .'[1] He was also told that it was preferable to shoot, rather than to hang, rebels. On 4 July Kitchener reported that he had confirmed the death penalty on two snipers.[2] Thereafter, Kitchener took a broad view of the discretion given to him by the War Office. Sniping, train wrecking, the burning of buildings, and, above all, the killing of Natives were treated as offences meriting death, and the penalty was extended from rebels to burghers of the republics.

From the beginning of the war it had been announced that this was to be a 'white man's war', and that the British had no intention of arming the non-White peoples except in their own defence. It was assumed that this meant only in the event of a Boer attack upon the native territories, especially Basutoland and the Transkei. This intention had been specifically confirmed by Brodrick in the House of Commons on 14 February. From the beginning of the war, however, each side had alleged that the other had made use of Native troops or auxiliaries. During the second invasion of the Cape, certain Boer commandants began to flog, and in some instances to shoot, Natives found with arms or judged guilty of spying. Kitchener, once again, took a broad view; he widened the interpretation of what constituted arming a non-White for his own protection. He used non-Whites as messengers, drivers, convoy guards and as watchmen in blockhouses. The Boers regarded these men as combatants. A cycle of reprisals was set in motion. Kitchener was evasive when repeatedly asked from London to give the number of non-Whites whom he had armed: eventually, in March 1902, he gave the total number of 10,053—2,496 Natives and 2,939 Coloureds in the Cape, 4,618 Natives in Natal, the Orange Free State and the Transvaal.[3] This was done on Kitchener's responsibility, with the strong disapproval of the Colonial Office.[4]

From the beginning of 1901, Kitchener authorized the summary execution of Boers captured while wearing British uniforms—a practice which many Boers had adopted once their own clothes had worn out, in ignorance that in so doing they had infringed one of the provisions of the Hague Convention.[5]

---

[1] War Office Confidential Telegrams, Nos. 550, 554.
[2] Ibid., No. 577.   [3] Ibid., No. 1004.   [4] Chamberlain PP, J.C. 11/6.
[5] Deneys Reitz, *Commando* (1929), *passim.*

IV

Such activities increased the bitterness of the struggle, but did nothing to solve the problem of how the Boer forces were to be brought to battle and defeated. By the middle of 1901, the War Office confessed itself to be barren of invention. A memorandum reviewed the means of ending the war, without much optimism. Three methods were considered: negotiations, a change of strategy, patience. Negotiations had been tried and failed. 'You cannot forever go on negotiating with various highwaymen.' No strategical innovations were likely to be profitable: there remained only patience.[1]

Patience did not appeal to Kitchener; he was always in search of a short cut. Early in May, he proposed the confiscation, after an announced date, of the property of all Boers still in the field. Milner was disposed to favour this proposal, suggesting that the property of a few selected leaders should be sold, not on the grounds that the annexations had made them rebels but on the general principle that the conqueror in war had a right even to the private property of the conquered.[2] The British Law Advisers stated that such a step would be an infringement of the Hague Convention: the Intelligence Department of the War Office gave its opinion that the operations of the commandos did not constitute guerilla warfare, that the Boer resistance, in the absence of effective British occupation, was legitimate and that confiscation, apart from its illegality, would be politically unwise, in that it would 'lead to the creation of a most dangerous class of white paupers who would probably be driven to lead the life of bandits for years to come and would lose no opportunity of raising the standard of revolt. To enforce confiscation in the case of particular men only, such as for example Louis Botha, would be unjust and would put against us in the future those leaders whose support is necessary to the peaceful settlement of the country'.[3]

In June Kitchener was recommending that all prisoners of war and their families should be permanently deported from South Africa: 'Settle on some island or country where we can safely establish the Boers, Fiji for instance, or get some foreign power to take them, such as France, to populate Madagascar. Send all the prisoners of war there and let their families join them; have no more

[1] J.C 11/4   [2] Ibid.   [3] Ibid.

voluntary surrenders and ship all as they are caught to the new settlement. We should then only have the surrendered burghers left and the country would be safe and available for white colonists . . .

These Boers are uncivilized Afrikaner savages with only a thin white veneer . . .'[1]

Kitchener, in short, was proposing to terrorize the enemy into defeat. 'Can nothing be done', he telegraphed with unconscious irony on 14 July, 'to bring it home to the Boers that they cannot carry on this state of affairs with impunity?'[2] He asked for permission to shoot every member of a small commando which had been captured in the Cape. The War Office refused; but the commandant, Lotter, was executed after a court-martial had convicted him on two charges of treason, two of murdering Natives, and one each of train-wrecking, marauding and 'disgraceful conduct'.

On 19 July Kitchener changed direction. He had conferred with General French at Middelburg, in the Cape, and had been impressed by two members of the Afrikaner Bond who assured him that only the fear of severe punishment deterred the Cape rebels from surrender. Kitchener proposed, therefore, to announce that those rebels who surrendered before 1 September should be treated leniently, and in no circumstances should be sentenced to more than one year's imprisonment, without confiscation of property; those who remained in arms should be dealt with most severely.[3] The Cape Ministry objected to this change of policy: they refused to limit the jurisdiction of tribunals, but were prepared to promise that the 'extreme penalty of the law' should not be inflicted upon those who surrendered before 1 September. They objected to Kitchener's proposal on the grounds that it would be interpreted as hesitancy, and would suggest that the British Government was offering new sets of terms.[4] Kitchener was exasperated, and complained that he was being hampered by political interference. Chamberlain was thoroughly unsympathetic: Kitchener, he inferred, was sulking because he could not have his own way. He had proposed, over the past few weeks, a series of drastic measures which were impracticable and absurd, illegal according to the laws of the Cape and Natal, and contrary to international usage. His last proposal was on different lines.

---

1 Magnus, *Kitchener* (1959), p. 185.
2 War Office Confidential Telegram No. 594.
3 Ibid. No. 608.   4 C.O. 417/349 f. 332.

He proposed to tell the rebels that if they came in before a certain date they should not have more than twelve months' prison but if they did not come in awful things would happen.

It was the last part of this that we chiefly objected to. We did not believe that they would come in and go to gaol for a year and if they did not we felt that we had no power to carry out any threats of wholesale punishment of a severer kind and should only make ourselves ridiculous by threatening what we could not perform. I am afraid Lord Kitchener attaches too much importance to 'bluff' but it is a very dangerous game when you do not hold the cards.[1]

Debarred, then, from wheedling the Boers, Kitchener turned once more to proposals of severity, this time involving the banishment for life of the leaders. Milner concurred: he wished to have power to remove irreconcilable enemies when peace came and, as he wrote to Chamberlain: 'Apart from everything else, it is a good thing if we can do *something* which Kitchener wants. It may steady him and give him fresh hope. His tendency to discouragement is, to my mind, one of the most serious features of the situation.'[2] The 'banishment proclamation' was issued on 7 August 1901. It read:

All commandants, field-cornets and leaders of armed bands, being burghers of the late Republics, still engaged in resisting Her Majesty's Forces, whether in the Orange River Colony or in the Transvaal, or in any other portion of His Majesty's South African Dominions, and all members of the Governments of the late Orange Free State and the late South African Republic, shall, unless they surrender before 15 September next, be permanently banished from South Africa; the cost of the maintenance of the families of all burghers in the field who shall not have surrendered by 15 September shall be recoverable from such burghers, and shall be a charge upon their property, moveable and immoveable, in the two Colonies.[3]

This was coupled with a proclamation, issued by Milner, legalizing the sale by public auction of the property of burghers still in the field, and the attachment of any bank balances which they might possess.[4]

These threats had no visible effect whatsoever; indeed, the military intelligence department at the Cape estimated that, if anything, more rebels had joined the commandos as a result. Sir Henry McCallum, who had succeeded Hely-Hutchinson as Governor of Natal, reported to Chamberlain that 'the leaders openly laugh at the idea of banishment as they say they are sure to be sent back as

[1] Chamberlain PP. J.C. 11/6. [2] Milner MSS., vol. 18.
[3] *Cape Gazette*. [4] C.O. 48/552, f. 716.

soon as a Liberal government is returned to power with the swing of the pendulum.'[1] Lord Roberts was more hopeful: he never expected, he said, that the proclamation would have any effect upon the leaders, who were too seriously committed to surrender, but he hoped that it would have a gradual effect upon the rank and file, once its terms had circulated throughout the country. 'In my opinion it would be better if the leaders did not surrender before 15 September as there might be a difficulty in dealing with some of them. Their banishment from South Africa for a term of years is, I consider, essential to the speedy settlement and future peace of the country, and this we need have no compunction in insisting upon if they continue hostile after the date named.'[2]

Once again, Kitchener took a wide interpretation of his powers, and brought down upon himself another rebuke. It had long been his contention that the Boer women were more implacable than the men, and that, in some way, they were responsible for prolonging resistance. He decided therefore to deport the wives of President Steyn and General de Wet. This was favoured neither by the Natal Ministry nor by the War Office. Kitchener cancelled the order, with reluctance; he thought, he told the Secretary of State for War, that he had discretion to deport anyone whose presence prolonged resistance: '. . . it seems to me . . . sentimental consideration ought not to be allowed to interfere with measures which seem necessary to us on the spot to check machinations of enemy and hasten the end. It is difficult for us to make use of discretion if steps taken under it are liable to be thus checked.'[3] Brodrick's reply was chilling: 'Sentiment would not have prevented our concurrence if real mischief was being done.'[4] Kitchener pressed the point; the women, he said, were an evil influence, and spread anti-British propaganda, and he had therefore selected six of the most irreconcilable to be deported as an example. On 22 November, Brodrick informed him that he had brought the matter before the Cabinet. 'The opinion expressed was unfavourable to the proposal.'[5] Kitchener next wished to have circulated lists of those liable to banishment, but complained that Milner refused to co-operate. Once more, he was denied: the banishment proclamation, he was told, was intended to refer only to leaders, and should not be unduly stretched but confined 'to men of

---

[1] C.O. 179/299.   [2] Milner MSS., vol. 45.
[3] War Office Confidential Telegram, No. 723.
[4] Ibid., No. 724.   [5] Ibid., No. 753.

real importance whom it is determined to banish and not merely to threaten'.[1]

V

The overshadowing event of 1901, however, was the mortality in the concentration camps. The camps had been established, sited, staffed and equipped by the military. They had been set up in haste and, after the policy of 'clearing the country' had become the principal activity of the British Army, Boers were deposited in the camps with unregulated speed. They died there in great numbers, largely from diseases such as pneumonia, measles, dysentery and enteric fever. The Boers estimated that 26,000 died in the camps, the British Blue Books gave the figures as 18,000.[2]

The conditions in the camps were publicized in England by Miss Emily Hobhouse, who visited those south of Bloemfontein on behalf of a voluntary organization, the South African Women and Children Distress Fund, early in 1901. Her report was, in essence, an account of inefficient administration, aggravated by shortages of supplies, especially fuel and soap, and exacerbated by ignorance and, in some instances, callousness and neglect. She was at pains to distinguish between conditions in different camps; some were well run, others were not. The 'amount of discomfort', she wrote, 'depends on various matters.

1. The style of commandant.
2. Natural conditions (proximity of wood and water).
3. Distance from a base store.
4. Presence of public opinion.
5. Date of commencement. The earlier camps, of course, had opportunities of getting many necessities which are no longer available.'[3]

Miss Hobhouse's account caused a sensation in England. Campbell-Bannerman described the British way of warfare in South Africa as 'methods of barbarism'; Lloyd George moved the adjournment of the House of Commons to consider 'the condition of the camps of detention in South Africa, and the alarming rate of

[1] Ibid., No. 800.
[2] G. B. Pyrah, *Imperial Policy and South Africa, 1902–1910* (1955), Appendix II.
[3] E. Hobhouse, *Report on a Visit to the Camps* (1901).

mortality amongst the women and children detained there'.[1]
He, and some of those who supported him, charged the Government
with pursuing 'a policy of extermination against children in South
Africa'. The overstatement of the case brought the matter within
the polemics of party strife; and to a certain extent the feeling of
humanitarianism was dulled in England. Brodrick defended the
policy behind the camps, while admitting that there were many
deficiencies in administration. There was much special pleading.
The charge was made that the Boer women were uncooperative, and
that their habits were insanitary. Lord Kitchener talked of charging
certain Boer mothers with manslaughter, on the grounds that their
own neglect had contributed to the death of their children. The report
of Dame Millicent Fawcett's committee of ladies quoted examples of
Boer ignorance. Every camp superintendent, the report stated, 'has
to wage war against the insanitary habits of the people'.[2] They
pointed out the reluctance of the Boers to use latrines, their 'horror
of ventilation', and their suspicion of the medical services. Instances
of bizarre treatment were quoted: a woman treated her children
for measles by daubing their bodies with green oil paint, so that
they died of arsenical poisoning; another varnished the chest of
her child; another administered cow-dung and sulphur. There were
instances of potions compounded in one instance of brick-dust and
brandy, in another of dog's blood and Reckitt's blue. But, as the
report mentioned, 'no doubt parallel horrors could be found in
old-fashioned English family receipt books of 150 or 200 years ago'.
Indeed, it seems that many of the inmates were resorting to variations
of the folk medicines preserved in the Voortrekker tradition. A
recent historian of early South African medicine has given an
account of some of these specifics, *e.g.*

Beest mest met asyn (cow's dung with vinegar): used as a poultice
for the pain of sprained joints, or to heal skin sores.

Bokken mest (goat's dung): used as an infusion to drink in measles,
and for severe chest pain.

Hoende bloed (dog's blood, obtained by ear puncture): used to
drink in severe inflammation and in convulsions.

Wolwe mest (wolf's dung): used as an infusion to drink in sore
throat, diphtheria and tonsilitis.[3]

In the main, British official reports bore out the essential criticisms

[1] Cd. 893.   [2] Cd. 893.
[3] E. H. Burrows, *A History of Medicine in South Africa* (1958), p. 192.

made by Miss Hobhouse. The Fawcett Committee concluded that
there were three causes of the high death rate:

1. The insanitary condition of the country caused by the war.
2. Causes within the control of the inmates.
3. Causes within the control of the administration.

Under the third heading, they pointed out that the military had not
taken account of the difference between catering for soldiers in
the field and women and children confined in a specific area. In
particular, the army provision of one bell-tent to 16 men was
inappropriate in conditions where more than five persons to a tent
amounted to overcrowding. Some of the sites were very badly
chosen indeed: the worst of them, in the committee's opinion, was at
Merebank, in Natal: 'It lies at the foot of a low hill, the water from
which drains into it. The flat, swampy ground on which the camp is
pitched slopes slightly from both sides towards a central drain or
little stream, into which all surface water from wash-houses, etc.,
runs, and which flows slowly into a large mere from which there is no
outlet. On that side of the camp which is towards Durban there
appears to be a big morass which drains towards the camp.'[1] In this
camp, grave-diggers found that they struck water at a depth of four
and a half feet.

For the rest, the committee noted that some officials had sunk
to a low order of decency and cleanliness; that there was a shortage
of doctors and nurses; and that a diet which was deficient in fresh
meat, milk and vegetables produced a lowering of vitality.

In essence, the same criticisms were made by Dr. Kendal Franks,
who visited camps in the Cape and Orange Free State at the end of
1901.[2] He, too, found it impossible to generalize; but he reported on
bad siting, neglect and ignorance. At Bethulie, the original site was
so placed that, in wet weather, storm water flowed from the native
cemetery into the supply of drinking water. The matron was quite
inexperienced, there was no system of inspection, and many cases of
illness were not reported to the medical authorities. Supplies of all
kinds were lacking, and the doctors were in scarcely better case than
the inmates. 'Each medical officer is provided with a bell-tent and a
bed *et praeterea nihil*.' The latrine system, he said, was disgraceful.
'The camp has been in the hands of the late superintendent since
18 April, and now at the end of nine months there are still no

---

[1] Cd. 893.   [2] C.O. 417/349, ff. 85 seqq.

buckets.' Conditions were much better at Aliwal North, at Spring-fontein they were better still, There, an imaginative superintendent (Captain J. H. Sinclair, a noted cricketer) had established a local health committee of a chairman and two men and two women selected from each block of tents, who conducted daily inspections. At Port Elizabeth, a camp for undesirables and prisoners of war, conditions were best of all. 'As far as the comforts of existing go, it is best to be an undesirable or a prisoner of war. Next to this, it is well to be a Boer refugee and to live in one of the "concentration camps"; but the least of all to be desired is to be a loyal refugee, with British blood flowing through the veins.'

Milner asked that this statement be omitted before publication. 'In the first place,' he minuted, 'it is nonsense; and in the second place it is highly undesirable to publish it, even if it were not.'

Milner disapproved of the policy of the camps, although he thought that, once it had been decided upon, it could not be changed. The camps were transferred from the military authorities to civilians in November 1901, and thereafter a remarkable transformation took place. A mortality rate of 344 per 1000 in October 1901 was reduced to one of 160 in January 1902, and 20 in May. But by then the damage had been done. Milner had no illusions about the extent of the calamity. Commenting on the death rate in the camps in the Orange Free State, he wrote on 4 December 1901:

The theory that, all the weakly children being dead, the rate would fall off, is not so far borne out by the facts. I take it the strong ones must be dying now and that they will *all be dead* by the spring of 1903!

Only I shall not be there to see as the continuance of the present state of affairs for another two or three months will undoubtedly blow us all out of the water.

I say this quite calmly and 'objectively'. It is impossible not to see that, however blameless we may be in the matter, we shall not be able to make anybody think so. And I cannot avoid an uncomfortable feeling that there must be some way to make the thing *a little less awfully bad* if one could only think of it.[1]

The deaths in the camps, taken with the clearing of the country, bred the suspicion that the British were seeking not merely to conquer an enemy but to exterminate a race.

Charles W. Eliot wrote from Harvard to Bryce in March 1902:

Isn't it a remarkable thing that three Christian nations at the end of the nineteenth and the beginning of the twentieth century should have adopted

[1] Milner MSS., vol. 19 f. 43.

a war measure which is really crueller than anything mankind has yet exhibited in a state of war—namely the concentration camp? It seems to be a method of race extermination by killing off the children. On a small scale, we have attempted in the Philippines precisely the same thing which the Spaniards did in Cuba, and you in South Africa . . .[1]

Apologists have pointed out that the death-rate in the camps, even at its peak of 43 per cent., did not compare outrageously with that of the poorest class in the worst slums of European cities of the nineteenth century. That may be true, but it is beside the point. It is also true that many of the inhabitants of the camps had insanitary habits. It is also true that the British Army suffered about four times as many deaths from disease in South Africa as it suffered in battle, and that medical science was inept in caring for large bodies of people in novel conditions in trying times. All this is irrelevant to the fact that the Boers in the concentration camps died under British responsibility, in places which the British had chosen and, in many instances, after they had been confined against their will. The camps were a gigantic blunder. They still form part of the mythology of extreme Afrikaner politics.

[1] Bryce PP., U.S.A. 1.

CHAPTER FIVE

THE FRAYING OF RESOLUTION

> The intellect of the nation is piling up on the other
> side . . .
>
> *Winston Churchill to Milner, 1901.*

THE Second Cape Rebellion and the continuation of the war, apparently without hope of rapid finality, produced in Britain a feeling of discouragement mixed with a certain humiliation. 'It is no use denying', Milner had written in a published dispatch of 6 February 1901, 'that the last half-year has been one of retrogression.'[1] At almost the same moment, Chamberlain was warning Milner that 'if some progress is not made before long I think public dissatisfaction may become serious and threaten the existence of the Government in spite of its enormous majority.'[2] In particular, a reaction began to set in against the policy of 'unconditional surrender', with which Milner was personally identified. This became more pronounced after the failure of the negotiations at Middelburg. Bryce suggested in the House of Commons that the British should offer peace terms as soon as they had gained another victory. 'This is not a case in which whatever is given to the enemy is taken from ourselves . . . Who are the conquered? They are the people we desire to make good British subjects, whom we desire to be loyal, against whom we do not wish to be obliged to keep an enormous garrison at an enormous expense, and to whom even the Government express themselves as desirous of restoring free government at the earliest possible moment.'[3]

The published disagreement between Kitchener and Milner fed the sentiment that Milner's intransigence was one of the barriers to peace. His friends began to hint delicately that he might soften his attitude. Haldane, one of the 'Oxford group' who had, in Morley's phrase, constituted themselves as a 'voluntary bodyguard' to Milner, wrote on 3 March in this strain, and went further still four

[1] Headlam ii. 193.   [2] Amery, *Chamberlain* iv. 28.
[3] 4th *Parl. Deb.*, vol. xcii, c. 123.

months later: 'Where you can help us to get you left unmolested at
the wheel is by being gentle in the little things that do not matter.'[1]
On 17 March, Winston Churchill (who had just made his maiden
speech in the House of Commons) wrote a letter of advice mixed
with admonishment, which offered 'stray gleams of light on some
accumulations of opinion here in England; for I am not altogether
out of touch with popular and political feeling'. What Churchill had
to say was not encouraging. There was a hopeful feeling that
'the end of this miserable war—unfortunate and ill-omened in its
beginning, cruel and hideous in its conclusion'—was in sight. Therefore he urged conciliation towards the Boers.

I look forward to the day when we can take the Boers by the hand and say
as Grant did to the Confederates at Appomattox, 'Go back and plough
your fields . . .'
I realize—imperfectly perhaps—the amazing difficulty of showing such
a spirit in South Africa . . . I know we have already quarrelled with the
Dutch and must not now quarrel with the British. We must be friends
with someone. But although every act of justice or generosity towards the
Boers will be regarded by the Loyalists as a personal insult to themselves,
you must not shut your eyes to the feeling in this country. The intellect of
the nation is piling up on the other side: the strength of the Government
cannot be measured by its large majorities. Thousands of voices silenced
by the warlike shouts of the crowd these many months will be heard again
when peace is restored.
I feel I ought not to write like this to you who have to face so much and
struggle against so many difficulties, that you should only hear words of
encouragement from those who are earnestly resolved to support you,
but I write it because I want exceedingly to hear some public pronouncement from you of a conciliatory character . . . And anything you might
be able to say in this direction would disarm enemies and what I daresay
are quite as tiresome—officious friends (like me!), and secure you the
undisturbed power which of course is necessary if you are to accomplish
anything in the way of reconstruction. Any kindly word that falls from
you in Africa will silence a chorus of jangling tongues at home: and win the
confidence of a swarm of honest doubters . . . [2]

All this, and much more of the same kind from other candid
friends, increased Milner's apprehension that a 'wobble' was to be
feared in British opinion, a fraying of resolution to 'see the thing
through', and a disposition to leave the task of breaking Boer power
half-finished. In May, Milner went to England on leave. His return
was widely reputed, among his growing band of enemies and
doubters, as evidence of a fall from favour. To dispel this, the

[1] Milner MSS., vol. 37.   [2] Ibid.

Government treated him, on his arrival, with signal honour: he was met by the Prime Minister, taken at once to an audience at the Palace and there (as he put it) 'jumped into the peerage' as Baron Milner of Cape Town and St. James's. On the following day, at a luncheon in his honour, he answered those who pressed conciliation upon him: 'Conciliate what? Panoplied hatred, insensate ambitions, invincible ignorance.'

In February, in the letter of warning already quoted, Chamberlain had reassured Milner that, if there were some progress in the war, the danger of wobbling resolution would diminish, 'provided that our policy is firm, clear and consistent, and that in carrying it out we do not raise new questions of a deeply controversial character'. One of those questions—that of the concentration camps—was deeply troubling the country. Milner did not bear the responsibility for this, but he suffered some of the odium. For the moment, however, Milner was more concerned with the obstacles to reconstruction placed in his way by the military authorities in South Africa. In particular, he was coming increasingly to deprecate, and even to distrust, the activities of Lord Kitchener. He did his best, in London, to secure some diminution or control of Kitchener's influence. He approached Roberts with the suggestion that the theatre of war in South Africa should be divided into three commands, with a senior general to decide where authority clashed—one command for Natal, Basutoland, the Orange Free State and part of the Transvaal, a second for the Western Transvaal and the Cape north of the Orange River, and a third for the southern Cape. The war, he argued, no longer had any unity, but had become 'a mass of scattered and petty operations which no single mind can grasp and the character of which varies considerably in the various localities'. In the past, he said, he had deferred to the wishes of the soldiers, but he thought that the time had come when civil considerations should have at least equal weight. Therefore, he asked that his right should be recognized to correspond directly with the military commanders, and to require them to provide him with information.[1] What Milner had in mind was a return to the policy of 'reconstruction under arms', and he hoped that Kitchener would soon be transferred out of South Africa: he favoured Neville Lyttelton as his successor. But Lyttelton was relatively junior, and Roberts made it clear that, until the war was over, there was no practicable alternative to Kitchener as

[1] Ibid., vol. 45.

commander-in-chief 'until it is possible to dispense with the services of French, Methuen, and all officers senior in rank to Neville Lyttelton'.[1] However, Roberts did write at length to Kitchener, putting to him Milner's general views on the increasing weight to be given to civil questions. But, Roberts assured Kitchener that there could be no diminution of his own authority until the war was over, and that only the commander-in-chief could be in direct communication with the High Commissioner.

Kitchener continued, however, to pay as little attention to political questions as he had ever done. In the latter part of the year, he quarrelled seriously with the Cape Ministry over the administration and extension of martial law. The second invasion and rebellion of the Cape produced, in the main, the same kind of complaints from the inhabitants as those that had been heard in 1900—that the administration of martial law was harsh and unimaginative, that commandants were stupid and sometimes vindictive, that the innocent and the guilty were sometimes treated alike, and that certain measures taken to limit the commandos, such as the requisitioning of all horses and mules, pressed hardly upon the farming population. At the same time, the failure of the British troops to prevent the passage of the commandos bred a growing resentment. Hely-Hutchinson sent to Chamberlain a report—typical of many—from a British farmer at Barkly East. There were Boers all over the place, he said, and no British troops showed any signs of attacking them. Authority in the area had practically passed into the hands of the Boer commandant, Wessels; and the farmer had been constrained to apply to him for a pass to visit the town in order to sue a Jewish storekeeper (an errand of which Wessels apparently approved).[2] The Cape Ministry resented the fact that the colonial troops and the volunteers raised within the Cape were under imperial command, and were used as part of the columns directed by General French, the officer commanding in the Cape, so that they were not available for local duties. Hence, protection was lacking where, in the Ministers' opinion, it was most needed.

The control of the Cape colonial forces was a matter of some complexity. At the outbreak of war, Schreiner's ministry had taken the view that all operations against the Boers should be carried out by imperial troops. They changed their attitude when the Cape was invaded, and called for volunteers, on the understanding

[1] Ibid.   [2] Chamberlain PP. J.C. 11/4, 5 November 1901.

that they would be used only within the Colony. However, the difference between the peace- and war-time pay of these men was met by the British Government, and when Roberts took over the command Cape troops were used wherever the commander-in-chief chose to send them. Fresh forces were raised during the second rebellion, but these came under imperial command: the Cape Government, therefore, had no effective forces under its own control except the untrained town guards. 'An army', Milner wrote to Hely-Hutchinson in February 1901, 'can deal with an army, but, as we have just seen, it is almost helpless against small scattered and highly mobile commandos, and unless there is some obstacle in their way, 500 men can ride through the Colony, as they have ridden through it, with 5000 ineffectually riding after them.'[1]

In July, after he had been rebuffed in his attempt to make terms with the rebels, Kitchener complained to the Governor that the Cape Ministry was uncooperative and was not assisting the military to the best of its ability.

Where I consider more might be done by your Government in dealing with the situation is:

By giving assistance in collecting horses.

By not refusing to extend martial law as was asked for by G.O.C., Cape Town.

By insisting on more active work by the local authorities throughout the Colony.

By taking more precautions against leakage of arms and ammunition in the hands of the local defence forces.[2]

Sprigg reacted sharply to these criticisms. On 27 July, Kitchener's charges were rebutted in detail, and the ministry made counter-charges of its own. They saw no reason for the extension of martial law, and they specifically complained against the requisitioning of transport animals in districts outside the theatre of operations, such as Worcester, Paarl, Malmesbury and Stellenbosch, where 'whatever may be the sympathies of a large part of the population, active rebellion does not exist'. They thought that martial law ought to be relaxed. They denied that there was a leakage of arms from town guards. 'Much leakage of ammunition is alleged to occur from the bandoliers of the regular military forces while on the march, but nothing of that kind has been brought to the notice of Ministers in relation to the local defence forces . . .' In particular,

[1] Milner MSS., vol. 20.   [2] C.O. 48/553, f. 432.

they complained of the manner in which the Cape forces were used, and indicated that they could do better themselves than the British Army. The Cape Police and the Cape Mounted Rifles, they said,

> are by their constitution and experience pre-eminently adapted to withstand and overcome the guerilla warfare which now prevails in so many Districts of the Colony. They understand the tactics of the enemy and how to meet them. They are prepared to move about the country, not encumbered with trains of wagons, but in small bodies in light marching order . . . Let the imperial military officers commanding large bodies of regular troops meet and drive back the invaders from the north of the Orange River and prevent their return, and Ministers feel confident, if the whole of the Cape Colonial Forces are placed under their control, of their ability to bring the rebellion to a close and to meet the cost involved in that undertaking.[1]

Kitchener took unkindly to the imputation of military incompetence. He pressed for an extension of martial law to the Cape ports. Ministers objected strongly. There had been a long-drawn quarrel between General Wynne, commanding in the western Cape, and James Rose Innes, the Attorney-General, on the details of military administration, in which Innes showed himself much the more skilled debater. Occasions of stupidity or excess of zeal could be multiplied: the order confining J. X. Merriman to his home in Stellenbosch, the civilian who had been fined £10 for saying that the commandant of his district was a damned fool, the British officer who had refused to permit a wedding gathering because he believed that marriage in the Dutch Reformed Church was not a religious ceremony. Ministers, therefore, were unsympathetic to Kitchener's complaints that the local civil authorities were 'too neutral', and did not sufficiently identify themselves with the military. They replied that without police, local magistrates were powerless. Kitchener refused to transfer any colonial troops to local control: 'That is a military question on which they will perhaps think that my opinion carries some weight; and I am convinced that there is no officer serving in the Cape Colony who would be able to make a better use of the troops in question than Lieutenant-General French.'[2]

On 27 August, the Ministry produced a detailed list of complaints to substantiate their opinion that the condition of the Colony was

---

[1] Ministers' Minute No. 1/214; ibid., f. 557.
[2] Ibid., f. 1050, 3 August 1901.

being aggravated by the manner in which martial law was administered. They made six specific charges, all pointing to the fact that commandants of districts were acting outside their authority as laid down in the general instructions issued in February and May, 1901.

1. Local inhabitants were forced to join the town guard or local defence forces, which were supposed to be maintained by voluntary recruitment, and those who refused had been imprisoned and treated as convicted criminals.

2. Men arrested on suspicion had been kept in prison for long periods without trial. They gave details of a case in Britstown in which a colonist had been under arrest since 30 June on a charge 'not yet formulated'.

3. Private property was commandeered indiscriminately. 'Whole areas of the Colony are gradually but surely being ruined, with the result that disaffected persons are gravitating to the enemy, and well-affected citizens are becoming sullen, indifferent and lukewarm. Thus on the one hand we find rebellion spreading, and men of substance joining it, in spite of the stern measures of repression recently undertaken, and on the other hand a want of enthusiasm on the part of many to whom the Government is entitled to look for aid in putting rebellion down.'

4. Many commandants were not fit to hold their offices. The Ministry asked that they should be consulted before appointments were made.

5. Officers commanding mounted columns were given too great a discretion, which was not wisely used, in dealing with civilians.

6. The military did not give sufficient co-operation to the civil magistrates.[1]

Complaints of the same kind were sent by the South African Vigilance Committee to Milner, of the abuse of authority 'filtering, as it frequently does, through a channel of petty and irresponsible officialdom'.[2] In particular, they drew attention to enforced attendance at executions, to commandeering without adequate compensation, and to signs that the process of 'clearing the country' was being extended to the Cape Colony.

On 29 August, the Ministry formally refused to agree to Kitchener's request that martial law should be extended to the ports. They would not, they said, agree to a step 'which would place the

[1] Ibid., f. 1015.   [2] C.O. 48/554, f. 33.

supreme court of the country and the principal public offices of the
Colony within an area under the control of the military'.[1]

This decision produced a brief but heated crisis. The controversy
turned upon points which could be regarded as affecting imperial
interests, and hence outside the exclusive competence of the Cape
Ministry, and as touching upon military requirements, which in
the conventions of the time were outside civilian control altogether.
Hutchinson, now Governor of the Cape, called upon Milner for
advice, proposing that he might induce the Ministry to accept a
restricted form of martial law—that Kitchener should give a written
undertaking that powers given to the military should be used only to
arrest undesirable persons, suppress disloyal publications, and
censor correspondence, and that no arrest should be made without
communication with the Attorney-General. Hutchinson would give
to the Ministry a written undertaking that, if martial law were used
for any other purpose, he would repeal the proclamation.[2] Milner
put the proposal to Kitchener, tactfully omitting the suggestion
that his undertaking should be in writing, and Kitchener agreed.[3]
The Cape Ministry would not budge; on 9 September they unanimously refused, stating that they would surrender no more power.
Two days earlier, Rose Innes had stated that he would no longer
allow the civil gaols to be used for the confinement of men arrested
under martial law against whom no formal charge had been made,
and that the military would have to make their own arrangements.

The Ministry next took a high constitutional line, claiming
that it was in their discretion alone whether or not to proclaim
martial law, and that discretion could be shared neither with the
commander-in-chief nor with the Secretary of State.[4] Kitchener
turned to the use of *force majeure*. On 15 September, he warned
Hutchinson that he was thinking of putting a cordon of troops
around every port, 'to prevent all ingress and egress whatsoever.'[5]
On the same day, he addressed a formal threat to the Ministry.

If Ministers consider that they alone are responsible for the introduction of martial law and can override the united opinions of the High Commissioner, yourself, the Secretary of State and myself, I presume they will
allow that I am just as responsible for the safety of the Army and the
carrying on of the war, both of which matters are so nearly affected by
their decision not to allow even modified martial law in the Cape ports,

---

1 Ibid., f. 28.   2 Ibid., f. 11.   3 Ibid., f. 1942.
4 Ibid., f. 349.   5 Ibid., f. 350.

and that it is my imperative duty to take all necessary steps in such matters; I shall therefore have to tell General Wynne on Monday to give certain instructions for giving passes on railways and for searching of luggage and merchandise on the frontier, as my information points to consignments of munitions of war being sent by train hidden in merchandise and private baggage of persons travelling who intend to join the enemy. I should be glad to have Ministers' final opinion with the least possible delay.[1]

Kitchener did not wait. On the following day, the Ministry learnt through a message received by the Postmaster-General from military headquarters in Pretoria, that Kitchener was proposing to divert the weekly mail vessel from Britain to Durban, and to close the port of Cape Town to civilian shipping. The Ministry appealed at once to the Colonial Secretary, asking him 'to stop this extraordinary proceeding', and hinting broadly that they would resign if he did not support them.[2] Chamberlain had, until that moment, been rather more than less in favour of the extension of martial law; but, he minuted on Hely-Hutchinson's dispatch: 'We may very likely have to put pressure on Cape Government, but *we* must do it and not Lord K. acting independently.' On 17 September, he instructed Milner to point out to Kitchener that no such action should be taken without the sanction of the British Government, which had every desire to support Kitchener's policy but would not allow its hand to be forced.[3] Chamberlain expressed his opinion of Kitchener's behaviour to Brodrick in outspoken terms: 'I am much annoyed at Kitchener's proceeding. I have no doubt it is 'bluff' as usual, but he has no business to threaten the Cape Government—through an individual Minister like the Postmaster—without a word to us . . . Let him stick to his military work and catch Botha or de Wet and leave us to decide political questions.'[4]

Kitchener took his defeat with an ill grace. On 19 September, in reply to a telegram from the War Office reporting that a consignment of rifles believed to be for South Africa was arriving in a German ship from Antwerp, he replied petulantly that he could do nothing about it. 'We cannot now prevent introduction of arms and ammunition for enemy through Cape ports owing to Ministers' refusal to proclaim martial law'[5]

In threatening resignation, the Cape Ministry were on firm ground; there was no practicable alternative government. Hely-Hutchinson,

[1] Ibid., f. 352.   [2] C.O. 48/554, f. 298.
[3] Chamberlain PP. J.C. 14/4.   [4] Ibid., J.C. 11/1.
[5] C.O. 48/554, f. 408.

who supported Kitchener in principle but not in method, reported that their resignation would involve the virtual suspension of the constitution, and that he would then have to govern directly, using the permanent heads of departments. He was by no means reluctant to take this responsibility: once again, Chamberlain took the view that only the extreme of military necessity would justify suspension. Lambert minuted that the resignation of Sprigg and his colleagues would mean the suspension of the constitution 'in an unpleasantly dramatic manner', in which the Cape Ministry could appear as the defenders of constitutional rights 'from the lawless invasions of the military and the Imperial Government'. Chamberlain sent a telegram to Milner, asking him to see Sprigg and either smooth him down or present the Colonial Office with an overwhelming case for accepting his resignation.[1]

The Cape Ministry was not easily to be smoothed. Sprigg refused to travel to Pretoria until the matter was settled. Rose Innes prosecuted with gusto his feud with General Wynne, and was able to take legitimate offence when Wynne told him that he was acting in a manner 'devoid of justice'.[2] By 20 September, they had ceased to correspond directly, and sent messages to each other through the Governor. On 26 September, the Ministry returned to the tactics of the counter-attack.[3]

Modified or restricted martial law, they said, was a contradiction in terms. Either the civil or the military power must be predominant, and the hybrid form suggested would lead only to misunderstanding, friction and confusion. They left Kitchener under no misunderstanding as to what they thought of his policy.

With respect to the Imperial aspect of the question . . . Ministers are now and have been all through the war alive to the fact that the real issue is British supremacy or republicanism in South Africa, and that unless the first of these alternatives be upheld the Cape Colony will not be a country in which a man of British extraction can remain. And Ministers are strongly of the opinion that the best means of maintaining the Empire in its supreme position is to accept the advice of those who have spent the best part of their lives in the Colony which is their home, and who by reason of their long and intimate connexion with its public affairs thoroughly understand its history, its capabilities and requirements, and the character of its population.

The immediate issue was settled in Pretoria, through Milner's mediation. Sprigg agreed to the extension of martial law to the

[1] Ibid., f. 412.   [2] Ibid., f. 764.   [3] Ibid., f. 830.

ports, on condition that a martial law board, of representatives appointed respectively by the Governor, the Ministry and the military, carried out a general supervision of its administration. However, friction continued. In November, they protested against a military order which prohibited the cultivation of foodstuffs over wide areas of the Colony, on the grounds that crops sooner or later reached the Boers. This, the Ministry said, was one more instance of 'making rebels'; whoever starved, the commandos would starve last. The order was relaxed in December.[1] Protests continued to the end of the war; and it required the intervention of Hely-Hutchinson to prevent the military from 'clearing the country' in the Cape. General Settle gave way with reluctance: he did not agree, he said, that this would have serious political effects; it seemed to him to be 'both legitimate and advisable'.[2] Kitchener's temper was wearing thin: on 25 February 1902 he wrote to Hely-Hutchinson complaining of the 'hostile tone' of the Ministry, and pointing out to it and to the Governor: 'that this war is an imperial matter affecting the whole Empire, and very largely the British taxpayer, and that it is not a merely local concern in which the interests of the Cape Colony alone might be considered.'

Hely-Hutchinson retorted tartly that Kitchener was mistaken if he thought that the Governor needed any such reminder. On 17 March Kitchener formally put on record that he had no intention of 'clearing' the Cape.[3]

III

In September 1901 Milner tried unsuccessfully to obtain some authority over the allocation of supplies which he needed for reconstruction—for the railways were under military control—and some voice in military policy. In November he wrote privately to Chamberlain, asking that Kitchener should be removed from command in South Africa: he complained that Kitchener's methods were likely neither to bring the war quickly to an end nor to make the best use of the conquered territories while the war was 'burning itself out'. He had repeatedly pressed his opinions on Kitchener, who was outwardly friendly, listened courteously and took no notice.

It is impossible to *guide* a military dictator of very strong views and strong character. He can only conduct the war in his own way. The most that

[1] C.O. 48/555, ff. 411, 1184.   [2] C.O. 48/558, f. 785.
[3] C.O. 48/559, ff. 92, 94, 243.

any man in my position could do, and that could only be done under very great difficulty, and possibly undesirable friction, would be very slightly to modify his operations.

The remedy, and the only remedy, if the results seem inadequate, is to change the command. The difficulty of this course appears to be that Kitchener does not want to go until he has finished the war. To remove him, against his will, seems to me, in view of the great services which he has undoubtedly rendered, to be next door to an impossibility.

Kitchener has not done badly. The great drawback to him is that he will look at the problem as a purely military one. It is not now purely or mainly military. What is the use of having cleared great areas of the country absolutely of the enemy if we still subordinate every consideration of policy to military exigencies, and make hardly any use whatever of the areas cleared? Yet to every effort to do this, Kitchener opposes an insuperable resistance. It is not a blank refusal, it is a whole host of minor difficulties and obstructions, often intangible, which have practically the same effect.[1]

In short, Milner proposed that Kitchener should be cozened out of South Africa—should be told that he was badly wanted in India, recalled, given a holiday, loaded with honours and sent to the command which he coveted. 'I am sure that we shall get on better without him, not because anyone else will conduct the war better, but because someone else *may*, if put in on that distinct understanding, obstruct the work of reconstruction less.'

This letter was circulated by Chamberlain to each member of the Cabinet. Their consensus was that Kitchener could not be recalled against his will, and that the Government could not, for political reasons, risk another clash with the Army at that stage. For there had been passionate controversy over the long-delayed dismissal of General Buller.

Buller, on his return to England in 1900, had gone back to the command of the First Corps at Aldershot, the appointment which he had held before his departure for South Africa. The decision to re-employ Buller had been taken by the Secretary of State for War in full knowledge of the incapacity which Buller had shown in Natal; but Brodrick had decided that, as Roberts had refused to dismiss Buller in 1900 and had left him in command of 50,000 men, there were no public grounds upon which Brodrick could refuse to restore to Buller his position at Aldershot.[2] In September 1901, it was announced that the first three army corps would be commanded by the men who would lead them in battle in the

[1] Chamberlain PP. J.C. 13/2.   [2] Salisbury PP.

event of a European war. At this period, L. S. Amery had just finished the second volume of his *Times History of the War in South Africa*, which ended with the battle of Colenso. The book was dominated by the purpose, in Amery's words, 'that the story of the war could be made the best instrument of preaching Army reform';[1] and in his opinion Army reform and General Buller did not go readily together. Amery's study of Colenso had convinced him that Buller had shown 'a sheer lack of determination and even a disastrous loss of morale'; furthermore, he was coming to believe in the existence of Buller's message to General White, advising the surrender of Ladysmith, which had been successfully kept secret until then.

On 28 September 1901 Amery wrote a letter to *The Times* over the *nomme de plume* of 'Reformer', rehearsing Buller's inadequacies as a commander and referring to the Ladysmith telegram as if it were a matter of general knowledge. This brought a surprising response—a public acknowledgement and justification of the telegram from Buller himself. On 10 October, in the course of a rambling after-dinner speech to the officers of the Queen's Westminster Volunteers, Buller explained how he had 'spatchcocked into the middle of the telegram' the suggestion of surrender, as a cover for General White. 'I was in command in Natal, and it was my duty to give my subordinate some assistance, some lead, something that in the event of his determining to surrender he would be able to produce and say, "Well, Sir Redvers Buller agreed".'[2]

This extraordinary pronouncement embarrassed the Government acutely. 'Reformer' at once wrote to *The Times* again, asking whether this was the kind of lead which England expected her corps commanders to provide. 'I must repeat my charge against this Government', the letter ended, 'that in appointing Sir Redvers Buller to the command of the First Army Corps, they have appointed one who, to their own knowledge and by his own admissions, is unfit to hold high command in the field.'

By a Cabinet decision, Buller was relieved of his command at Aldershot and put on half-pay; but the stated reason for his dismissal was that he had committed a breach of the Queen's regulations by speaking publicly of official secrets. The Army professed itself to be deeply shocked. (There may have been some who thought that the

---

[1] L. S. Amery, *Days in the Sun, passim.*
[2] Annual Register, 1901, p. 203

right thing had been done for the wrong reason.) It was argued that the Government had victimized a senior officer, of officially unblemished reputation, because of a newspaper agitation. An unexpected consequence of the success of Amery's Buller-trap was to make it impossible for the Government to remove Kitchener. The Secretary of State for India, in his reply to Chamberlain's circular, spoke for the majority of the Cabinet: 'Kitchener on top of Buller would make the Army unmanageable.'[1] Salisbury wrote to Chamberlain:

. . . If you desire to move in the direction in which Milner is pulling, you must make him set down his demands and—if we approve of them—urge them upon Kitchener. I do not say that the results of this mode of action will be free from embarrassment; but any other course, adverse to Kitchener, seems to me, in the present state of affairs, impossible. The Buller affair has very much modified our power of taking action of this kind.[2]

Milner returned to the attack in February 1902. His relations with Kitchener were friendly enough on the surface, he said, but:

co-operation in any true sense of the word is out of the question. Personally I do not think there ever has been, or ever could be, co-operation between Lord Kitchener and any other man, who was not either distinctly his subordinate or distinctly his superior. In our respective tasks, wherever they touch each other, we are always pulling different ways . . . [But] I am quite resolved not to have a Kitchener–Milner controversy on top of a Buller–Roberts one . . .

As I see the position, things are constantly being done which will make our future task more difficult, while on the other hand golden opportunities of strengthening ourselves now in the deserted country are being thrown away. Kitchener won't go, unless he can do so with glory and saying that he finished the war. But the war can only be formally finished either by a compact—which Heaven forbid!—or by his catching the last Boer, which may take years.[3]

Milner was in a circle of frustration: Kitchener could not beat the Boers; yet, unless the Boers were beaten, Milner could not make headway with his plans for reconstruction.

[1] Salisbury PP.   [2] Ibid.   [3] Chamberlain PP. J.C. 11/4.

CHAPTER SIX

THE PEACE OF VEREENIGING

We must not sacrifice the nation itself on the altar of independence.

J. C. Smuts, 30 May 1902.

'A TEDIOUS war is a great educational instrument', Leonard Courtney wrote to L. S. Amery in 1899, 'and the views we entertain today are not those we held six weeks ago and may be different from those we shall hold six weeks hence.'[1] In August 1900 Mrs. Courtney wrote in her diary: 'The English public is getting weary of the war! There is a great change! The heroics are over—there is left a bitter determination to get something out of it we can *call* success.'[2] On 7 February 1901 Chamberlain warned Milner that 'if some progress is not made before long I think public dissatisfaction may become serious and threaten the existence of the Government in spite of its enormous majority'.[3] By the end of 1901 the direct cost of the war had amounted to nearly £200,000,000, and outright victory seemed to be as difficult as ever to achieve. It was clear that the British Army was unable to catch and beat the Boers in open battle; Kitchener's attrition was certain of success in the long run, but it involved a double cost—devastation before the enemy's surrender, reconstruction afterwards—and it produced hardships which, outside the area of combat, pressed upon the loyal and the disloyal together. 'The Orange River Colony is virtually a desert . . .', Milner wrote in September 1901. 'At a liberal computation *there are not more than 6,000 Boers* still in arms against us. They are ill-mounted, ill-clad, ill-armed, the most wretched objects conceivable, and constantly on the run. Still they keep on, deluded by the persistent lying of their leaders, and it may take a long time yet to catch them in twenties and thirties. It is a miserable business.'[4]

Miserable business it might be; but it was preferable in Milner's opinion, to any weakening of resolve which might allow the Boer

---

[1] Courtney MSS., vol. 7, f. 113.   [2] Ibid., vol. 29.
[3] Amery, *Chamberlain*, IV. 28.   [4] Milner MSS., vol. 26, 11 September 1901.

leaders to avoid unconditional surrender. Milner had not been able to go as far as he would have wished with 'reconstruction under arms' (and for this he blamed Kitchener), but the unity of Afrikanerdom was visibly disintegrating. The policy of separating 'tame' from 'wild' Boers in the prison camps was beginning to show results: more and more prisoners were demonstrating an eagerness for peace and a disposition to blame their misery upon the commando leaders who were prolonging a war in which eventual defeat was certain. By March 1902 nearly 2000 prisoners had taken service with the British as 'National Scouts' in the Transvaal and 'Volunteers' in the Orange River Colony. Their value to the British was out of proportion to their scanty numbers: they knew the country, they knew the habits of the commandos, and they were particularly valuable as guides and scouts. Furthermore, they were increasing in numbers. Burghers of Potchefstroom, at a meeting in January, resolved to send a letter to General de la Rey exhorting him to surrender; after an appeal by General Andries Cronje, sixteen men volunteered as National Scouts.[1] Two hundred Boer prisoners in Ceylon offered to serve in the British Army; from Bermuda and St. Helena there were reports that the prisoners there were willing to take oaths of allegiance if they were allowed to return home. Early in 1902 one of Hofmeyr's supporters in Cape Town published an appeal to General Botha to lead the way to submission. 'Oh surely, surely he cannot be so blind as not yet to see the hopelessness of continuing the struggle, nor so bigoted as not to acknowledge that every day is adding to the degradation and ruin of his people. Are his ears closed like those of the adder that he hears not the piteous cry of the widows and orphans in the concentration camps or the pleadings of his banished compatriots . . . ?'[2] The 'breaking of Afrikanerdom' was nearer at hand than the military situation suggested. At Durban, Milner suggested in a public speech that there might be no ending to the war, in a formal sense, but that it would gradually flicker out as the Boers were forced, piecemeal, to submit.

In England, however, 'unconditional surrender' was becoming a discredited slogan. Pressure for peace was building up within the

[1] Ibid., vol. 44. Letter of 8 January 1902 from W. S. Duxbury, Resident Magistrate of Potchefstroom.
[2] H. W. Fourie, *An Afrikaner's Appeal to Afrikaners to Assist in Bringing about Peace in South Africa.* (Cape Town, 1902), pp. 13–14.

Government. The longer the war lasted, the greater was the accumulation of evidence that the British Army needed a thorough reorganization; but reorganization must wait upon the promised commission of inquiry, and the commission could not begin its work until the war was over. The Chancellor of the Exchequer was becoming stiffer in his demands for economy. In January 1902, Kitchener estimated that if the war ended with 'acquiescence on the part of the enemy in peace', the future garrison of South Africa could be reduced from 20,000 troops (assisted by 10,000 constabulary) in the first months to 15,000 or less within two or three years; if peace came 'as the result merely of exhaustion or incapacity to carry on the struggle', South Africa would require 'a minimum of 50,000 troops and 15,000 Constabulary, and . . . subsequent reduction or increase would depend on circumstances impossible to foresee'.[1] Kitchener himself was ardent for peace, lest the India Command escape him. The King did not wish his coronation to take place while part of his dominion was at war. Meanwhile, repeated hints from the Netherlands suggested that the exiled Boer Deputation was anxious for peace if only humiliation could be avoided. In July 1901, Salisbury had rejected an offer from Rosebery to open negotiations through a German intermediary.[2] In August, Edouard Lippert, the original holder of the dynamite concession in the Transvaal, had brought to England from the Netherlands proposals for peace on the basis of an amnesty to rebels, reconstruction of farms and the recall of Milner.[3] In January 1902, Sir Thomas Lipton reported to Chamberlain that Leo Weinthal, the former proprietor of the *Pretoria News* who was on parole in Britain, had offered himself as an intermediary. In November, F. W. Fox, a Quaker philanthropist, wrote to Chamberlain that, on a private visit to the Hague, he had seen the Dutch Prime Minister and Foreign Minister and had ascertained that the Dutch Government would be prepared to mediate if they knew in advance that the British would welcome such an offer. He had also seen Grobler, a relative of President Kruger who was a semi-official member of the Boer Deputation, and had learnt from him that the Boers would accept terms which included a confederation, to be known as the Dominion of South Africa, with the Transvaal and the Orange River Colony as self-governing

[1] W.O. Conf. Tel. No. 484: Kitchener to Secretary of State, 20 January 1902.
[2] Chamberlain PP. J.C. 11/4. F. W. Fox to Chamberlain, 28 November 1901.
[3] Salisbury PP.

states within it, equal in status to the Cape Colony and Natal.[1] To all these overtures, the reply was given that any peace negotiations must be in the hands of official men: Chamberlain told Fox, in the third person, that His Majesty's Government 'cannot conduct communications on public affairs with the Governments of foreign nations except through the recognized diplomatic channels'.[2]

Lord Rosebery, in his Chesterfield speech of 16 December 1901, expressed a growing sentiment in the country when he suggested, obliquely, that peace could be had at once if only the British Government would show a more accommodating temper. Rosebery explicitly denied that he wanted Milner's recall, but he condemned the policy of continuing the war until the last commando had been driven into the last corner—'a policy against which I venture to offer the most emphatic protest in my power'.[3] He appealed to self-advantage by enumerating 'four separate and distinct reasons' why the war should be brought to an end. 'In the first place it is an open sore through which is oozing much of our strength. In the next place it weakens our international position and reduces us to a standpoint in international politics very different from that which we are accustomed to occupy. In the third place it stops all domestic reforms (cheers), and in the fourth place it adjourns and embitters the ultimate settlement of South Africa.' He uttered the conventional platitude that the war should be carried on vigorously to its natural end, 'But I believe that its natural end is a regular peace and a regular settlement—not unconditional surrender or interminable hunting down of an enemy proclaimed outlaws and rebels.' Britain should not make advances, but she might let it be known that she could be wooed: 'some of the greatest peaces . . . in the world's history have begun with an apparently casual meeting of two travellers in a neutral inn, and I think it might well happen that some such fortuitous meeting might take place under the auspices of His Majesty's Government and of the exiled Boer Government which might lead to very good results.'

The pacific spirit showed itself in Parliament when the session opened in January. Cawley, for the Opposition, moved an amendment to the Address to the effect that the Government's actions and attitude had 'not conduced to the early termination of the war and the establishment of a durable peace . . . No one [Cawley said] can

---

[1] Chamberlain PP. J.C. 11/4
[2] Ibid., 2 December 1901.   [3] *The Times*, 17 December 1901.

look forward with equanimity to a prolonged hunting down of our enemies until armies are replaced by small bands, and the bands finally break up into desperate individuals. Distinction will then be impossible between the fighting burgher and the bushranging robber, and the war will end in a blood-stained series of executions and reprisals'.[1] Balfour shrugged off the amendment by implying that the initiative to peace must come from the enemy. 'The Boers say, as far as we know, "we are not going to surrender our independence." We say "You are going to", and there the matter stands. And until one of those parties is subjugated the war is to go on, and we do not mean to be the party that is to be subjugated.'[2]

Harcourt referred to another source of uneasiness—the virtual suspension of the Cape Colony's constitution by the repeated prorogation of Parliament; this, he said, was the policy of the Stuarts.[3] Chamberlain replied that, although he agreed with the advice which the Cape Ministers had given to the Governor not to summon Parliament, it was none of his business; 'it would be an impertinence for me to interfere with the responsibility of the Cape Government . . . unless imperial interests are concerned.'[4] Later in the debate, however, he showed a more conciliating spirit. He softened the outline of unconditional surrender: what it amounts to, he says in effect, is that 'we decline to be bound at the time of surrender to any special conditions which may embarrass us in the future. We have, however, expressed our hope, our intention, our expectation, as soon as possible to grant to the people whom we have conquered full political rights, and meanwhile, we have promised them that from the first they shall have equal justice and equal privileges with the other white races'.[5] On 25 January the Dutch Government made a formal offer to mediate, offering its own services and suggesting, as an alternative, that members of the Boer deputation to Europe might be given safe-conducts to visit the commandos and return, as a preliminary to peace negotiations. Lord Lansdowne replied on 29 January that the British Government held to their resolve not to admit foreign intervention; and peace negotiations must take place in South Africa between the commander-in-chief and the Boer leaders in the field: but the correspondence was sent to Kitchener, with instructions that he should pass it on to Vice-President Burger.

[1] 4th *Parl. Deb.*, vol. 101, cc. 328–9.   [2] Ibid., c. 117.
[3] Ibid., c. 145, seqq.   [4] Ibid., cc. 157, 159.   [5] Ibid., c. 378.

Kitchener wrote to Burger on 4 March and received a reply, dated 10 March, in which Burger asked for a safe-conduct to consult President Steyn. In the meantime, on 7 March, the Boers won their greatest success since Colenso, when General de la Rey defeated and captured General Methuen at Tweebosch, in the western Transvaal. This defeat strengthened rather than weakened the desire for peace in Britain. 'We are [Chamberlain wrote of Methuen's defeat] to a certain extent discredited abroad by these constant failures, and the pressure both financial and otherwise in consequence of the prolongation of the struggle is very great. I suppose no civilian can understand why 200,000 men and a million and a half a week are required to put an end to the resistance of 8,000 farmers who probably do not possess £10 apiece.'[1]

Indeed, it was becoming evident that if once the Boer leaders met the British at a conference table, it would be difficult for the British to justify any breaking off of negotiations unless the Boers showed themselves to be utterly obstinate. On 29 March Salisbury told Chamberlain that Hicks Beach had asked that, if any peace proposals were received, the Cabinet should be summoned to consider them 'at whatever inconvenience', before a reply was sent; the King, he added, 'talks about the length of the war emulating the Thirty Years' War in Germany'.[2] Chamberlain was exasperated.

I think Beach's intervention was wholly unnecessary. It is inconceivable that I should deal in any way with proposals for peace without consulting you and the Cabinet.

But the King with his Coronation and Beach with his Budget are both too eager for 'Peace of a sort'. I have spoken several times to the King and thought each time that I had satisfied him that while we were all most anxious to finish the war, nothing would be more dangerous for the country and for his own popularity than that any responsible person should appear ready to sacrifice essential points and show weakness at this stage.

I have an idea that the Rosebery clique and perhaps Rosebery himself have been assuring him that an honourable peace was possible if only we were rid of Milner—and perhaps—although he did not say so—of the Colonial Secretary.[3]

II

On 23 March, Burger and members of his Government entered the British lines at Kroonstad, from where two Boer dispatch riders were sent in search of President Steyn. They found him three days

[1] Chamberlain PP. J.C. 13/3 (9 April 1902).   [2] Ibid., J.C. 11/6.
[3] Salisbury PP. Chamberlain to Salisbury, 1 April 1902.

later, not in the Orange River Colony but in General de la Rey's *laager* near Lichtenburg, whither he had gone for treatment, from de la Rey's doctor, for a nervous disorder which was affecting his eyes. Steyn suggested a meeting in the Transvaal, and on 9 April the two Governments met at Klerksdorp.[1] The Transvaal was represented by Schalk Burger, General Botha, General de la Rey; two former generals who were members of the Executive Council, L. G. Meyer and G. C. Krogh; F. W. Reitz, the State Secretary, and L. Jacobsz, the acting State Attorney: the Orange Free State by President Steyn, General de Wet, General Hertzog, General C. H. Olivier, and W. J. C. Brebner, the acting State Secretary.

From the first meeting, the old division of opinion between the Transvaal and the Orange Free State—a division which was to remain until almost the end—reappeared in the discussions. Formally, both Governments were bound by the joint declaration issued in June 1901—that no peace would be made which did not secure the independence of the Republics and the safety of the Colonial rebels. The Free Staters still held to the letter of this declaration. They had entered the war, on a point of honour, as the allies of the Transvaal; on their country had fallen the brunt of the devastation; they were homeless, proscribed, bereaved: it seemed monstrous that, after their sufferings, they should be, as it were, deserted by those to whose aid they had come. This, in brief, was the attitude of President Steyn. General de Wet was equally implacable; but he may have had a more personal reason for his fortitude, for he had been indirectly accused of complicity in the murder of Morgendal, a member of the Burgher Peace Committee, who had been shot in cold blood by men under de Wet's command.[2]

The Transvaalers saw the problem in a different light. They had now lost hope of retaining independence, and with every month of war that passed Milner's hold on the Transvaal was tightening.

[1] There are three contemporary accounts, from the Boer side, of the meetings at Klerksdorp, Pretoria and Vereeniging—C. R. de Wet, *Three Years War* (London, 1902); J. D. Kestell, *Through Shot and Flame* (London, 1903); and J. D. Kestell and D. E. van Velden, *The Peace Negotiations between Boer and Briton in South Africa* (London, 1912). These have been cited hereafter respectively as *Three Years War*, *Through Shot and Flame* and *Peace Negotiations*. They have a common origin in the notes taken by Kestell, chaplain to Steyn and de Wet, who, with van Velden, was appointed joint secretary to the two Governments—a post, he explained, which he accepted 'not for the position, but in order to get material for my book'. (*Through Shot and Flame*, p. 227n.).

[2] Cd. 903, pp. 79–81.

Whatever happened, the Dutch would remain a majority in the Orange Free State; but a new Transvaal was beginning to emerge, populated by Uitlanders and 'hands-uppers'. Timely surrender might be the only means left of preserving the core of *Afrikanerdom*; otherwise, with the chosen leaders of the *volk* sentenced to perpetual banishment, the remnants of the nation would be left at the mercy of the conqueror. Let them, therefore, make what terms they could while they were still strong enough to bargain, and trust in Providence and their own exertions thereafter: tomorrow, in the words of the Dutch proverb, was another day.

The Free Staters were not to be moved by the argument of growing weakness, and they had gained a valuable supporter in de la Rey, flushed with the victory of Tweebosch and exposed, over the past weeks, to the masterful personality of Steyn. The nation should fight until it could fight no longer, Steyn argued, and then it should surrender unconditionally—submit vengefully, rather than make terms.

The discussions at Klerksdorp swayed backwards and forwards, over this ground, for three days. Steyn was opposed to making any peace proposals whatsoever: it was for the enemy to suggest terms, he said, and he would not take any initiative in submission. Burger and Reitz argued that, for tactical reasons, the first proposals should come from the Boers: it would be harder for the British to whittle away proposals from the Boers than for the Boers to modify terms framed by the British. De Wet said that 'before he conceded an iota of their independence he would allow himself to be banished for ever'.[1] Botha spoke of the compressing effect of the British system of blockhouses. 'There was nothing', he said, 'that urged him personally to terminate the struggle. He could flee about as well as anybody else, but when he considered the circumstances he was bound to say, "We are becoming weaker" ... They were becoming so weak that he was afraid that they would afterwards no longer be considered a party that had to be reckoned with. It was not impossible that they would afterwards be declared rebels, and then a mutual murdering would take place.'[2] Meyer suggested the acceptance of an 'encumbered independence'; Hertzog, the former judge, said that constitutionally the Government had no right 'to meddle with the independence'; that authority could only come from 'the people'. Reitz suggested that they should not mention 'independence'

[1] *Peace Negotiations*, p. 26.   [2] Ibid., p. 29–30.

but demand 'self-government', and that 'the people' should elect representatives to express their views to the Governments. Steyn, broken in health but not in spirit, showed throughout a fiery tenacity which compassion made it difficult to counteract. However, on 11 April, it was decided to ask for a personal meeting with Kitchener, and a sub-committee of the lawyers present drew up proposals for peace with independence.

Proceeding from the basis that they do not recognize the annexation, the two Governments are prepared to conclude peace by conceding the following matters:

1. The concluding of a perpetual Treaty of friendship and peace, including:

(a) Arrangements relative to a Customs Convention.
(b) Post, Telegraph and Railways Union.
(c) Fixing of the Franchise.

2. Dismantling of all State Forts.

3. Arbitration in all future differences between the contracting parties, an equal number of arbitrators to be appointed by each party from their subjects, with an umpire to be chosen by both parties.

4. Equal educational rights for both the English and Dutch languages.

5. Mutual amnesty.[1]

Kitchener agreed at once to a meeting, and the delegation left in two trains that night. In Pretoria, they were lodged apart—the Transvaalers in a house near Kitchener's headquarters, the Free Staters in a more distant suburb. Kitchener had taken steps to inform himself of the Boers' private discussions: an officer who spoke Dutch (unbeknown, it was hoped, to the Boers) was in attendance throughout the formal discussions, and officers who spoke Dutch were instructed to mingle, outside the conference chamber, with the younger Boers who had come as *aides-de-camp* or attendants. On 12 April Kitchener met the two Governments. 'It seems best as you propose', Brodrick had telegraphed on 11 April, 'that you should see the Boers alone and receive their proposals'; and in a second telegram on the same day he added: 'The word "alone" referred to your not being accompanied by Milner. You will be, no doubt, careful to have witnesses present.'[2]

Here, present and recognized, is the lack of sympathy, and the argument from slanting purposes, which were to characterize

---

[1] Ibid., p. 28.   [2] W.O. Conf. Tel. Nos. 1070 and 1071.

the relations between Kitchener and Milner throughout the negotia-
tions—a divergence which the Boers were quick to recognize. On 10
April, in a 'private and personal' addendum to a telegram to
Chamberlain, Milner had written:

I do not at all relish idea of interview between Kitchener and Boer delegates. Under whatever conditions it is held it will virtually be a commencement of negotiations. For a military surrender Kitchener would be the
proper person to conduct them. But Boers are sure [to ask?] a number of
things profoundly affecting political future. Kitchener is not a very good
judge of the effects of such proposals and he is extremely anxious to end
the war and get away. Under these circumstances he is quite likely to make
dangerous concessions without quite realizing the extent of them, and
though of course this would not bind His Majesty's Government, who
will reserve decision, it might be very compromising.
I happen to know for instance that Kitchener thinks there is no great
objection to fixing a date for self-government. Personally I think such a
stipulation quite intolerable, and there are other points on which he is, in
my opinion, inclined to be very lax.[1]

This telegram was printed for circulation to the Cabinet. On 12
April, Chamberlain replied that the British Government could not
give instructions to their representatives until the Boers had submitted proposals in writing. 'We have never', he added, 'contem-
plated negotiations as possible except with your participation.'[2]
   The meeting of 12 April was private and the secretaries were
excluded; but an account of the proceedings was taken down
immediately afterwards by Kestell from Hertzog's dictation, and
the transcript was then revised by Steyn and Brebner.[3] Kitchener
opened the discussions 'as one with a grievance', complaining that
after the Middelburg negotiations with Botha he had been unjustly
described as one who wished to exterminate the Afrikaner people;
then, abruptly changing his mood, he asked for the Boer proposals.
These were read by Burger, and interpreted by Reitz. Kitchener
'showed surprise' when he realized that the Boers were demanding
independence. Steyn interjected that 'the People must not lose their
self-respect'. There could be no question of a loss of self-respect,
Kitchener replied, for men who had fought so bravely; to send such
terms to London would harden opinion against them, and he advised
the Boers, as a friend, to accept the British flag and then try to

---

[1] C.O. 417/350, f. 641. Headlam (ii. 328) quotes the first sentence of the
'private and personal' message.
[2] Headlam, ii. 329.   [3] *Peace Negotiations*, p. 33.

bargain for the best possible terms regarding self-government. Steyn asked whether the self-government would be like that of the Cape Colony, and Kitchener replied, 'Yes, precisely so'. Steyn retorted that the situation of the Republics was not analogous to that of the Cape: the colonists there had never lost their freedom. 'The Afrikaners in the two Republics were an independent people. And if that independence were taken away from them they would immediately feel themselves degraded, and a grievance would arise which would necessarily lead to a condition of things similar to that in Ireland. The conditions in Ireland had arisen mainly from the fact that Ireland was a conquered country.'[1]

Some desultory argument followed on Irish history, in which Kitchener professed to speak as an Irishman himself. Then, returning to the role of candid friend, he said that military rule would be followed by self-government 'and then the Boers could annul any measure or law passed by the military authorities'; he urged them, therefore, to make some proposal short of independence. The Boers replied that they had no constitutional power to do so, and Kitchener than agreed to send their terms, in a modified form, to London. With the assistance of Reitz, he struck out the preamble, which explicitly rejected annexations, and an agreed telegram was sent to the Secretary of State for War.

The Cabinet rejected the Boer terms, but instructed Kitchener and Milner to press for further proposals. Hicks Beach urged conciliation upon Chamberlain.

I would suggest for your consideration [he wrote on 13 April] whether it might not be worth while for you to tell Milner your own opinion (whatever it may be) on two points of which he can know nothing unless he is told. (1) The strength of the desire for peace here among those who have supported the war throughout. (2) the condition of the army. Brodrick seems almost in despair about the latter—and other reports are also bad. And, though our people would decidedly support us in resisting any proposals that could clearly be shown to be dangerous for the future, they would, I think, take a very different view if we rejected an agreement with the Boers on what they would consider merely minor grounds. If I am right in this, Milner might see, more than I imagine he does now, that Kitchener's desire to get away from South Africa is not the only reason for not being too stiff on the present occasion.[2]

Chamberlain did, in fact, encourage Milner to go to the limits of safety. He referred to his speech on the Address as giving a general

---

[1] *Through Shot and Flame*, p. 285.   [2] Chamberlain PP. J.C. 11/4.

indication of terms—recognition of defeat, a large amnesty, self-government in the future, equal rights for white men, but no conditions binding on the British; but he added that he would not shrink from inconsistency if local opinion encouraged Milner to further concession. 'The enormous cost of the war and the continuous strain upon the Army make peace most desirable, but we cannot buy it by concessions which may encourage future rebellion or which would justify the loyal section in saying that they had been betrayed.'[1] This telegram was sent on Chamberlain's personal responsibility, without being shown to the Cabinet.[2]

III

On 14 April, the Boer Governments returned to Kitchener's headquarters. The intervening period had been one of anxiety for them, for reports began to circulate of General Ian Hamilton's limited victory over part of de la Rey's force, under General Kemp, at Roodeval on 11 April. Steyn's determination, at least, was unweakened. Milner was present for the first time, and the Boers took note that he addressed the President of the Orange Free State and the Vice-President of the Transvaal respectively as 'Mr. Steyn' and 'Mr. Burger'. (Later, he accorded them the title of 'President'.) The British Government's refusal to recognize independence was read out, and the Boers were pressed to put forward further proposals. This they refused to do. 'You ask too much', Botha said. 'You say . . . Surrender and then let us discuss further terms. We earnestly desire peace. If we go to the People and say "We have certain proposals to make to you" the People will say, "No, you have given away Independence without our authority, we will not listen to you".'[3] But who were 'the People'? An exchange took place between Milner and Steyn, which Kestell reported in these words:

Lord Milner: May I ask if the prisoners-of-war will also be consulted?
President Steyn: Your Excellency surely cannot be in earnest in putting this question?
Lord Milner (in a tone of annoyance): Yes, certainly.
President Steyn: How can the prisoners-of-war be consulted?—they are civilly dead. To mention one practical difficulty; suppose the prisoners should decide that the war should be continued, and the burghers on commando that it should not—what then?

---

[1] C.O. 417/350, f. 646.   [2] Ibid., f. 646.
[3] Milner MSS., vol. 49; Notes of Meeting of 14 April.

Lord Kitchener and Lord Milner, seeing the absurdity, laughed aloud. They quite agreed with President Steyn, and admitted that the difficulty raised by him was to the point.[1]

Nevertheless, the debating point won by Steyn was of some significance: the British had tacitly admitted that the 'People' were to be defined as members of the commandos still in the field—that the prisoners, and, *a fortiori*, the 'hands-uppers' and the National Scouts, were to be excluded from influence. This was to have considerable importance in the future.[2]

The British had instructions to put forward no proposals: the Boers declared that to put forward proposals was beyond their power. Deadlock seemed to have been reached. Kitchener suggested an adjournment, so that the Boers might debate in private; and he and Milner withdrew. When the meeting resumed, the Boers presented a resolution, asking for an armistice 'to consult the People' and for a safe-conduct for a member of the Deputation in Holland to 'come over to them'. Kitchener said that it would be better to ask the British Government 'to make proposals which could be regarded as compensation to the Boers for the surrender of their Independence.'[3] An agreed telegram was sent to London, pointing out the Boers' constitutional difficulty, and asking the British Government to offer terms which the Boers could lay before 'the people'. The Boers had won another tactical victory.

Milner at once sent a 'secret, private and personal' telegram to Chamberlain. He distrusted all negotiations, he said, but as they were favoured by public opinion in England 'we must do the best we can'. He suggested that, as a basis, terms should be offered similar to those rejected at Middelburg, with certain modifications. He asked for instructions on three points (a definite instruction would deprive Kitchener of the power to make concessions): there was to be no treaty or convention; no date would be fixed for the introduction of self-government; English would be the official language, with toleration for Dutch in the schools and courts of law. On amnesty, Milner was prepared to relax, to the extent that rebels still in the field who had been guiltless of criminal actions should suffer disfranchisement only.[4]

The British reply was received on 17 April: it followed Milner's suggestions. Kitchener refused a general armistice on military

---

[1] *Through Shot and Flame*, p. 290.   [2] See chapter 7, below.
[3] *Through Shot and Flame*, p. 292.   [4] Headlam, ii. 334–5.

grounds, but promised to give facilities for the Boers to hold meetings of all commandos outside the Cape Colony. The request for a visit from a member of the Deputation was likewise refused: Kitchener said that the Boers could take his word that nothing to their advantage was happening in Europe. On this note, the Boers dispersed having undertaken to return with full powers to negotiate.

In their separate diagnoses of the Boer attitude, in telegrams to their political chiefs, Kitchener and Milner concurred that the question of peace or continued war would turn upon the personality of two or three leaders. Kitchener told Brodrick that he had allowed Steyn to see a doctor of Steyn's choice in Pretoria, as 'the doctor was very anxious, for his own purposes, to get the war over'. (The result had been discouraging: Steyn had been told that he would die if he did not rest, and had replied that he must give his life for the people, if necessary.) 'The Free Staters are doubtful,' Kitchener concluded, 'but they cannot go on alone, and we have so chaffed the Transvaal that they are being led by the nose by the smaller State that I really think that they will stick it out this time.' He reported, as the opinion of the younger Boers, 'that if no terms are made and they are forced to unconditional surrender they will hold themselves absolutely free to begin again when they get a chance and see England in any difficulty.'[1] Milner thought that three-quarters of the Boer representatives wanted to submit, but that no one was prepared to take the lead. Hertzog was 'quite irreconcilable', and Steyn would be 'most dangerous' but for the state of his health. 'De Wet is wavering. He is afraid of what we may do to him. A good deal may turn ultimately on our being able to reassure de Wet as to his personal safety in case of surrender, but this would have to be very carefully done and if possible quite privately. Though a good fighter, he is a low fellow and will put his own interest first.'[2]

Milner had already told Chamberlain, once more, that the 'great difficulty' was Kitchener. 'He is extremely adroit in his management of negotiations, but he does not care what he gives away.'[3] On 21 April, in reply to a suggestion from Chamberlain, Milner asked that an identical telegram should be sent to Kitchener and himself, stating that the British Government was not prepared

---

[1] Arthur, *Kitchener* II. 93, n. 1.
[2] Milner MSS., vol. 49, Milner to Chamberlain, 16 April 1902. Quoted in part in Headlam, ii. 336–7.
[3] C.O. 417/351, f.

to make concessions on points of policy. This was done on 22 April. It ran: 'You will have understood from our secret telegrams that we are entirely opposed to political pledges or conditions which may embarrass in the future and may lead to recrimination. We are ready to be liberal on all personal matters, but the Boers are not in a position to demand conditions of peace which would tie our hands in future administration.'[1] The example to be followed, the telegram ended, should be the capitulation of Lee at Appomattox.

By April, the British Government had made its decision on Natal's claims on the border districts of the Transvaal and the old Orange Free State, and proposed to transfer Vryheid and part of the Wakkerstroom district of the Transvaal to Natal. Kitchener thought that the publication of this news would discourage the peace party among the Boers. L. S. Amery, who was present in Pretoria during the negotiations, wrote later that 'Kitchener . . . was all for any kind of surrender. He liked his opponents personally. He was desperately anxious to get away and was little concerned with the political consequences. Lastly, with his rather Oriental outlook, he believed that once the Boers were disarmed we could interpret the terms of surrender in our own way.'[2] On 5 May, without consulting Milner, Kitchener telegraphed to the Governor of Natal, Sir Henry McCallum: 'I hope you will stop all correspondence being published about transfer of territory . . . and if possible do something to throw doubt on the arrangements which have been published.' McCallum informed Milner at once of this request, and Milner unburdened himself privately to Chamberlain in the strongest language which he had yet used about Kitchener.

This is not a matter which I can take up officially, as if I did, it must lead to a most frightful row. But I think you will recognize that it is a difficult thing, in handling such delicate matters, to be yoked to a person, who not only acts behind your back but is capable of suggesting to another gentleman, that he should try to deceive people by 'throwing doubts' on the action of his own Government. The intention is obvious—to keep the Boers in the dark about Vryheid and Utrecht until they sign a peace, and to let them find it out afterwards . . . This is the sort of diplomacy to which I profoundly object . . . Heaven knows how much of it is going on all round me today—not a little, of that I am very certain. I am beginning to think that those who sow the seeds should stop to reap the harvest.[3]

[1] W.O. Conf. Tel. No. 1109, Secretary of State to Kitchener.
[2] Amery, *My Political Life*, p. 165.
[3] Chamberlain PP. J.C. 13/3. Milner to Chamberlain, 9 May 1902. Chamberlain endorsed it: 'This letter has been seen by nobody but me.'

IV

Meanwhile, Milner had been sounding the Governments of the Cape and Natal on the details of the Middelburg terms. He found them in agreement that strict equality should not be granted to the Dutch and English languages; but, on the treatment of rebels, Milner had outrun the magnanimity of the Colonial Ministers. Sir Robert Hime said that it would be 'utterly impossible' to pass an amnesty Bill through the Natal Legislature: the only way in which rebels could escape prosecution for high treason would be for them to remain perpetually out of Natal (including the territory to be annexed to Natal).[1] The Cape was prepared to distinguish between the rank and file and those who had held office, either in the rebel forces or under the Cape Government; the former would be punished only with disfranchisement for life, the latter would be tried for treason and would suffer such penalty as the Court might decide, with the proviso that no sentence of death should be inflicted.[2]

On 5 May, forty 'leading citizens' of the Witwatersrand (led by Sir Percy Fitzpatrick) sent to Milner an appeal that only the unconditional surrender of the Boers should be accepted: 'we feel bound to say that in our judgement the conceding of any conditions at all— entirely apart from the principles in them—is undesirable and impolitic, and the granting of terms which would form a kind of convention is absolutely inadmissible.' They had no objection to a general statement of the manner in which the Boers would be governed:

But we do feel:

1. That any conditions referring to the political future of the country and its government will in effect form another convention which will be claimed as the groundwork of the constitution, and be deemed of force superior to any subsequent enactment, and will therefore constitute a lien upon a self-governing people, causing endless trouble in the future,

[1] C.O. 417/351, f. 212.
[2] Ibid., f. 356. The differential treatment of rebels decided upon by the Cape Government followed the Treason Act of 1900 and the Proclamations of Lord Roberts; it was held to be unwise in the Colonial Office. Lambert minuted: 'As a matter of equity there is nothing to be said against it. But as a matter of policy it is open to doubt. As long as we specially penalize the leaders we make it to their interest to hold out, and the Dutch have undoubtedly shewn through-out a great attachment to their leaders.' Chamberlain commented: 'I am inclined to agree.'

overriding their will if they submit, or making them and His Majesty's Government liable to charges of breach of faith if they repudiate it.

2. That a granting of conditions will erect into a party within the colony a particularly resolute and hostile body of men deeming themselves entitled by treaty to special rights; will give to this party much prestige; and will place the men who are still in the field, and whose intercepted correspondence shows that they will only make peace to husband their resources for the continued pursuit of their racial ambitions, in a position morally, if not materially, superior to those burghers who surrendered . . .

Self-government, they added, should come only when there was 'a loyal majority' in the new colonies, or when South Africa had been united in a federation. 'We do not and cannot believe that His Majesty's Government will knowingly take the chance of having to break faith or yield to the ballot what they have held from the rifle. But it is not unnatural that the Boer leaders should wish to see them placed in that dilemma.'[1]

V

On 15 May, the Boer Assembly of the People—thirty delegates each from the Transvaal and the Orange Free State, elected by the commandos—met at Vereeniging, on the Vaal River forty miles south-east of Johannesburg. Kitchener had undertaken not to attack any commando which sent its commandant to the Assembly; in consequence, the delegates were nearly all senior officers, and the war came unofficially to a halt. The war party had suffered one severe loss, and the peace party had gained one powerful advocate: President Steyn was now so weak that he could not dismount from his spider without help, and the Transvaalers (with Kitchener's accord) had recalled General Smuts from the far north-western Cape, where he was besieging the town of O'okiep.[2]

Before the discussion on peace or war began, one important preliminary question had to be decided: in the election of representatives some commandos had insisted upon a 'mandate' for no terms short of independence.

It appeared that at the meetings held by General L. Botha and most of the Transvaal officers, and at those held in the Orange Free State by Judge

1 Ibid., f. 255, seqq.
2 *Through Shot and Flame*, pp. 297–8; Deneys Reitz, *Commando* (London 1929), p. 315. Reitz (whose account was written in 1903) notes than when the news spread among Smuts's burghers that the general had been summoned to a peace conference, 'they were convinced that the British were suing for terms and were ready to restore our country.'

Hertzog, the Delegates had been fully empowered to act on behalf of the People according to circumstances, and even to come to a final decision. On the other hand, at the meetings held by General de Wet in the Free State, and by General de la Rey in the South African Republic, the People had given to their Delegates a fixed and limited authority, whatever else might be decided, in no case to relinquish the independence of the States.[1]

After Burger's opening speech, which was to the effect that the real decision was not independence, which the British would not concede, but whether to continue the war or not, Botha refused to proceed further until the question of the representatives' powers had been settled. Hertzog spoke to this point, with the authority of his civil office: legally, he said, a representative was no mere mouth-piece, but had a general power of acting in accordance with his best convictions. Smuts, the State Attorney of the Transvaal, supported Hertzog; and the sense of the meeting was in their favour.

The greater part of that day and the next was taken up with reports from the representatives of conditions in the areas in which their commandos were operating. As the discussions developed, two dominating themes began to appear—hunger and the growing menace of the Natives.[2] Botha, who made the first report, dwelt on the shortage of maize and cattle, the exhaustion of his horses, the plight of the women still with the commandos whom the British would no longer accept into the concentration camps, and the belligerency of the Native tribes. Since the previous June, he had lost over 6,000 burghers killed and captured; he still had 10,800 under his command, but nearly 3,300 were without horses and hence useless for operations. He described in detail an attack by Natives upon a commando in the Vryheid district, when 56 burghers had been 'murdered . . . by Kaffirs who came from the English lines'.[3] C. Birkenstock, the representative from Vryheid, added: 'That peace must be made at all costs is the opinion of all the families in my district, and I feel it my duty to bring this opinion before you.'[4]

Before the end of the first day's debate, it was clear that the split between the two Governments was reflected in a split between the

[1] *Through Shot and Flame*, p. 301.

[2] Kitchener told Brodrick that, during the discussions in Pretoria in April, he had taxed the Boers with their treatment of the Natives. 'They are much afraid of a Native rising, and I have told them they are entirely responsible if such an event occurs . . . They did not much like this, and Botha was a good deal impressed.' Magnus, *Kitchener*, p. 188.

[3] *Peace Negotiations*, p. 54.   [4] *Three Years War*, p. 412.

representatives of the Transvaal and the Free State: the former were for peace without independence, the latter for a fight to the bitter end. No argument of growing weakness made any impression on the Free Staters, who had taken their tone and temper from Steyn. They were supported, from the Transvaal, by General Beyers and General Kemp: food could be taken, Beyers said, from the Natives by force.[1] Smuts told the Assembly that there was no hope of a general rising in the Cape: even where the Dutch were sympathetic, he said, they were prevented from joining the commandos by the shortage of horses and the fear of punishment for rebellion. Both sides cited the Scriptures to their purposes. Vice-Commandant Breytenbach of Utrecht said that the men of his commando would fight no more unless he could assure them that the struggle could be carried on to some purpose; and had made up his mind that he could not give that assurance. 'Yet we can understand', he said, 'the answer God has given to our prayer—that prayer which we offered with Mausers in our hands when the war began.'[2]

On the second afternoon, Reitz proposed a compromise: the Republics should accept a British protectorate, give up independent foreign relations, and cede the Witwatersrand goldfields and Swaziland. This had sufficient appeal for the Assembly to appoint Hertzog and Smuts as a committee to draft proposals in this sense. In the meantime, the debate continued, with increasing passion. That evening, Burger answered those who still hoped for foreign intervention; of that, he said, there was no chance whatsoever. 'I emphatically state that the war cannot be carried on any longer; and I ask if there is any man here who can maintain with a clear conscience that the struggle can be successfully continued.' He warned his comrades against making speeches directed at proving their courage to posterity. 'Have we not arrived at the stage of our history, when we must pray, "Thy will be done"? . . . Perhaps it is God's will that the English nation should suppress us, in order that our pride may be subdued, and that we may come through the fire of our troubles purified.'[3]

Botha spoke again, pointing out that the discussions had shown that at least ten districts in the Transvaal must be abandoned, because they could no longer feed a commando, and explaining the

---

[1] In 1901 Smuts had written of Beyers that he could not stomach 'the wonderful combination of prayer and pillage practised by his forces'. Hancock, p. 126.
[2] Ibid., p. 418.   [3] Ibid., p. 422.

military consequences of this withdrawal: they had been able to survive because the commandos were so dispersed that the British had been obliged to divide their own forces; now it would be possible for the British to concentrate against them in overpowering strength. Beyers had spoken of taking food from the Natives' kraals in the Northern Transvaal; but that would be possible only while the Natives were still divided in opinion. If the Boers retired to that area and the British followed them, the Natives would rise. 'We have heard much talk about fighting "to the bitter end". But what is "the bitter end"? Is it to come when all of us are banished or in our graves? Or does it mean the time when the nation has fought until it can never rise again?'[1]

He spoke next of the deaths in the concentration camps and of the Boers who had joined the National Scouts. 'If matters go on as at present, there will shortly be more Afrikaners fighting against us than for us.'[2] It was clear to him that they could resist no longer with any hope of success; they must accept terms while they were still strong enough to bargain. They could still obtain rights for their language and a promise that their 'old ideals and customs' would be respected; they could hold the British to their promise of self-government; and they could provide for the debts of the republics. To insist upon surrendering unconditionally, as a matter of pride, would be to betray the nation.

De la Rey, the victor of Tweebosch, now brought to Botha's side the massive weight of his own support. He referred to his own recent successes to show that his commandos could continue; he had, he said, a mandate from his burghers not to give up independence: nevertheless, since he had heard of the conditions in other theatres of war he had become convinced that the time had come to ask for terms. Echoing Botha, he said: 'Fight to the bitter end, it is said. But has the bitter end not come?' As for Reitz's proposal to cede the goldfields, Britain would never agree lest it be said that she had gone to war only for the mines.

De Wet, throwing logic to the winds, answered his comrade-in-arms with angry defiance. England, he said, could send only one-third of her army to South Africa. The Boers had one-third of their own forces left. Therefore, the scales were still evenly balanced. He would fight to the end, and would surrender neither territory nor independence. The fact that there had been no European inter-

1 Ibid., p. 426.   2 *Peace Negotiations*, p. 85.

vention on the Boers' behalf was proof that it was not the will of God that intervention should happen: 'Does it not show that He is minded to form us, by this war, into a nation worthy of the name? Let us then bow to the will of the Almighty . . . For me, this is a war of religion and thus I can only consider the great principles involved. Circumstances are to me but as obstacles to be cleared out of the road.'[1]

On 17 May the Assembly passed two resolutions, the first empowering the two Governments to conclude peace on the basis of Reitz's proposals, the second appointing a commission—consisting of Botha, de la Rey, Smuts, de Wet and Hertzog—which, if these proposals should be refused, should negotiate for peace and submit the draft terms to the Assembly for ratification. The Boers, then, would not return to Pretoria with plenary powers, but the British were not disposed to make an issue of this omission. Colonel Henderson, Kitchener's Director of Military Intelligence, had telegraphed from Vereeniging on 18 May: 'Smuts considers that responsibility thrown on Delegates by necessity of ratification will make for complete peace, whereas if Commission had plenary powers minority might later repudiate any agreement made by Commission. If terms are ratified by Delegates, arrangement will be complete and final.'[2]

VI

On 19 May the Boer commissioners met Milner and Kitchener in Pretoria.[3] There were cross-currents below the surface on either side. Of the commissioners, Botha and Smuts were for peace, and de la Rey had joined them; de Wet (outwardly at least) was farouche and implacable; Hertzog, confused and distressed in spirit, inclined definitely neither to one side nor the other. For the most part, however, the Boers showed a united resolution in the formal sessions; a keen ear could note the discordance between the tones of Milner and Kitchener.

The Boers put forward, as a basis for negotiations, three proposals:

(1) We are prepared to surrender our independence as regards foreign relations.

(2) We wish to retain self-government under British supervision.

(3) We are prepared to surrender a part of our territory.

They requested formally that these proposals should be sent to

[1] *Three Years War*, p. 431.   [2] Milner MSS., vol. 49.   [3] Cd. 1096.

London; and when Milner replied that he had no hesitation in rejecting them on his own responsibility, Botha asked whether, when Lord Salisbury had declared that Britain sought no territory, he did not mean what he had said. Milner retorted that circumstances had changed, and tried to pin the Boers down to the terms offered at Middelburg. In an atmosphere of quickening hostility, the Boers argued that there was no necessary contradiction between their proposals and the Middelburg terms: they would go no farther until they had been given an answer from London. Milner, with sternness, recapitulated the course of the negotiations:

You came and made a proposal. The British Government gave you a distinct answer—they refused to accept it . . . At the same time, they said, 'We are anxious for peace; will you make other proposals?' You then said, 'No! we have no power to do so; we must first consult the nation.' We admitted that argument. Then you said, 'Let the British Government make proposals.' The British Government did so, and they are fully entitled to an answer . . . You come back with a totally fresh proposal, and do not say anything about ours. This is not fair treatment to the British Government, and we are not bound to take your proposal into consideration.[1]

At this point the meeting adjourned, and during the recess Smuts had an informal talk with Milner and Kitchener. At the resumption, Milner produced a document which was a bare, even stark, acknowledgement of Boer defeat. It required the leaders of the 'burgher forces in the field' to accept, 'on behalf of themselves and the said burghers', the annexation of the republics, to recognize themselves as British citizens, to lay down their arms and to cease from further resistance; to this, Milner said, a schedule might be added, containing a modification of the Middelburg terms. Once again the negotiations approached a deadlock. The Boers wished the British to draft the schedule. Milner refused: the Boers might draft it alone, or he would act with them, but he would not, considering past experience, draw up new documents for the Boers 'to cut up and alter'. De Wet said that he could not imagine how any acceptable schedule could be drafted: there was no chance 'of putting a body on such a head', and he added that he did not think that the Boers would accept a government in which either Milner or Kitchener had authority. Kitchener then suggested that the military members should withdraw: this removed him from the discussions, but it also removed de Wet. The Boers agreed, and appointed

[1] *Three Years War*, p. 442.

Hertzog and Smuts as a sub-committee to work with Milner (assisted by Sir Richard Solomon) on the schedule.

This work lasted for two days. The Boer lawyers argued with persistence. No minutes were kept, but Kestell wrote:

> The two men who constituted the sub-committee did much. They opposed all endeavours to make the oath of allegiance obligatory. They succeeded in arranging that no judicial steps, either civil or criminal, should be taken for acts done during the war. They insisted that the Governments of both States, if a treaty of peace were made, should sign it as the Governments respectively of the South African Republic and of the Orange Free State, and thus virtually forced the British Government to treat the 'annexations' of the two Republics as non-existent, and to negotiate not with late Republics but with existing States, whose official names, and not the new names given in the annexation proclamation, it would recognize through the signatures of its Representatives.[1]

The draft schedule was presented to the full conference on 21 May. It contained twelve clauses. The first four required the Boers still in the field to lay down their arms and to recognize the King 'as their lawful Sovereign', provided for the repatriation of prisoners, and safeguarded the personal liberty and property of those who surrendered. Clause 5 stated: 'No proceedings, civil or criminal, will be taken against any of the burghers so surrendering or returning for any acts in connexion with the prosecution of the war.'[2] Clause 6 stated: 'The Dutch language will be taught in public schools in the Transvaal and the Orange River Colony where the parents of the children desire it, and will be allowed in courts of law when necessary for the better and more effectual administration of justice.' Clause 7 permitted Boers to be armed, under licence, with rifles for their personal protection. Clause 8 stated: 'Military administration in the Transvaal and Orange River Colony will at the earliest possible date be succeeded by civil government and, as soon as circumstances permit, representative institutions, leading up to self-government will be introduced.' Clause 9 stated: 'The question of granting the franchise to Natives will not be decided until after the introduction of self-government.' Clause 10 stated that there would be no special war tax upon landed property, Clause 11 provided for the payment of government notes issued by the South African

---

[1] *Through Shot and Flame*, p. 318.

[2] Chamberlain cabled to Milner on 24 May: 'If object Clause 5 was to secure de Wet cannot this be arranged by Kitchener and your personal guarantee that he shall not be prosecuted?' Chamberlain PP. J.C. 13/3.

Republic, and Clause 12 provided for commissions to assist in re-patriation and rehabilitation.

Botha immediately objected to Clause 11: it was unsatisfactory he said, because it took no account of the receipts issued by Boer officials in the field for goods which they had commandeered for war purposes. A long argument followed. Milner was, at first, not willing to make any concession: he described Botha's proposal as 'very extreme', and said that it amounted to a demand that 'the British Government must pay all the money borrowed by the Republics to fight them'.[1] Smuts pointed out that the Middelburg terms had contained an offer to pay for receipts up to a limit of £1,000,000; Milner replied that the Middelburg terms had re-pudiated the liability for Government notes, and that the existing proposal was as far as he was prepared to go. The Boers made it clear that, in that event, the Assembly would not accept terms. De Wet repeatedly declared that they must 'have weapons in their hands' when they went back to meet the burghers, and that 'the honour of every officer is affected'. Botha said that it would be cheaper for the British Government to pay for the receipts than to break off negotiations. Kitchener openly sided with the Boers, and Milner gave way.[2] An addendum to Clause 11 provided that receipts might be presented to a Commission, 'and if found to have been given *bona fide* for goods used by the burgher forces in the field, will be paid out to the persons to whom they were originally given,' up to a limit of £3,000,000.

Milner emphasized that the Middelburg terms were now to be regarded as entirely superseded, and that the British Government would be bound by nothing which did not appear in the schedule. The draft was telegraphed to London that afternoon: de Wet said, before the meeting dispersed, that he did not approve of the document and did not think that the Assembly of the People would accept it.

In London, the Colonial Office refused to accept the principle of payment embodied in Clause 11 and the addendum, on the grounds that to do so would involve, in equity, large and unspecified

[1] *Peace Negotiations*, p. 120.

[2] Kitchener telegraphed to Brodrick on 28 May that he hoped that 'if my telegrams are published in a Blue Book or elsewhere you will kindly see that they are carefully edited so that they do not show any divergence of views between Lord Milner and myself. Of course I do not mind the vital necessity of subject of Clause 11 being put down to me if it is advisable.' C.O. 417/351, f. 790.

compensation to loyalists; and Chamberlain carried his point in Cabinet. Clauses 11 and 12 of the draft were struck out, and a new clause substituted which provided for the appointment of rehabilitation commissions, at the disposal of which the British Government would place a sum of £3,000,000; notes and receipts might be presented to these commissions, and, if accepted, would be regarded as evidence of war losses, which might entitle an applicant to relief. There was no mention of payment as of right, but the new clause stated that the British Government would be prepared to make loans, free of interest for two years and repayable thereafter with interest at three per cent.[1]

No other alterations of substance were made to the draft. Clauses 2 and 3 were thrown into one, and an exception was added to the former Clause 5 excepting from the amnesty persons guilty of 'acts contrary to the usages of war' whose names had been notified to the Boer generals: in effect, this referred only to three men accused of murder. There was only passing comment in London on the critical change in the clause relating to the Native franchise, which had been altered from the undertaking, given at Middelburg, not to consider the question before the grant of representative institutions to the pledge that the matter would be postponed until after the grant of self-government: Graham minuted, 'The Native franchise is I think the only point worth hesitating about. As [the clause] stands the Native will never have the franchise. No responsible government will give it to him.'[2]

The amended terms were telegraphed back to Pretoria on 27 May: on the suggestion of Milner and Kitchener they were now presented in the form of an ultimatum, to which the Assembly of the People must give the answer 'yes' or 'no' before 31 May. Botha asked whether the Assembly could delete any clause, and contended that it had this right by virtue of the fact that the Boers could, if they wished, surrender unconditionally. Milner replied that no alterations would be permitted. Kitchener then read the provisions relating to the rebels—trial in Natal and for office-bearers in the Cape, disfranchisement only for the Cape rank and file.

VII

The Assembly of the People began its last session on 29 May. The debate ranged over familiar ground: but it was clear that the

[1] Headlam ii. 359.   [2] C.O. 417/351, f. 394.

essential issue was no longer whether or not the war would be continued but whether the Transvaal and the Orange Free State delegates would stand together in defeat or would part in anger. The terms were read and explained to the Assembly.[1] Burger then said that there were three choices before them—war, acceptance, and unconditional surrender. Steyn, in a final plea, said that there was a fourth choice, 'to insist upon our cause being decided in Europe by persons empowered, and sent thither by us.'[2] But, he added, he was too ill to take any further part in the struggle, and hence probably had no right to speak further. Two of the Free State commandants pressed for an immediate vote on their proposal that the terms should be rejected, in the hope of taking advantage of the emotion of the moment; but the Assembly decided to debate further. If was now evident that, with the exception of three or four, the Transvaal delegates were solidly determined to accept the terms. General du Toit said bluntly that, even if there were a majority vote for continued resistance, the majority would have to yield to the minority, for those who were outvoted would fight no longer and the remainder, without them, would be forced into piecemeal surrender. Faith, he added, must have its grounds. 'When Abraham went to sacrifice Isaac, he knew that, even if Isaac were killed, God's promise would nevertheless be carried out. If we believe that God will ultimately deliver us, we must use our brains.'[3] De la Rey was blunter still: 'You may say what you will, resolve what you will; but whatever you do, here in this meeting is the end of the war.'[4] De Wet once again challenged de la Rey: the British had negotiated once, and if the Boers continued to fight the British would negotiate again. Nothing was known of what was happening in Europe: 'our information . . . comes only from newspapers, and "jingo" newspapers at that.'[5]

The debate continued far into the night. Next morning the

---

[1] It was clear from the explanations given that the Boers had not appreciated the significance of the alteration of the clauses referring to the notes and receipts.
[2] *Through Shot and Flame*, p. 326.   [3] *Peace Negotiations*, p. 150.
[4] *Through Shot and Flame*, p. 333.
[5] Cf. Harold Spender: 'I remember asking the Republican Generals after the war whether they had really been encouraged in their resistance . . . by the arguments of the British Radical Press. They informed me that, as they obtained all their newspapers from the belongings of captured officers, their reading had been almost solely confined to the British Conservative Press, which certainly could not be accused of giving them encouragement.' *General Botha* (London, 1916), p. 135 n.

Assembly began its session in high emotion, when Burger announced the resignation of Steyn from the presidency of the Orange Free State and the appointment of de Wet as acting-president in his place. Burger then, on behalf of the Government of the South African Republic, handed to de Wet a sum of money for the use of Steyn, who was destitute. This action, wrote Kestell, 'drew the heart of the Free Stater closer to that of the Transvaaler than before.'[1]

The debate was then resumed, and continued all through the day. Botha disclosed the figures which Kitchener had given him in Pretoria, showing the full extent of Boer losses—20,000 dead in the concentration camps, 3,800 killed in the field and 31,600 taken prisoner (of whom 600 had died in captivity).[2] The nation could endure such punishment no longer: further resistance was impossible, and unconditional surrender would mean destitution. Hertzog said that it had been a mistake to hold the meeting at all, because it had revealed the divisions among the people and discouraged those who would otherwise have been resolute. He gave no clear opinion, but said that each man should decide as his conscience moved him.

Smuts spoke on the afternoon of the second day. He was not a delegate, he said, but he must give his voice and take his responsibility as 'one of those who, as members of the Government of the South African Republic, provoked the war with England.' There was a danger that the question before them would be decided on purely military grounds. The war, it was true, could be continued because the Boer army was unbeaten in the field.

But it is as a nation, and not as an army, that we are met here, and it is therefore for the nation principally that we must consult . . . One and all, we represent the Afrikaner nation, and not only those members of it who are now in the field, but those who rest beneath the soil, and those yet unborn who shall succeed us. From the prisons, the camps, the grave, the *veld*, and from the womb of the future, that nation cries out to us to make a wise decision now . . . We must not sacrifice the nation itself on the altar of independence.

Independence, he went on, was lost. They could fight on, but without hope of success. There would be no foreign intervention on their behalf, and there would be no rising in the Cape Colony. Kruger had exhorted them to fight until all means had been exhausted; that time had come. The country was ruined; let them

---

[1] *Through Shot and Flame*, p. 327.   [2] *Three Years War*, p. 493.

stop before the people, too, were ruined. The end was at hand, an end more bitter than they had ever imagined.

The future is dark indeed, but we will not give up courage, and hope, and trust in God. No one shall ever convince me that this unparalleled sacrifice which the Afrikaner nation has laid upon the altar of freedom will be in vain. It has been a war for freedom—not only the freedom of the Boers, but for the freedom of all the nations of South Africa. Its results we leave in God's hands. Perhaps it is His will to lead our nation through defeat, through abasement, yes and even through the valley of the shadow of death, to the glory of a nobler future, to the light of a brighter day.[1]

By the end of the second day, there had been thirty speeches made. Twenty-one Transvaalers had spoken, twenty of them in favour of accepting terms, one in favour of stopping the war but surrendering unconditionally. Of the nine Free Staters, Hertzog was undecided, another spoke for unconditional surrender, and the remainder were for continuing the war. Burger spoke in a tone of sombre finality. The nation, he said, was divided. He was sorry that it should fall to the Transvaal to declare that it could go no farther; but the Transvaal had no choice. On that note the Assembly adjourned.

Early the following morning, Botha and de la Rey called on de Wet in his tent. No record has been published of what was said there; but it is likely that the Transvaalers urged on de Wet the importance of unity.[2] In any event, it was announced when the Assembly gathered that the two delegations would, for the moment, deliberate separately, and the Free Staters met in de Wet's tent. That afternoon, the Assembly met for the last time, to vote upon a resolution, drafted by Hertzog and Smuts, which amounted to an acceptance, under protest, of the British terms. This was a document for posterity. It listed six reasons why the Boers could not continue the war: the devastation of the countryside, the deaths in the

1 *Three Years War*, p. 495, seqq.

2 On 22 May, Kitchener telegraphed to Brodrick: 'Botha came round this morning to see me. He says de Wet is still rather sulky, but he thought it would be all right if the proposals were not altered by His Majesty's Government. I said, if the terms are approved as they stand by His Majesty's Government, will you tell de Wet before you get to Vereeniging that after the way you have been treated by us, and after leading us to suppose that the proposals were acceptable, that if de Wet intended to refuse them, you and de la Rey would leave him to his fate, that he and his people may cut their own throats if they like, but that they shall not by such action ruin the Transvaal. He said he would tell him this before reaching Vereeniging with the proposals.' W.O. Conf. Tel. No. 1166.

concentration camps, the fact that Natives had been armed and were taking part in the struggle, the proclamations which threatened banishment and confiscation, the inability of the Boers to keep the prisoners whom they captured, and the realization that a remnant of the nation was in danger of starvation and confronted by an overwhelming force. This was the manifesto of a people unbeaten in battle, but worn down by attrition. The resolution deplored the fact that the British Government had refused to recognize the independence of the Republics, and concluded: 'This Assembly expresses its confidence that the conditions called into being by accepting the proposal of His Majesty's Government may soon be so improved that our Nation will attain the enjoyment of those privileges which it considers itself justly entitled to claim.'[1]

This resolution was put to the Assembly, and carried by fifty-four votes to six. Three Transvaalers (General Kemp, J. J. Alberts and J. Naude) and three Free Staters (A. J. Bester, C. C. J. Badenhorst and C. A. van Niekerk) voted in the minority. A second resolution established a committee to collect funds for the destitute and the bereaved, and deputed Botha, de Wet and de la Rey to travel to Europe for that purpose.

The last words were spoken by Burger. 'We stand here at the graveside of the two Republics. Much remains for us to do, even though we cannot do what lies before us in the official positions which we have hitherto occupied. Let us not withdraw our hands from doing what is our duty. Let us pray to God to guide us and to direct us how to keep our people together. We must also be inclined to forgive and forget when we meet our brothers. We may not cast off that portion of our people who were unfaithful.'[2]

The terms of surrender were signed in Pretoria that night, shortly before eleven o'clock. Reitz, before he wrote his name, declared that he signed in his official capacity only.

The number of burghers who surrendered was 21,256 (11,166 in the Transvaal, 6,455 in the Orange River Colony, 3,635 in the Cape) —double the number estimated by Kitchener, three times the number estimated by Milner.

---

[1] H. Lambert minuted that the resolution showed not only that the Boers gave up reluctantly 'but that their last act was to fling at us every sort of accusation of barbarity and to hint not obscurely that they do not regard the arrangement as final.' Graham added that, in its context, the resolution 'points clearly to a desire for the restoration of independence at some future date.' C.O. 471/352, f. 121.

[2] *Three Years' War*, p. 501

NOTE

It has become customary to refer to the document signed in Pretoria on 31 May 1902 as 'The Treaty of Vereeniging'. The original document has no heading, and declares in the preamble that the signatories 'agree to the following Articles'. Kitchener, after the signing, used the phrase 'Terms of Peace'; Milner insisted upon the phrase 'Terms of Surrender'; the Boers talked of 'The Treaty of Vereeniging'. J. E. B. Seely relates that when, as Under-Secretary of State for the Colonies, he was in charge of the South Africa Bill of 1909 in the House of Commons he referred to the 'surrender' of Vereeniging in conversation with King Edward VII, who replied: 'Never say that . . . General Botha is a great man. I know what he would wish it to be called in order to heal the breach between the Boers and the British—the Treaty of Vereeniging.'[1]

[1] J. E. B. Seely, *Adventure* (1930), p. 91.

CHAPTER SEVEN

THE FAILURE OF MILNERISM

> The case of the Transvaal is urgent, for it is the nerve
> centre of South Africa. It is the arena in which all
> questions of South African politics—social, moral,
> racial and economic—are fought out; and this new
> country, so lately reclaimed from the wilderness, with a
> white population of less than 300,000 souls, already
> reproduces in perfect miniature all those dark, tangled,
> and conflicting problems usually to be found in popu-
> lous and old-established European states.
>
> *Winston Churchill, 31 July 1906*

THE first direct challenge to Milner's administration in the Transvaal
came not from the Boers but from the British. For the first year or so
after the peace, the Boers were too occupied with the business of
personal survival to have time to spare for political exercises. They
were absorbed in the task of rebuilding their private lives and re-
settling their families; literally, they were constrained to cultivating
their gardens, or what was left of them. The returning Uitlanders,
on the other hand, found little to their liking in benevolent auto-
cracy; they had no doubts about their own competence to govern
nor about their conviction that only those with long experience of
the country knew what was in its best interests. They tended to think
that the war had been fought exclusively for their benefit; as victors,
they considered themselves entitled to the spoils, including those of
office. Milner had misunderstood the nature of the prestige which
he had accumulated in the days when he had been the champion of
the British interest against the Boers. With the coming of peace, a
champion was needed no longer and gratitude slipped silently away.
His administration was castigated as expensive, wasteful, aloof and
over-regulating. It was given credit for few of its successes, but
blamed for almost every misfortune from cattle sickness to the fall in
gold shares. His officials were regarded as brash and juvenile
intruders; Merriman spoke in the Cape Parliament of a 'kindergarten'
of young men from Balliol, and the name stuck.[1] The Transvaal

---

[1] As a matter of record the influence of New College was predominant.

Political Association was formed in Pretoria within a few weeks of the peace, to press for representative government; in January 1903 one of its spokesmen lectured Chamberlain publicly at a banquet on the shortcomings of Downing Street and said that the Transvaal wanted a 'little less "Crown" and a little more "Colony" ' about its government.[1] In Johannesburg a few days later Chamberlain received an address from the Transvaal province of the South African League —which described itself as 'having for its chief cardinal principle the support, maintenance and defence of British supremacy in South Africa'—setting out its complaints under four headings. The League said that Milner was too conciliatory towards the Boers, that it disliked imported officials, that it was not consulted about legislation, and that it feared that Native policy would 'not be in harmony with Colonial ideas'.[2] (Its alarm about negrophilism, on closer examination, rested mainly upon the abolition of flogging for offences under the pass laws.) It observed that 'comparisons between the methods of the Boer and British Governments, greatly unfavourable to the latter, are continually heard', and it asked for the immediate grant of representative government. Similar requests were made by the Transvaal Political Association and the Johannesburg Chamber of Commerce.

Milner saw clearly the immediate danger to his grand design in the aspirations of the British. For the moment he saw no threat from the Boers. Their leaders he regarded as incorrigible, but he looked on the rank and file with not-unkindly contempt. 'The average Boer', he wrote at the end of 1902, 'really is the most good-natured manageable creature in the world as long as he clearly realizes that you have got the thick end of the stick.'[3] To him they were simple souls, earth-bound and materialistic, who were not interested in abstractions such as national independence and republicanism. Once they were separated from the malign influence of their generals, they would settle down to learn English ways and the English tongue under the guidance of a latter-day Lord Durham. (Milner, Smuts wrote to Emily Hobhouse, 'has dreamed a dream of a British South Africa—loyal with broken English and happy with a broken heart . . .'[4]) The British, however, could not be denied indefinitely the right to govern themselves.

1 Julian Amery, 304.   2 C.O. 529/1.
3 Milner MSS., vol. 26. Milner to Dawkins, 10 November 1902.
4 Anna R. Fry, *Emily Hobhouse: a Memoir* (1929), p. 27.

In a memorandum written to guide Chamberlain in the Transvaal, Milner said:

> My own view is, that it is inevitable that a Crown Government should be unpopular in a community like this, and that its accumulated unpopularity must ultimately lead to a change. The whole question is, at what pace the unpopularity accumulates? If it grew sufficiently slowly to tide the country over the next three or four years, a point may have been reached when popular institutions may be granted with safety. It is therefore of supreme importance, not indeed to make Crown Government popular, which is impossible, but to make its unpopularity grow as slowly as possible, or, in other words, not to use up faster than necessary the influence, which is still considerable, of its principal agents.[1]

In short, he believed that he had a personal reserve of influence which he was deliberately prepared to expend for the sake of his grand design; he would use it to build up 'an administration so competent and so imposing as to enforce an unwilling respect—a system which self-government, when it comes, is not likely altogether to destroy.'

The general plans for reconstruction were discussed and approved in general terms in a series of long conversations which Milner held with Chamberlain in Johannesburg and Bloemfontein. He obtained a loan of £35,000,000 to be raised by the Transvaal and Orange River Colony under Imperial guarantee. Of this, £5,000,000 were allotted to the building of new railways. Milner united the administration of the railways of the two new colonies under the Inter-colonial Council, which also administered the South African Constabulary. He set up a South African Native Commission, to attempt to frame a unified policy for non-Whites. He assured the water supply of the Reef by the establishment of the Rand Water Board and the exploitation of the Vaal River. He established a Forestry Department, and he encouraged, through the work of Lionel Curtis, the creation of self-governing municipalities. He and his young men worked with unrelenting energy. 'I have now', Milner wrote in his diary on 31 March 1903, 'got into the habit of being called at 6.30, getting up at once, and working till 8, then bath and dressing and breakfast, which last collectively about an hour, then working on till 1.30. This gives me nearly six hours work by myself before luncheon . . .'[2] The labours thus begun would commonly last well into the night; and Milner would then relieve his tensions in letters of formidable

1 Headlam, ii. 429.   2 Ibid., 455.

length to his friends. His energies were immense, but the grand design was not prospering, and his reserve of popularity was exhausting itself more quickly than he had expected.

Prosperity was slow in coming. The 18 months which followed the peace saw depression and drought. The mines were slow to increase production. The figures for gold production on the Witwatersrand were:

$$
\begin{aligned}
1899 &\ldots \ldots £15,452,000 \\
1900 &\ldots \ldots £1,481,000 \\
1901 &\ldots \ldots £1,097,000 \\
1902 &\ldots \ldots £7,297,000 \\
1903 &\ldots \ldots £12,622,000
\end{aligned}
$$

At the end of 1903, 3000 stamps and 5000 skilled workers were in involuntary idleness. The 'overspill' which was to lift the new colonies was not forthcoming; the expected immigration did not happen. The depression was popularly ascribed to the shortage of unskilled Native labour; in 1899 the mines had employed 96,000 Native workers, in 1903 the figure was 63,000. The majority report of the Labour Commission of 1903 estimated that there was an immediate shortage of 129,000 Native labourers.[1] Attempts to find new sources of supply elsewhere on the African continent failed. In these circumstances the Transvaal Government proposed and the British Government sanctioned the importation of indentured labourers from China.

The issue of 'Chinese slavery' brought odium upon the Unionist Government, ended Milner's personal immunity from criticism by the leadership of the Liberal Party, divided the British in the Transvaal, and provided the occasion for the return of the Boers to organized politics. Milner had not deviated from the course which he had described to Chamberlain in 1900. He had then written: 'I do not think the reconciliation of the two races hopeless, but the Dutch must be made to feel from the first that it is a question for them of a change of attitude or political extinction. Either they must accept our flag and membership of the British Empire in good faith—thus making equal rights practicable—or we shall have to keep up a system of autocratic rule till their opposition to the new order of things is completely broken.'[2]

[1] Cd. 1896.   [2] Milner MSS., vol. 5, f. 85.

Reconstruction, then, would be carried on with the assistance of the Boers if possible, without it if necessary. Government would in either event be for an indefinite period by executive discretion tempered by local advice. The Executive Council—the Governor, the Lieutenant-Governor and the heads of the principal departments —would have as its adjunct a Legislative Council in which the Executive would be joined by twelve nominated citizens, Boer and British. Seats on this council were offered to, and declined by, Botha, de la Rey and Smuts. They doubted, they said, whether the time was ripe even for a nominated legislature, feeling being what it was; and the Government must accept sole responsibility where it had sole power. In other words, they were not going to compromise themselves with their own *volk* by collaborating where they would enjoy only a dubious influence. Thus with courtesy they returned the poisoned chalice to Lord Milner, and the Boers whom he found willing to take office were men of small standing with the commando leaders. Milner had hardly expected co-operation; but he had perhaps underestimated the subtlety and the persistence of the resistance which he encountered. He found his policy questioned in a multitude of individual complaints, about compensation, repatriation, the return of prisoners of war from abroad, and the discouragement of the use of Dutch in schools. It was clear that the work of extinguishing a rival loyalism must be done anew, this time by the surer hand of a civilian. The Boers, it seemed, were determined to remain irreconcilable, and he drew fresh evidence for this conviction from the reports, sometimes crude and usually unsophisticated, of his secret service. He had created a civilian secret service in 1902, appropriating for its payment £10,000 in the colonial budget under the heading 'miscellaneous'. Writing to Chamberlain for approval on 6 July, he said: 'Beyond the Treasurer, myself and you, nobody, not even my staff, will know of the existence of such an organization.'[1] Some of Milner's agents seem to have been less discreet than he could have wished. A year later Merriman wrote to Bryce: 'I wish I could tell you anything about the Trans-Orange, but I can add little to what you know otherwise. Owing to the noisome system of espionage still carried on, correspondence is tabu.'[2]

How accurate was Milner's diagnosis? Formally, the Boers expressed their desire to live in peace. A document prepared by

[1] Chamberlain PP. J.C. 13/3.   [2] Bryce PP. 18 Augus 1903

Smuts for transmission to Chamberlain in 1903 states that the Boer notables 'have learnt with the greatest pleasure that it is your object to reconcile the races and to bring contentment and prosperity to South Africa. The undersigned give you the assurance that they identify themselves completely with that object and will heartily co-operate for its attainment.'[1] But the co-operation which was offered assumed a system of 'equal rights'; the Boers were not prepared to assist in the extinction of their language or their political identity. Moreover, it takes two to make a reconciliation and many of the former Uitlanders had returned to the Witwatersrand determined that the Boers should suffer the full humiliation of defeat.[2] The importation of Chinese for the first time made possible the building of a bridge between British and Afrikaners in the Transvaal. Chamberlain, in a public speech in Johannesburg in 1903, had tried to soothe the disgruntled British by depicting Crown Colony government as the least of possible evils. 'You do not desire,' he said, 'to put into the hands of your opponents the power to gain by political agitation what they have failed to secure by the sword . . . Neither Boer nor Briton, in the Transvaal, would wish to get rid of Downing Street in order to substitute Park Lane.'[3] Park Lane and Downing Street now appeared to many as equally odious.

II

At the time of Chamberlain's visit, Botha had undertaken not to start a political association without consulting Milner. When Chinese labour became an issue in 1903, Botha gave notice that, as circumstances had changed, he proposed to hold 'some meetings' of former burghers. The letter to Milner was signed by Botha but drafted by Smuts, and from this period onwards Botha and Smuts worked in the closest accord. The relationship between them was more than a political alliance: it was a partnership of the mind, mutually rewarding, almost a symbiosis.[4] Sir Keith Hancock has disposed of the legend, built upon the indiscreet publication of a wild letter to Emily Hobhouse—a single letter in a voluminous correspondence—that Smuts had 'relapsed under Milner's rule into a mood of embitterment, ennui and despair.' On the contrary, this

[1] Hancock, p. 191.
[2] Lionel Curtis, *With Milner in South Africa* (1951), *passim*.
[3] Julian Amery, 326.   [4] Hancock, ch. 10.

was the period in which hard work at the bar brought him the money, invested in land, which gave him independence to devote himself to politics. At Milner's court he was regarded as irreconcilable, but Smuts was no crude racialist and it is likely that pride and reserve were mistaken for indiscriminate hostility. To Smuts, the enemy was not the British, but 'Milnerism'. Now he began to see how Milnerism could be overthrown. The first of the Boer meetings, held at Heidelberg in June 1903, passed resolutions which denounced the 'capitalist plot' to import Asiatics to the detriment of the white man, demanded equal treatment for the Dutch and English languages and the local control of education, and protested against the promise given by the 'magnates' of a war contribution.

The resolutions were skilfully chosen. Two of them—those concerning language and education—appealed exclusively to Afrikaners; those concerning Asiatics and the war contribution touched upon grievances which were shared by many of the British. Chamberlain had obtained from representatives of the mining industry a promise to raise a loan of £30,000,000 to be paid to the Imperial Government in three instalments as a contribution to the cost of the war. In the event, nothing was paid and the British claim was waived after the grant of self-government to the Transvaal; in the meantime, the promise to pay rankled, and the British could claim that they were being taxed without representation.

Milner had reluctantly convinced himself that Chinese labour was necessary, partly because what was left of his grand design would collapse if mining profits did not increase, and partly to anticipate an alliance of Boers and British demanding compulsory labour for Natives and (because this would never be permitted by the existing administration) self-government to put it into force. He wrote to Chamberlain on 13 July 1903 that arguments were abroad that indigenous labour could be found for the mines if only the Government would show a little realism.

Now this is untrue. Personally I am convinced that, if you sent out an army to flog all the natives out of their locations into some sort of work for whites, we should still be short of labour . . . But public opinion here is so feather-brained, people are so impatient and unable to see an inch before their noses, that I am quite certain, if the labour strain continues very much longer, we shall have, *among the meaner sort of British*, a clamour, not in so many words for slavery but 'for some means or other of making the nigger work', and for self-government in order to accomplish this . . . The likeliest combination to produce a strong party in favour of [self-government] is the combination of the bulk of the Boers with a section of the British on the Compulsory Labour Platform.[1]

Milner went on leave to Europe in August 1903. In September Chamberlain resigned. Milner refused the offer of the Colonial Secretaryship, and the office went to Alfred Lyttelton. Chamberlain had on occasions overruled Milner, but always with circumspection. Lyttelton was of softer resolution and regarded himself rather as Milner's pupil than his superior. 'In the world of shadows,' he wrote to Milner in 1906, 'I was called your political chief. But in the world of realities you must know that I always thought of you as mine, and that I shall always think of you as a leader.'[2]

On his return to South Africa at the end of 1903, Milner found himself the object of a converging attack. The Afrikaner Bond in the Cape had adopted a policy of outright opposition to the importation of Chinese, and were joined in this by some Progressives. Milner dismissed this as pure electioneering, an attempt by both sides to win the non-White vote in the Cape.[3] Agitation was growing in the Transvaal. Milner had now made up his mind. On 28 December 1903, the Legislative Council passed a motion proposed by Sir George Farrar, requesting the Transvaal Government to introduce a draft ordinance permitting the importation of 'indentured unskilled coloured labourers . . . under such restrictions as will ensure their employment as unskilled workmen only and their return to their native country on the completion of their contracts.' Of the unofficial members of the Council, nine (including four Afrikaners) voted for the motion, four (all British) against. Milner claimed that these figures represented the balance of opinion in the country, and represented the choice as one between stagnation and economic revival.

Officials in the Colonial Office felt that Milner had moved too fast, and had in effect committed the British Government in advance. Sir Montagu Ommanney, the permanent secretary, doubted whether

---

[1] Milner MSS., vol. 41, f. 21. Headlam (ii. 465) quoted part of the letter but omitted this passage. On the British attitude, compare a letter from Seward Bryce, K.C., in the *Rand Daily Mail* on 16 December 1904, in which the writer advocated a Native policy 'in the true interests alike of the coloured people as of the white,' which might involve the 'subordination of the native . . . and the utilization, paternal and compulsory if need be, of his energies so far as required by the State which protects him.'

[2] Headlam ii. 561. 27 February 1906.

[3] C.O. 291/68. Milner to Lyttelton, 3 January 1904.

public opinion in the Transvaal had been tested. 'I think that it is quite possible,' he minuted, 'that His Majesty's Government, if it gives its assent at this stage, may find that a very strong anti-Chinese feeling will have to be dealt with when the first introduction of these aliens takes place, and that it may take an inconvenient and even a violent form.'[1] Lyttelton disagreed; the ordinance could always be vetoed and he expressed himself as impressed by the strong support of 'representative Boers' and by the sensitiveness of the Legislative Council to public opinion. The representativeness of the Afrikaner councillors may be doubted, however; Botha was emphatically opposed to the measure, and a mass meeting of Boers at Lydenburg on 30 December 1903 protested and asked for a plebiscite to test the feeling of the Colony. This request was taken further in a statement signed by six Boer leaders (Schalk Burger, de la Rey, Smuts, Botha, C. F. Beyers and P. R. Viljoen), which hoped that the Colonial Secretary would 'not remain under the mistaken impression that the Boer people is in favour of a measure which it looks upon as a public calamity of the first magnitude . . .'[2] Once again, there were suggestions in the Colonial Office that the matter should be reconsidered. H. W. Just drew attention to the standing of the signatories, and questioned Milner's assumption that only the majority opinion of the Transvaal British should be considered. He minuted:

I think that this expression of opinion renders it difficult, and practically impossible to justify the sanction of His Majesty's Government to the Ordinance without further consideration. If the opinion is to be thrown aside, it must be treated as unrepresentative and dishonest, and Lord Milner's advice to that effect be published as endorsed by His Majesty's Government. It will follow that the Transvaal will be a pure Crown Colony, not governed in accordance with local wishes and local opinion, but in the interests or according to the voice of the majority of the British.

Milner objected to a plebiscite or referendum; there were no voting lists for the countryside, he said, and it would take six months to prepare them. Furthermore, 'as far as the Boers were concerned it would not be a vote for or against imported labour but a vote for or against the present form of government.'[3] Once again Lyttelton sided with Milner. He dismissed the Boers' protest, and refused 'to admit the claim of its writers to speak on this subject on

[1] Ibid., minute of 5 January 1904.
[2] Ibid. Milner to Lyttelton, 11 February 1904, No. 1.   [3] Ibid. No. 2.

behalf of the great majority of the Boer population.'[1] The British Government withheld its veto, and the Ordinance passed by the Legislative Council on 10 February thereupon became law.

III

There was no denying the growth of unrest in the Transvaal. Reports from resident magistrates indicated the excitement in the country districts at the news of the outbreak of war between Russia and Japan in February 1904; rumours were afoot that, if Britain were involved, the Transvaal would either be given back to the Boers 'or they would have no trouble in taking it.' Milner reported that 'Even the National Scouts are now being approached with a view to reconciliation.' On the other side, resolutions in favour of self-government were passed by trades unions and labour organizations. In April at a meeting at Fordsburg, in the centre of Johannesburg, Botha announced his intention of calling a convention of the Boer people. In the same month a British meeting at Potchefstroom, under the chairmanship of Harry Solomon, demanded immediate self-government.

On 2 May 1904, after the Fordsburg and Potchefstroom meetings, Milner wrote to Lyttelton that the demand for self-government had spread so widely that it could be controlled 'only by humouring it to some extent . . . If the Government of the Colony itself takes the initiative we may be able to retard the pace, and perhaps to provide against some of the dangers.' He proposed therefore that election should be substituted for nomination in the Legislative Council. 'I assume that in that case the attempt to keep a Government majority . . . would be frankly abandoned.' Sooner or later, what was given to the Transvaal would have to be given also to the Orange River Colony; but 'granted that we have to try an experiment which at best is somewhat risky, there is surely obvious common sense in trying it first under the less dangerous conditions.'[2]

This was an admission of defeat. The grand design had failed: and Milner underlined his failure in a dispatch of 9 May in which he gave his final advice, while in office, on the closer union of South Africa. He did not think that it would come soon or that it should be accelerated.

---

1 Ibid. Lyttelton to Milner, 13 February.
2 C.O. 291/70. Quoted in part by Headlam, ii. 521.

It is the common criticism of my own policy, that I am trying to 'hurry Federation'. I do not mind such an object being attributed to me—the notion may have its uses—but, in my innermost mind, I see far more obstacles to Federation than any of my critics have yet thought of. And as far as the interests of the Empire are concerned, I cannot conceive why we should desire to see the establishment of a Federal Government until we are quite sure that it cannot fall into the hands of men opposed to the Imperial connexion. It would be bad enough if any of the Local Governments fell into such hands. But it would not be fatal. But I do not see how a Federal Government in the hands of the Afrikaner Party could lead to any other result except separation or another war.[1]

In recommending an elected council, Milner was thinking of throwing a sop to Cerberus; at the same time, the Colonial Secretary was thinking of 'dishing the Whigs'. Milner's dispatch of 2 May crossed a private letter from Lyttelton which forecast that there would probably be a dissolution of Parliament in the spring of 1905, 'when almost inevitably we shall be beaten'. The Liberals might then grant to the Transvaal 'self-government *sans phrase*'. Would it not be wise therefore, Lyttelton asked, to make a cautious movement forwards, 'under your and our guidance', rather than to leave the initiative to 'men who seem very reckless of the essential interests of South Africa'?[2]

Milner's proposals found little favour among officials in Downing Street. 'Crown Colony Government, in the Transvaal at all events, has been a failure,' Graham minuted on the dispatch of 2 May.[3] The consensus was opposed to yoking a popular assembly to an irremovable executive. It was pointed out that wherever this 'vicious system' had been tried in the past, it had always led to friction and sometimes to deadlock. 'The difficulty is that the Government [of the Transvaal] have got a bad name for extravagance and incompetence, but that is a reason for self-government at one stride and not so much for an official minority'; under Milner's plan, 'with the Government in a minority, the mining industry would have it all its own way, for it would combine with the Government against the Boers and with the Boers against the Government, just as suited its interests and convenience.'[4] Nor was there any enthusiasm for Milner's supplementary proposals of 9 May to safeguard 'essential imperial interests' by transferring the customs

---

[1] Ibid., 9 May 1904.   [2] Headlam, ii. 520–1.
[3] C.O. 291/70. Minute on dispatch of 2 May.
[4] Ibid. Minutes by H. W. Just on dispatches of 2 and 9 May.

revenues of both colonies to the Inter-colonial Council, on the grounds that with the railways, the armed forces (the South African Constabulary was a para-military organization), and security for the guaranteed loan beyond the reach of a representative assembly, it would not matter very much if domestic affairs fell into doubtful hands. This was dismissed as ingenious but impracticable: for how long, it was asked, would an elected legislature acquiesce in the continuance of the Inter-colonial Council as it was already constituted? These exceptional checks, it was felt, would be unnecessary if the Crown retained an official majority in the Legislative Council.

On 20 May Milner telegraphed that the census returns showed that 'on any fair basis of representation' the Boers would have a small majority in an elected council, but that this could be neutralized by placing in the Legislature unofficial members to the number of a quarter or a fifth of the whole, so that the Government, with the assistance of the British members, would 'command a majority on any vital political question'.[1] The Colonial Office remained unconvinced. What, asked Graham, made Milner so certain that the British would be united or, if they were, that it would be in support of his administration? 'Before the war we used to think with dread of the Transvaal becoming a British Republic . . . If we can keep Cerberus quiet for a year or two by the sop of an elected minority, circumstances may have changed so much as to admit of complete self-government geing given. But in less time than a year, we may hope that financial prosperity will have returned to the Transvaal, and in that case the cry for self-government will be much less heard.'[2]

On 4 July Milner telegraphed asking urgently for action. Four days later Lyttelton authorized him to announce that the constitution would be amended to include elected members in the legislative council. Once more the Government had sided with Milner against the Office. 'The Cabinet rather inclines,' Lyttelton telegraphed privately, 'to a moderate elected majority in the Transvaal Council but for the difficulty which would in that case arise in the Orange Free State.'[3] In a formal dispatch on 20 July, Lyttelton gave his reasons for the constitutional change in language which was designed both to appease and to warn the Transvaal British. The disadvantages of a system which combined representative legislature and unrepresentative executive were emphasized by reference to the experiences of the Cape between 1852 and 1872, Western Australia

[1] Headlam, ii. 528.   [2] C.O. 291/70. Minute of 7 June.   [3] C.O. 291/71.

before 1890 and Natal between 1856 and 1893. However, it had been proved to be 'workable, if not easily workable, and at least to be a good school for full self-government and a means of bringing citizens together in political co-operation.' But, imperfect or not, it marked the limit of concession for the time being; and, lest this mood of modified rapture be misunderstood in the Transvaal, the dispatch ended: 'His Majesty's Government . . . believe in the good sense of the Boer population and are confident that in time all regret for the incorporation of the country with the Empire and all desire to reverse the decision will disappear, and give place to sentiments of the opposite kind, but it would be folly to assume that [this change] had actually taken place or to run any risk of the renewal of a conflagration which cost so much trouble and suffering'[1] In short, the British were offered a means of consultation, with the implied assurance that their wishes would be granted where they did not endanger an 'imperial interest.' There was to be no change in the constitution of the Orange River Colony.

Milner was invited to make specific proposals for consideration in London. They were sent forward at the end of that year. In the intervening months, with the consciousness of defeat sour in his soul, Milner was occupied with the last frenetic burst of activity before he gave up his labours. His desire to retire, often vaguely expressed, had been sharpened into intention by the knowledge that the life of the Unionist ministry might be measured only in months. 'I get daily more disinclined to write "official" dispatches about South Africa. I cannot deal with the *most material* points officially, and I am afraid of my last words on South Africa falling into the hands of the enemy, as my official communications might. I regard the Opposition, quite frankly, as wreckers in so far as South Africa is concerned; and inside information given to them simply would be material supplied to the Powers of Darkness.'[2] He wanted his successor to be appointed soon, 'in order that the Enemy may find a

---

1 Ibid. Graham minuted on 15 July that he had written a new draft of part of the dispatch, referring to the Boers: 'it seems to me better to say frankly what everyone knows is the only objection to complete self-government. The dispatch is written to meet a cry from the Johannesburgers who seem to think that we went to war solely on their behalf, and that they are therefore entitled to get everything they ask . . . It seems to me desirable to remind the Johannesburgers that there are other people to be considered besides themselves, and this we can do in pointing out the objections to giving complete self-government to either Colony and in any case an elected majority to the Orange River Colony.'

2 Milner MSS. South Africa: Box 12. Milner to Lyttelton, 25 July 1904.

decent man in possession, whom they cannot well oust.' He favoured Lyttelton himself—the job, he commented, required 'cast iron *force of character*'—but the suggestion was not made in Cabinet and the Colonial Secretary felt that he could hardly propose himself. As a second choice, 'Selborne himself would, in my opinion, be absolutely the fittest man for the job, if you hunted the whole Empire through.'[1]

IV

The census of 1904 showed that there were, in round figures, about 300,000 Whites in the Transvaal and Swaziland. Their distribution was uneven, ranging from 69 persons to the square mile in Johannesburg to 0·2 in the desolate areas of the north. To the complexities of varying distribution were added those of differing composition between town and countryside. The white population of the Witwatersrand was 117,000, of whom 84,000 lived in Johannesburg. On this figure, the Witwatersrand could claim rather more than one-third of the total of representatives. But if the total population were disregarded and only the number of adult men taken into account, the electoral map changed shape. The rural Boers married young and bred fast; the urban British contained a high proportion of men who, for one reason or another, lived singly: there were only sixty-one women to every hundred men in Johannesburg.

It is clear from these figures that the grand design had failed: the Boers were in a numerical majority which would be likely continually to increase. The inference was as plain to Smuts as it was to Milner.[2] However, it might still be possible to contrive a British majority in the Legislature. Milner's census officers, by considering names, birthplaces and stated religious affiliations, had made for him an estimate of the racial composition of the population, information which the returns did not directly reveal.[3] On these calculations, there were rather fewer than 58,000 British adult men, about 34,000 Boers, and 15,000 aliens who could be disregarded for electoral purposes. Of the total of about 91,000

[1] Ibid. Milner to Lyttelton, 12 September 1904.   [2] Hancock, p. 196.
[3] 'The more we can obliterate such distinctions [of race] the better,' Milner wrote, 'and any classification of the people according to race in official records would only tend to maintain them.' The estimate of the composition of the population is included in a dispatch from Selborne of 28 May 1906: C.O. 291/99.

potential voters, more than half were concentrated on the Witwaters-rand and in Pretoria, and of these 46,000 were thought to be British. Delimitation of constituencies on the basis of voters would throw power into the British towns, on the basis of total population into the Boer countryside.'[1]

On 5 December Milner submitted his proposals on the franchise and the constituencies in a dispatch fifty pages long.[2] It was too soon for self-government, he said once more, but to allay discontent some means must be found of giving the community a sense of participation in public affairs. 'The representatives of the people must be numerous enough, not only to voice public opinion, but to determine the character of the laws and, except where vital Imperial interests are concerned, practically to direct the policy of the Administration.'

Racial animosities, he hoped, might not wholly dominate the first elections, but he recognized that the ties of language and religion would bind together the Afrikaners.

On the other hand, it would require some very potent and exceptional influence to unite the non-Dutch population in support of anything. Differing widely to begin with in origin and traditions—home-born British, South African British, and British from other Colonies, together with a large admixture of naturalized foreigners—they are further split up by numerous cross-divisions arising from business rivalry, from class antagonism, or from local jealousies. Mining interests versus commercial interest, Capital versus Labour, Pretoria versus Johannesburg, Town versus Country, each of these antagonisms, and others which might be enumerated, tend to divide the Europeans of more recent advent, and would make co-operation between them, except in the actual presence of some grave catastrophe threatening them all, almost inconceivably difficult.

The problem was to distribute power, of a limited kind, fairly among the different sections. 'What use they make of it is their own affair. The Dutch are clearly entitled to the advantages of their common origin and capacity for acting together. The non-Dutch

---

[1] Cf. Winston Churchill: 'It is only in the Transvaal, this country of afflicting dualities and of vicious contradictions, where everything is twisted, disturbed and abnormal, that there is a great disparity between the distribution of seats on the basis of voters and on the basis of population. The high price of provisions in the towns restricts the growth of urban population, and the dullness and inaccessibility of the country districts appear to be favourable to the growth of large familes.' 4th *Parl. Deb.*, vol. 155, c. 841 (5 April 1906).
[2] C.O. 291/74.

must take the consequence of their original heterogeneity and fissiparous disposition.' He proposed that the franchise should be fixed at a low property qualification (lower indeed than the existing municipal franchise)—the occupation of property valued at £100 or rented at £10 a year, or the receipt of wages of £100 a year. This would bring in almost the whole of the adult urban population, but it would exclude some in the countryside, such as *bywoners* (share-croppers) and young men working for their keep on their fathers' farms. The vote should be extended, therefore, in addition to those not otherwise qualified who had been full burghers of the South African Republic—i.e. entitled to vote for the First Volksraad.

The critical decision was the number and distribution of seats. 'The tranquil, or to speak more accurately, the *comparatively* tranquil progress of the country for a long time depends upon it.' Nothing that could be confected would satisfy everyone. Milner put foward two schemes. Scheme A disregarded history and total population: it divided the Transvaal mathematically into large constituencies equal in voting strength, each to return three members elected by proportional representation. Scheme B departed from strict voting equality by recognizing, as far as possible, the old magisterial divisions; it was based upon single-member constitu-encies with simple majority vote, which ranged in the number of voters from 1,100 to 3,200. 'If the principle of respect for existing units is to be upheld, I am convinced that, with only a limited number of seats at our disposal, no system can be devised under which the irregularities will be smaller.' Under Scheme A there would be thirty representatives, under Scheme B thirty-five. Milner was not wedded, he said, to one or the other, but he rather preferred Scheme B. There should, then, be a Legislative Council of thirty-five elected members and from six to nine officials, and a way should be left open through which elected members could be brought into the Executive Council.

The dispatch was received in the Colonial Office with shocked surprise. This was not the 'moderate elected majority' which Milner had been instructed to devise; it was the 'vicious system' at its worst. Ommanney wanted to know 'how the King's Government is to be carried on under such a constitution as Lord Milner proposes. On this vital point he maintains a quite singular silence.'[1] Such a council would be certain to oppose the Government on nearly every

[1] Ibid., minute of 11 January 1905.

matter 'vital to imperial interests'—on the treatment of Natives
and Asiatics, on the functions of the Inter-colonial Council, and
on the war contribution. Legislation of which the Government did
not approve would be proposed and carried, and it would be
oppressive and even dangerous to make repeated use of the power of
veto. To admit elected members to the Executive would be equivalent
to giving seats in the British Cabinet to the Opposition. Graham
went further, in what amounted to a condemnation of all Milner's
work. None of this need have happened, he minuted, but for the
agitation in the Transvaal: 'and the root of it all is the present
Crown Colony Government which has made Downing Street stink
in the nostrils of everyone. In that alone, all parties are agreed.
Nowhere else in the British Empire has "Downing Street" been so
unanimously condemned, though in no Crown Colony has it
interfered less.'[1] Milner, he suggested, should be instructed to return
to Britain and justify his proposals in detail.

V

In Downing Street, then, it was agreed among officials that
Milner had overstepped the limits set for him in Lyttelton's dispatch
of 20 July, 'to concede the utmost liberty compatible with safety'.
Indeed, each batch of news from the Transvaal strengthened the
conviction that the colony could not be entrusted with its own
management. One thing was clear: Cerberus was not going to
swallow his sop. In May 1904 the Boer congress of the people had
met in Pertoria, had asked for the redress of grievances and had
elected a committee of seven to prepare a scheme of permanent
organization. In November 1904 two British parties were formed in
Johannesburg, the Transvaal Progressive Association and the
Transvaal Responsible Government Association. They were agreed
on the principle of 'one vote, one value'—equal constituencies
delimited according to voters and not total population—and on
the slogan that the Transvaal should remain 'a white man's country',
but on little else. The Progressive Association resembled a political
action group of the mining industry and its list of office-bearers
and sponsors read like a reunion of the Reform Committee of 1895:
its president, Sir George Farrar, had indeed been sentenced to death
for his part in the Jameson Raid. Its binding sentiment was fear
of Afrikaner nationalism, and it was content that the Colony should

[1] Ibid.

remain for the time being under imperial protection, at the cost of having its affairs managed by the Crown. Alone among the organized groups, it did not ask for immediate self-government. Abe Bailey, who had been a member of the Reform Committee, wrote in the *Transvaal Leader* of 8 February 1905: 'Despite their protestations, the policy of the Dutch party is not "South Africa for the South Africans" but South Africa for the Dutch and those who will subordinate themselves to their ideas' R. Orpen, another Progressive, was reported to have said at a meeting in Klerksdorp: 'It was not a question of want of trust in the Boers. He had the most implicit trust in the Boers and their ability to run the government of this country according to their own ideas, but he also recognized them to be the most clever nation in the world in politics. The Boer would be found as able with the vote as with the Mauser, as formidable with a portfolio as with a Long Tom.'[1] The Progressives, in short, called up the spectre of the Pan-Afrikaner Conspiracy.

The Responsible Government Association was led by prosperous men from commerce and the professions, who were vehement in criticism of Milner's administration, disliked the mining magnates and were disturbed but undecided about Chinese labour. Their sharpest difference with the Progressives was in their attitude to the Boers. The British, their leaders said, had laid upon themselves the obligation to trust the Boers when they had insisted upon an oath of allegiance in the Peace of Vereeniging; the Boers would be wholeheartedly loyal when they had 'attained their legitimate desires'.[2] The Boers cannot be trusted, said the Progressives, because they do not accept the Empire; the Boers never will accept the Empire, replied the Responsibles, until they are trusted. The Responsible Government Association, then, stood for full and immediate self-government and was prepared to run whatever risks there might be in the presence of a large Afrikaner party in the legislature. The moving spirit of the Association was E. P. Solomon, brother of the Harry Solomon who had taken the chair at the Potchefstroom meeting; and he drew at least moral support from a third brother, Sir Richard Solomon, Milner's Attorney-General. Sir Richard had drawn up a memorandum criticizing Milner's proposals of 5 December: its theme was that racial harmony among Whites would be achieved only under self-government. 'If the people

[1] *Johannesburg Star*, 4 February 1905.
[2] *Rand Daily Mail*, 3 February 1905.

of this country are not at the present time to be trusted with full self-government, they are not to be trusted with such a form of representative government as you propose in your dispatch.'[1]

Divisions among the British did not end with these two parties. All along the Witwatersrand, Labour organizations appeared, quarrelsome in leadership, not easily to be combined. They preached a strident 'all white' socialism with strong Australian associations, which was hostile alike to capitalists, Natives and Asiatics. They wanted universal suffrage, and they wanted self-government at once.

At the turn of the year, after the solemn and evocative ceremonies which surrounded the return of Kruger's body from Europe and its burial in Pretoria on 16 December—a day set apart annually to commemorate the anniversary of the victory of the Voortrekkers over the Zulus at Blood River in 1838—the Boers moved into the field with the creation of their own party, Het Volk—'The People'. From one aspect Het Volk resembled a commando in *laager*, an Afrikaner community drawn together for defence against the renewed advance of the Uitlanders of the Progressive Association. It seemed indeed that the basis of enmity was unchanged—that the Transvaal had learned nothing and forgotten nothing. But this was a superficial impression. Het Volk exercised a discipline over its members and commanded an obedience which resembled conditions in the commandos of 1902 rather than in the Republic of 1899. It published at first neither manifesto nor statement of principles; its purpose was the reunion of Afrikanerdom, and few Afrikaners needed to be told what their party stood for. Its statutes concentrated power in the Head Committee, which could dissolve subordinate bodies if, in its opinion, they fell under 'detrimental or hostile influences'. The chosen leader was Louis Botha, and the appearance of Het Volk marks the success of Botha's quiet but unceasing efforts to damp down the feuds among the Boer people After the war, the 'hands-uppers' and the National Scouts had been neglected by the Government, ignored by the British settlers and ostracized by the 'bitter-enders'. Botha had urged that they should be forgiven after they had done penance for their sins against the *volk*. They should be treated, he said, exactly like blind sheep; an old Afrikaner remedy for this condition was to paint the eyes with a caustic fluid. Now, they had been readmitted into the fold, and it was significant that some of the recruiting committees of Het Volk were

[1] C.O. 291/74. Memorandum of 19 December 1904.

composed in equal numbers of 'bitter-enders', former prisoners and National Scouts.

In December and January Botha and Ewald Esselen toured the country, forming branches of Het Volk in each of the old field-cornetcies. They had, they said, never asked for a change in the constitution, but if there were to be a change they would accept nothing short of the promises made at Vereeniging—full self-government, equal treatment for the Orange River Colony. Addresses to this effect, in identical words, flowed into the High Commissioner's office from each new branch. Botha's speeches dwelt on the need for reconciliation between the British and Afrikaners, varied with thrusts at Sir George Farrar and his friends; he had never, said Botha, heard of a party calling itself 'progressive' which admitted that it was not fit for responsible government.[1] But although Botha avoided recrimination about the war, some of his lieutenants seemed to be looking backwards rather than forwards. Smuts talked about a united nation from the Zambesi to Cape Town and recalled to the minds of some of his hearers the closing words of *A Century of Wrong*. Esselen said in Pretoria that 'they were not assembled that day to say to England, "You have killed my wife and you have slaughtered my cattle", but they were there to say that they would not have a bastard form of government'—a speech in which one may catch an echo of the cry 'Don't nail his ears to the pump!' General Beyers made violent harangues in the Northern Transvaal. At Pietersburg he came out strongly against 'kaffirs', the compensation committees, Lord Milner, English schoolteachers, Johannesburg capitalists and veterinary surgeons. The Boers, he said, were being driven to despair by a hostile administration, and after a reference to the rebellion at Slachter's Nek in 1815, he added: 'It will lead to another war in South Africa, if the Government does not treat us more fairly.'[2] A few days later he said at Louis Trichardt that the Boers 'had fought for their rights, but by divine will had been beaten. Now they would make another fight for their rights another way.' Botha repudiated Beyers's statements but, in the ears of many British, the reverberations of menace lingered on.

But such incidents were not enough to check the slow growth of understanding between Het Volk and the Responsible Government Association, and as these two parties moved together the Transvaal Government was thrown back upon its only friends—the

[1] *Johannesburg Star*, 6 February 1905.   [2] Ibid., 13 February 1905.

mining industry and the Progressive Association. It was clear to one official in Downing Street that the 'Rand malcontents' (as he called the Responsibles) were now certain to combine with the Boers, and that the rest—'which will really be the mining industry'—would probably be in a minority in an elected legislature. 'I think we must make up our minds,' he went on, 'however much we may dislike "capitalists" and "magnates", that it is on the mining interest that not only the prosperity of the country, but the British connexion, really depends.'[1]

By the end of January Milner had lost faith in the proposals which he had made in early December. 'I have no confidence,' he wrote to Lyttelton, 'that the lines on which we are at present going will command a sufficient amount of popular support to give even temporary stability to the proposed structure.' All his predictions of how the Trasnvaal would behave had gone awry, and now he thought it better to delay than to take a false step. 'The worst that can happen is that the framing of a constitution would then fall into the hands of the Liberals who would probably grant immediate self-government. But that disaster is equally imminent if a more restricted constitution is introduced by us and is badly received from the outset.'[2] For once Lyttelton did not bow to Milner's judgement. The Cabinet felt that matters had gone too far to be halted and the Lyttelton Constitution (as it came to be called) was promulgated by Letters Patent on 31 March 1905.[3] Its timing had been arranged to coincide with Milner's retirement as High Commissioner.

Milner left South Africa with the knowledge that his work had fallen short of its purpose. The Transvaal had not been transformed into an outpost of England. The Boers had neither been cowed nor persuaded into acceptance of the Empire; indeed they were better organized and more subtly led than ever before. He had failed either to consolidate or to inspire the British. The enthusiasm which he evoked from his colleagues did not extend far beyond the small circle of the administration. He could point to remarkable achievements—to new railways built and planned, to improvements in irrigation and agriculture, to the foundations of local government, on the English pattern, in the towns, to telegraphs and telephones, to better police and prisons—but these represented only the

---

[1] C.O. 291/74. Minute by H. Lambert on dispatch of 5 December 1904.
[2] Milner MSS. South Africa: Box 12. 31 January 1905.   [3] Cd. 2400.

beginning of the grand design. His last address in Johannesburg contained a plea, almost plaintive in tone, 'to those—perhaps they are not very many—who are good enough to place confidence in me . . . To them I would say: "If you believe in me, defend my works when I am gone" . . .'[1] In private, he regarded the Afrikaner as an enemy of the imperial connexion; in public he could do no more than exhort British and Boers to sublimate their quarrels in a higher loyalty.

When we, who call ourselves Imperialists, talk of the British Empire, we think of a group of states, independent of one another in their local affairs, but bound together for the defence of their common interests, and the development of a common civilization, and so bound, not in an alliance— for alliances can be made and unmade, and are never more than nominally lasting—but in a permanent organic union . . .

And see how such a consummation would solve, and, indeed, can alone solve, the most difficult and most persistent of the problems of South Africa, how it would unite its white races as nothing else can. The Dutch can never own a perfect allegiance merely to Great Britain. The British can never, without moral injury, accept allegiance to any body-politic which excludes their motherland. But British and Dutch alike could, without loss of dignity, without any sacrifice to their several traditions, unite in loyal devotion to an Empire-State, in which Great Britain and South Africa would be partners, and could work cordially together for the good of South Africa as a member of that greater whole. And so you see the true Imperialist is also the best South African.[2]

Milner, who had done more to force the pace in South Africa than any man of his generation, found at the end of his labours that he could look in hope only towards the possibility that time would heal bitterness. (South Africa, General Butler had said in 1899, needed rest, not surgery.) For the most part, Milner blamed his failure upon developments which he considered outside his control— to faction, to the growth of the party spirit, to criticism which turned into agitation, on the perversity of his opponents, especially the British. In his farewell speech in Pretoria he claimed that 'serious injury' had been done to the 'best interests' of the Transvaal

by this trick—and very often it is nothing more than a trick—of perpetual fault-finding, this steady drip, drip of depreciation, only diversified by occasional outbursts of hysterical abuse. I perfectly understand, and I am not now referring to, the abuse of people who attack the present Government merely because they hate all that it represents. That is simply political business—disagreeable perhaps, but natural and to be expected.

[1] *The Nation and the Empire*, p. 85.
[2] *The Nation and the Empire*, pp. 90–1.

But I should have thought that the mere fact that the present Government was inevitably a target for the attacks of this section would have induced a little more moderation in the strictures of those who are, or at least ought to be, its friends.[1]

In only one respect did Milner admit publicly to error: he referred obliquely to Article VIII of the Peace of Vereeniging when he said in Johannesburg that he believed 'as strongly as ever that we got off the right lines when we threw over Mr. Rhodes's principle of "equal rights for every civilized man".'[2] Milner had not been able to avoid the dilemma which he had described to Asquith in 1897: that any move to establish the equality of the races would produce a united opposition from British and Afrikaners.[3] Milner, therefore, had never been prepared to move far in advance of 'colonial sentiment', and colonial sentiment was hardly prepared to advance at all. He had improved the administration of Native affairs, he had revised the pass laws and mitigated the harsher punishments; but he had not been able to persuade the South African Whites to distinguish between the civilized and the uncivilized African. He had hoped that, by exempting the educated African from the requirements of the pass laws, that gradually White opinion would change and that the 'superior' African would be admitted to something approaching equality, if not in political at least in personal rights.[4] He had done little to improve the position of Indians; indeed, they complained to Chamberlain that their lot was, if anything, worse under the British than it had been under the Boers. Both policies were equally restrictive, but whereas Boer administration had been lax, British was efficient.

VI

The Lyttelton constitution was based upon Scheme B in Milners' dispatch of December 1904. It provided for an elected council of between thirty and thirty-five members, to be elected in single-member constituencies, to be determined by electoral commissioners, with six to nine officials. The instructions to the electoral commissioners contained a section that was to become an important precedent[5]:

In dividing the Transvaal into districts the Commissioners shall give due consideration to
    (a) Existing boundaries of wards, municipalities or magisterial districts, or other like divisions . . .

---

1 Ibid., p. 70.   2 Ibid., p. 89.   3 See above, p. 11.
4 Headlam, ii. 314.   5 See below, p. 195.

(b) Community or diversity of interest.
(c) Means of communication.
(d) Physical features.

The commissioners were empowered to vary the electoral quota by a maximum of ten per cent.—five per cent. upwards or downwards.

The Progressives announced that they were grateful for the constitution, Het Volk announced that it was unacceptable, the Responsibles announced that they would make it unworkable. In August 1904 Smuts had written to Miss Hobhouse: 'So long as we are distrusted we don't want anything, and if we are not distrusted why retard self-government?'[1] This constitution, in the opinion of the Boers, had the trail of distrust all over it, and they let it be known that they would not come within its pale. The Responsibles threatened sabotage. E. P. Solomon said:

> If this form of government is given to us, at the very first election which takes place, we, who are in favour of Responsible Government, will stand as one man in this country. We will elect men to the Parliament who will support the immediate introduction of self-government . . . We will return a majority in that Parliament, and where are they then? You pass a resolution to adjourn the House. You block every measure the Government introduces, you stop their supplies until you force them to come to what the majority of the House is resolved upon.[2]

In April the Responsibles published the terms on which they had concluded an electoral alliance with Het Volk, against the day when self-government were achieved. The two parties had agreed to differ on the principle of 'one vote, one value' and on the future of the Chinese labourers. They had reached a compromise on education. They had agreed that a decision on the war contribution should be deferred until the first instalment fell due for payment; that the representation and the franchise should be confined to white men; and that there should be the same control and restriction upon Asiatics as there had been in the South African Republic. The statement ended: 'The Responsible Government Association claims, as the outcome of these negotiations, to have eliminated the racial question from the politics of the State.'[3]

The Lyttelton constitution gave no hope of representation to any non-Whites: the British Government had accepted the Afrikaner definition of the word 'native' as used in Article VIII of the terms

---

[1] Hancock, p. 188.   [2] Ridgeway Report, para. 6. (C.O. 291/112).
[3] *Johannesburg Star*, 20 April 1905.

of the Peace. On 3 February 1905 the Association of Coloured Peoples of the Witwatersrand had sent to the High Commissioner, for transmission to London, a resolution setting out their grievances and trusting that the British Government would 'not forget the just rights of His Majesty's coloured subjects or allow them to be tampered with.'[1] Article VIII had excluded 'natives' from the franchise until self-government had been conceded; but who exactly were 'natives'? What was a British Indian? The issue, it was now realized, had been prejudged by the Transvaal Municipal Councils Ordinance of 1903, which had confined the franchise in local elections to Whites; it was noticed for the first time in Downing Street that Milner had not reserved this ordinance for the consideration of the Crown—as his instructions required—as one laying special disabilities upon coloured British subjects. One brief attempt was made to reopen the door. Ommanney suggested that the Letters Patent should be so worded as to extend the franchise to 'civilized' Indians—to 'coloured British subjects, not natives of South Africa, who on grounds of education, profession or trade, are exempted by Proclamation No. 35 of 1901 from the Pass Law.' Lyttelton agreed. 'Try this in the Letters Patent', he minuted. 'It should work.'[2] Milner demurred. He had no intrinsic objection, he said, to enfranchising Indians, but to do so would be to give 'another slap in the face' to the Cape Coloured people, who would have to be excluded because they had always been classed as Natives in the South African definition of that term.[3] On 21 March at a conference in the Colonial Office, Sir Richard Solomon gave his opinion that to Afrikaners a Native was any person who was not white, and quoted Smuts as his authority. Faced with these objections from the men on the spot, Lyttelton tried no longer to widen the interpretation of Article VIII. It was not desirable, he minuted, to risk an accusation that the terms of surrender had been broken or evaded for the sake of a measure which would 'bring no real benefit to the persons in question'.[4]

There was no possibility of holding elections in 1905, for the laborious business of compiling a register had first to be completed. One provision and one omission in the Letters Patent caused friction. The vote was to be given to those men not otherwise qualified who

[1] C.O. 291/80.   [2] Ibid. Minute of 14 February 1905.
[3] C.O. 291/81. Milner to Lyttelton, 18 March 1905.
[4] Ibid. Minute of 21 March.

had been 'enrolled on the latest list of burghers'. Unhappily for the Transvaal Government, the latest list, devised for the election of 1898, was notoriously defective; it omitted, for instance, the name of General de la Rey. Het Volk argued that, as the list was incomplete, it should in justice be enlarged; and that, if this principle were admitted, there was no reason why the line of qualification should be drawn in 1898. They asked for the enrolment of men lacking in property who had come of age since 1899 and would have been able to vote in the South African Republic if they had been born earlier. They made out a case for including aliens who had been given the right to vote if they joined the commandos. ('This is monstrous impudence,' Graham commented. 'They were enfranchised to fight against us.') The High Commissioner was instructed to point out that the purpose of the clause had been to recognize acquired rights and not to create a separate qualification for Boers only.

The second cause of friction was the result of pure omission: no one had remembered explicitly to disqualify the soldiers of the British garrison and, as the Letters Patent stood, it could be contended that most of them were eligible to vote. The Progressives argued that the soldiers were resident British subjects, and thus automatically entitled to be enrolled. Het Volk was indignant, made reference to 'hired foreigners', and spread the rumour that the Government had it in mind to swamp the vote of the 'old population' by quartering the military by thousands in selected constituencies. It had never been the British Government's intention to enfranchise the garrison, but the mischief in the Letters Patent was beyond the remedy of a simple Order-in-Council. The Transvaal law advisers gave an opinion that soldiers were not *bona fide* occupants of premises or earners of wages within the Colony; but the courts might decide otherwise. If they did, the British Government decided privately, the Letters Patent would have to be amended. This flaw in the instrument was to have a certain importance later.[1]

Lord Selborne, Milner's successor, though a man of gentler disposition, was no less determined than Milner to uphold 'imperial interests'. His duty as he saw it drew him towards the 'British party', and his relationship to the Progressives' leaders became cordial and confidential. This did nothing to endear him to the Responsibles, the Labour sects or Het Volk. Selborne rapidly

[1] C.O. 271/83 *passim*.

came to the same conclusion as the Progressives: it was too early for self-government. At the same time, he had no confidence in the Lyttelton constitution; it was predestined to failure, he thought, because it was based upon the fallacious principle that British institutions were universally transplantable. 'Every day that I stay in South Africa, the more convinced I am that the British system of responsible government is quite unsuited to the Boer population of the two new Colonies . . . and in the Transvaal, with the exception of Mr. J. C. Smuts and Mr. Ewald Esselen, I do not think it is an exaggeration to say that the Boer leaders do not in the least comprehend the working of our responsible government system.'[1] He conceded that the proposed constitution had merit in that it would provide a period of apprenticeship for responsible government; but what, he asked, was the point of training the Colony for something which it would never be able to perform. If British institutions would be a failure in the Transvaal, they would be a calamitous failure in the Orange River Colony, where conditions were even less favourable. He had been impressed by the virtues of the constitution of the Orange Free State, as expounded to him by J. G. Fraser, and he suggested that this constitution should be modified and restored, with the Governor substituted for the State President: the great advantage, he thought, would be that the legislature would have only an indirect control upon the executive. 'The only objection in principle to this idea, of which I can think, is that there is no precedent for such a constitution within the orbit of the British Empire; but the fact is that there is no precedent within the British Empire for the Orange River Colony itself . . . I repeat my deep conviction that the British colonial responsible government system is unsuited to the people and conditions . . . I believe that the grant of responsible government would be dangerous to British supremacy.'[2]

All this produced no response. The British Government had made up its mind about the Transvaal. At least one official detected in Selborne's enthusiasm for the *Grondwet* of the Orange Free State a certain naïvety; the former burghers would hardly mistake a Governor appointed from London for an elected President and, anyway, Selborne had incompletely understood the extensive powers of the Volksraad.[3] Het Volk had already insisted, almost

[1] Ibid. Dispatch of 4 August 1905.   [2] Ibid.
[3] Ibid. Minute of 11 September by A. B. Keith.

ad nauseum, that the Terms of Surrender had promised identical treatment for the Transvaal and the Orange River Colony; and Lyttelton decided that any proposal such as Selborne had in mind would be considered only if it were suggested in a large and representative petition.[1]

However, it was more than ever clear that the only friends whom the Lyttelton constitution still possessed in South Africa were to be found in the Progressive Association. Before the end of 1905 even that support had crumbled. On 21 November Sir George Farrar and his *alter ego*, Sir Percy Fitzpatrick, called upon Selborne to warn him confidentially that their followers were now convinced that they could win a majority in the elections to the Legislative Council. 'If, when the Legislative Assembly meets', Selborne reported, 'His Majesty's Government is not in sympathy with their political views it will, in Sir G. Farrar's and Sir P. Fitzpatrick's opinion, require only the slightest inducement to lead the Progressive Party into an immediate agitation for full self-government, a movement which these gentlemen will be obliged to lead as the only alternative to losing all influence over the members of their own party.'[2] This news meant that the constitution was doomed before it ever went into operation. The Progressive leaders now asked that the number of elected members should be increased from thirty-five to fifty: in a larger assembly, they reasoned, there would be a greater preponderance of members from the Witwatersrand, where the Progressives' strength was concentrated. Selborne sent forward this proposal, recommending it on the grounds that to make the enlargement at once would diminish the chance of a fresh controversy over the franchise and the constituencies when (as now seemed to be inevitable) the constitution was altered to provide for responsible government.

The Unionist Government had no time in which to consider this new and startling development. On 4 December Arthur Balfour resigned and on the following day Sir Henry Campbell-Bannerman took office. Lord Elgin succeeded Lyttelton as Colonial Secretary, with Winston Churchill as Under-Secretary and spokesman for the colonies in the House of Commons. The expectation was general in South Africa that a Liberal government in Britain meant immediate self-government in the Transvaal. The Boers hoped that their

1 Ibid. Minute of 6 September.
2 C.O. 291/87. Dispatch of 27 November 1905.

sojourn in the wilderness was now coming to an end. Sir Arthur Lawley, the Lieutenant-Governor, wrote to Elgin that the Boers had no doubt that the change of ministry 'must of necessity mean the advancement of Dutch as opposed to British ideals', and added: 'It is impossible I think to look for any permanent tranquillity in South Africa so long as there is no continuity of Imperial policy.'[1]

But where was continuity to be found amid the flux and confusion of the past nine months? Lord Elgin when he took office was confronted with what now seemed to be a general demand for self-government from the white people of the Transvaal, and to have inherited the responsibility for a dormant constitution which no one wanted and which the Colonial Office had heartily damned. It is true that, with the Liberals in office, Ommanney had decided that he preferred the Lyttelton constitution, warts and all, to trusting the Boers; but his minutes were in the files to weaken the force of his pleadings. Selborne was of the same opinion as Ommanney, but Selborne now had less than ever the ear of the Government. Would it be wise, he asked, to introduce responsible government at once? 'I unhesitatingly answer, "no".'[2] He repeated the objections with which he had bombarded Lyttelton. The Boer did not understand parliamentary government according to English conventions: 'the only way in which he will work it will to be elect the Central Committee of Het Volk as his Cabinet, if he can, and leave them absolutely uncontrolled authority to do what they please.' A government in the Transvaal drawn from the British would not be much better, considering British inexperience; and both racial groups were selfish and exclusive.

I do not think that a British government, under the responsible government system, would treat the Boers, their wants and prejudices, with as much sympathy as the present government does. The British are an unimaginative people, and, unfortunately, their interests here are almost entirely urban and industrial or commercial or professional while those of the Boers are almost entirely rural and agricultural.

If, on the other hand, the majority were Boer and a Boer government was formed, then I think the British would give much trouble, and not without some excuse. Not only have they bitter recollections of Boer government, but they are conscious that the interests which they mainly represent pay at least 90 per cent. of the taxes of the country, and that the

1 Milner MSS. South Africa: Box 12.
2 C.O. 291/88. Selborne's memorandum of 23 December 1905.

Boers would spend this money with a limited consideration for British wants or requirements.[1]

In short, I think that, at the present moment, the British would govern the Boers badly and the Boers would govern the British badly, but that the Boer misgovernment of the British would be greater in degree and more dangerous in its effects than the British misgovernment of the Boers. I think that the experience both parties would gain by sitting side by side for a few sessions in a representative chamber would be invaluable to both alike and would make a vast difference in the conduct of either party when entrusted with the full responsibility of government in a few years' time.

Ommanney added his voice to Selborne's. None of the reasons against self-government set out in Lyttelton's dispatches, he said, had lost its cogency. The combined advice of Milner and Selborne was ardent against it, and the Government would be taking a dangerous risk and a heavy responsibility if they disregarded the considered opinion of the men on the spot. 'As strongly as I can,' he urged that the Lyttelton constitution should be allowed to go into operation at least as a foundation for further development.[2]

But the Lyttelton Constitution, as it stood, was full of admitted errors: the Letters Patent might have to be altered, in any event, to deal with the matter of the military vote, and there was in addition the new proposal, pressed by Selborne, to increase the size of the Legislative Council. 'Both these questions', Churchill minuted on 18 December, four days after he had taken office, 'make it desirable to amend the Letters Patent. The position seems to have therefore come when His Majesty's Government may review and reconsider the position adopted by Mr. Lyttelton in his dispatch of 31 March.'[3]

VII

It has been necessary to describe in some detail the state of the Transvaal situation when the Liberals took office, because there has been a disposition to dramatize and in the process to distort the role of Sir Henry Campbell-Bannerman in the granting of self-government. One interpretation suggests almost an overnight conversion after a meeting with General Smuts. Smuts had hastened to England

[1] Cf. Fitzpatrick's opinion that to give way to the Boers would mean that they would 'remove the Civil Service and put back the old one, re-man the railways with the old staff, take control of the Education Department and allow us the privilege of paying for it, raise ten millions at our expense to give it to the poor burghers, establish Protection in the form in which it would be most serious for us and effect the Bond–Het Volk domination throughout South Africa.' J. P. R. Wallis, *Fitz* (1955), p. 113.

[2] C.O. 291/88. Minute on Selborne's telegram of 12 December.   [3] Ibid.

after the change of government, armed with a memorandum in which he set out the case for self-government and a change in the Lyttelton franchise.[1] His first conversations—with Morley, Lloyd George, Elgin and Churchill—were disappointing. He saw the Prime Minister twice,[2] and Smuts has described the end of the second interview, on 7 February, in these words: 'I could see Campbell-Bannerman was listening sympathetically. Without being brilliant he was the sort of sane personality—large-hearted and honest—on whom people depend. He reminded me of Botha, Such men get things done. He told me there was to be a Cabinet meeting next day, and he said: "Smuts, you have convinced me".'

'That talk', says Smuts, 'settled the future of South Africa.'[3]

It was indeed on the following day that Campbell-Bannerman carried the Cabinet with him on the question of the new colonies after a speech which Lloyd George used to describe as the finest that he had ever heard. But it is possible that Smuts, in pardonable exhilaration at the result, overestimated the importance of his interview.[4] There is no need to search for an apocalyptic explanation for Campbell-Bannerman's decision, or to assume that he acted on impulse or under the domination of another man's mind; moreover the doctrine that Smuts relied upon in his memorandum—that consent was likely to be a more enduring bond than constraint—was one that Campbell-Bannerman had been preaching for years. (The memorandum reads largely like an anthology of Liberal statements.) It is probable that the meeting of the two men had its largest consequence in its influence not upon Campbell-Bannerman, but upon Smuts. Certainly, in the years ahead, Smuts regarded the Transvaal settlement with the protective affection which a man may give to something which he regards as partly his own creation. Beyond that, his meeting with Campbell-Bannerman may have altered his opinion of British statesmen.

[1] The Smuts memorandum has been analysed by Pyrah, *Imperial Policy and South Africa, 1901–1910* (1955), pp. 165–71, and more critically by L. M. Thompson, *The Unification of South Africa, 1902–1910* (1960), pp. 25–26.

[2] Hancock, p. 214.

[3] S. G. Millin, *General Smuts* (1936), i. 213.

[4] For an example of how a public man may, in good faith, mistake his influence on decisions taken in the *arcanum imperii*, compare the account of the passing over of Lord Curzon in favour of Stanley Baldwin as prime minister in L. S. Amery's *Thoughts on the Constitution* with that given in the documents published by Robert Blake in *The Unknown Prime Minister: The Life and Times of Bonar Law*.

There were general reasons why the Liberals should jettison the Lyttelton constitution, in view of its unpopularity and its imperfections. Furthermore, their earlier pronouncements had led men to expect a change, and it could hardly have been forgotten that Gladstone's tardiness in abandoning a policy which he had condemned while he was in opposition had been one of the factors making for war in the Transvaal in 1881. There was, in addition, a pressing specific reason: immediately on taking office, Campbell-Bannerman had announced that the importation of Chinese labourers into the Transvaal was to cease forthwith. He had indeed gone farther than was legally possible; it was discovered that the licences already issued formed a contract which could not be broken; but this was an intervention from Downing Street more drastic than anything done by Chamberlain in the Transvaal Colony. There was every reason, therefore, why Campbell-Bannerman, if he were not to be accused of apostasy in his colonial policy, should couple this demonstration of the authority of the 'imperial factor' to a grant of self-government. The announcement that this was to extend both to the Transvaal and to the Orange River Colony was made in the speech from the throne on 19 February 1906.[1]

However, although it may be shown that there was little else that a Liberal Government could have done without inviting a charge of bad faith, it would be misleading to depict them merely as the prisoners of circumstance. Churchill said in the House of Commons:

There is a profound difference . . . between the schools of thought which exist upon South African politics in this House. We think that British authority in South Africa has got to stand on two legs. Hon. Gentlemen opposite have laboured for ten years to make it stand on one. We on this side know that if British dominion is to endure in South Africa it must endure with the assent of the Dutch. We think that the position of Agents and Ministers of the Crown in South Africa, should be just as much above and remote from racial feuds as the position of the Crown in this country is above our party politics.[2]

This implied a great deal more than the obvious fact that the new Government would look for other allies in the Transvaal besides the Progressive Association and the mining industry. In condemning

[1] For Campbell-Bannerman's attitude to the Lyttelton constitution, see J. A. Spender, *The Life of Sir Henry Campbell-Bannerman*, vol. 2, c. 29. Spender does not mention the interviews with Smuts.
[2] 4th *Parl. Deb.*, vol. 155, c. 848. 5 April 1906.

the Lyttelton constitution, Churchill said that, if it had been put into operation:

Is it not certain . . . that the Assembly would have been infuriated, that parties differing from each other on every conceivable question, fiercely divided by race and religion and language, would have united in common hatred of the interference of the outside Power and the Government of bureaucrats . . . ? There would have been a swift transition. The Legislative Assembly would have converted itself into a constituent Assembly, and it would have taken by force all that the Government now have it in their power to concede with grace, distinction and authority.[1]

In these words one may, without straining the vision, discern the outlines of the great principle of political conduct which, to the Victorians as they looked back at the history of their island, seemed to explain how England, in a century of turmoil, had reconciled order with progress: 'we can enjoy a wise conservatism because we have displayed a timely liberality.' It was by this principle, as the events were inspected in tranquillity, that the basis of agreement in Britain had been enlarged by the emancipation of Catholics in 1829, the reform of the House of Commons in 1832, the repeal of the Corn Laws in 1846, and the widening of the franchise in 1867 and 1884.

In the reaction that followed the last great manifestation of the jingo spirit, the Anglo-Boer War in retrospect began to appear as an episode that was shameful, costly and profitable only to capitalist interests: the theme of J. A. Hobson's writings began to circulate and to influence opinion. As the British surveyed the shortcomings of their army as revealed to the Esher Committee, the claims of the navy in response to the challenge of Germany on the high seas, the darkening of the European prospect and the new commitments to allies in fact and allies in all but name, it became evident that another colonial war was out of the question. Was there not something better to be done with the Empire than to garrison it? Bernard Shaw had written in 1900 that the war in South Africa had shown that without constitutional rights and guarantees 'every sturdy citizen of a British province overseas may at any moment cost us the expedition thither of seven of our soldiers: two for him to shoot, two to die of enteric fever, and three to wrestle with him for his gun, and to wrestle, in the long run, unsuccessfully.'[2] Campbell-Bannerman had never deviated from the prediction that the Empire

1 Ibid., cc. 837–8. 2 *Fabianism and the Empire*, p. 34.

could not be retained by force. 'If we are to maintain the political supremacy of the British power in South Africa', he had said in one of many variations upon the same theme, 'it can only be by conciliation and friendship; it will never be by domination and ascendancy, because the British power cannot, there or elsewhere, rest securely unless it rests upon the willing consent of a sympathetic and contented people.'[1]

One of the unresolved problems of imperial governance is that opinion seldom moves in the same direction and at the same speed both in the provinces and in the metropolitan country, so that a change of policy may reach a distant dependency with disrupting impact, in the manner in which a wave gathers force as it traverses an ocean. The Transvaal British had, for the most part, received the news of Balfour's resignation with alarm, that of the election results with consternation. Insulated as they were from the controversies that had preceded this vast transfer of power, they knew little or nothing about the quarrels over education, or over the Taff Vale judgement, or about the deeper significance of Chamberlain's resignation and the fiscal debate. They did not appreciate that the issue of 'Chinese slavery', with the chance which it gave to a fragmented Liberal Party to draw together upon an issue which could be depicted as morally wrong and therefore as simple, had an import that was as much domestic as imperial. It appeared to them that this election, like that of 1900, had been fought primarily on the Transvaal question, and they regarded its outcome as a triumph for the 'pro-Boers'. They felt themselves betrayed and abandoned in the land which they called 'home'. What might appear in Britain as justice and preserving concession to the Boers was regarded by many Transvaal settlers as a surrender, detrimental to themselves, of privileges to a people who would abuse what they were given. These fears were fed by speeches in London. Lord Milner, breaking his silence in the House of Lords, said: 'What I cannot understand is how any human being, not being a "pro-Boer", can regard with equanimity the prospect that the very hand which drafted the ultimatum of October 1899 may within a year be drafting Ministers' Minutes for submission to a British Governor who will have virtually no option but to obey them.'[2]

---

[1] Address to the Eighty Club, Oxford, 2 March, 1901.
[2] 4th *Parl. Deb.*, vol. 152, c. 710. 26 February 1906. The allusion is to Abraham Fischer, leader of the Oranje Unie.

Balfour said, with all the authority of his office: 'The question you have to ask is—Human nature, be it Dutch or English, being what it is, can the political institutions you are now going to give them be made a substitution for the military organization, cannon and all the rest of it, which brought them honourably into the field . . .?' He refused, on behalf of the Unionist Party, to take any responsibility 'for what I regard as the most reckless experiment ever tried in the development of a great colonial policy.'[1]

VIII

Could these fears be regarded as extravagant? Campbell-Bannerman and his colleagues had no intention of relinquishing British supremacy in the Transvaal or anywhere else in South Africa. What they were seeking to do was to achieve by influence and by 'timely liberality' what Milner had failed to achieve by power. But, one may ask, were they not acting as if a single stroke of policy could make amends for the war and for what had been done during and after the war? Was there something universal in 'liberal-conservatism', or had it been successful only with a certain people at a certain time? Was there not, underlying the belief in its efficacy, the assumption that reasonable men would generally reach the same conclusion, whether they lived in London or Pretoria—that there was, in short, a natural harmony of interests? If there had been something in Krugerism which could be preserved only in isolation, was there not something in neo-Krugerism which depended for its survival upon the memory of oppression? Could the mystique of Afrikanerdom, toughened in resistance to Milnerism, be destroyed by offering the Boers a partnership, but a partnership under the Crown and on British terms? Could the memory of the lost re-publics be dismissed so easily? Was there not something solid in the contention that the Boers would, in the long run, be satisfied with nothing less than predominance and, considering their discipline under leadership, that they might find the British system of govern-ment, plucked from its setting and its conventions, to be favourable to a racial oligarchy acting under constitutional forms? Had it not already been shown, elsewhere in the world, that liberal principles seldom prevailed when they were challenged by a vigorous national movement? In short, had the Liberals any reason to believe that 'magnanimity' had more than blind faith to commend it? These

[1] Ibid., vol. 162, cc. 802, 804. 31 July 1905.

questions, in one form or another, were asked in the dispatches of Milner and Selborne, in the Colonial Office, and in the speeches of the Unionist opposition.

Here one should not overlook the import of one event in the Transvaal—the alliance of 1905 between Het Volk and the Responsible Government Association. This had been viewed with alarm in the Colonial Office and by Lord Selborne, because it was directed towards immediate self-government and because it split the 'British party'. But from another standpoint it could be viewed with relief, as a sign that Afrikaners and British were beginning to find some political issues upon which there could be co-operation across the boundaries of race.

One of Campbell-Bannerman's closest counsellors on South African affairs was James Bryce, and Bryce drew local knowledge and some opinions from his correspondence with Merriman, which had begun in 1892, and was to continue until Bryce's death. On 18 August 1903 Merriman had written that, in the Cape, 'matters are settling down in a far better way than even the most sanguine could have expected. Parliament and discussion in Parliament have been a great safety valve. Political electricity finds a conductor and gets dissipated. New subjects for division present themselves, and interests common to both Dutch and English call for settlement on other than race lines.'[1] In this cross-alignment, Merriman saw the only hope for the reconciliation of the white races in the future. He dismissed the appeals for amity made by Chamberlain during his South African tour as having done more harm than good. He continued:

I have much more faith in the progress of time and in the gradual growth of great questions upon which Dutch and English will feel not as rival nationalities but as South Africans. As you do not want a pamphlet, I can only briefly illustrate my meaning. There is for example the one which dominates all others—viz. the introduction of Asiatic cheap labour to work the mines . . .

Preferential tariffs are another thing. These are condemned by all intelligent Englishmen and they are loathed by the Dutch.

The War Loan [sc. contribution] is another. No free man whether he is Dutch or English is going to pay tribute if he can help it, and you will have the first note of refusal from the latter rather than the former—but when the time comes they will be solid irrespective of race on a point like this.

The rule of the capitalist is another thing to which both races are equally resolved not to submit.

[1] Bryce PP.

It is to the growth of a common political feeling on subjects of common interest that moderate men look as the best hope for the future, and it is to the shaping and guiding of this opinion that those who wish well to South Africa will address themselves. It is a matter of deep regret to me that the official position of the Liberals at home does not seem to me to recognize that free communities like to manage their own affairs, and that they are still full of the unreasonable apprehension of a 'Dutch' majority, just as they used to be in Canada.

When he returned to this theme three years later, Merriman found the outlook much less hopeful, and he blamed the deterioration on to the British Government.

There has been a good deal of disappointment about the Transvaal Constitution, and still more at the non-inclusion of the Orange River Colony. If I were to tell you what I really think, it would be, that a great opportunity has been lost, and a fatal blunder made, in telling the Dutch that you fear them so much that you will not give them free government. The result will I fear be very grave, for these people have long memories and are not demonstrative. Every Dutchman in South Africa thinks that we have broken the terms of the Vereeniging pact in spirit if not in letter. They won't say much about this but it does undoubtedly strengthen the hands of those who point out that no fair dealing is to be expected from England.[1]

These were arguments which Liberals could hardly ignore. In 1905 it seemed that the exclusiveness of Transvaal politics was beginning to be broken. Het Volk and the Responsible Government Association had reached a rough understanding not only upon the desirability of self-government but upon activity in common thereafter. There was indeed evidence before the Liberal Government upon which they might fairly conclude not only that delay might be dangerous but that timely concession would be favourable to racial co-operation. Magnanimity, in Burke's words, might be the truest policy.

[1] Ibid., 2 July 1905.

CHAPTER EIGHT

THE CAMPBELL-BANNERMAN CONSTITUTION

> Speaking with full knowledge and with profound
> conviction I say that, if the British Government will
> fully and unreservedly trust my people, they will not
> be disappointed; they will find their confidence repaid
> in a thousand ways and will have in the Boer people a
> source of strength for the British Empire.
>
> *Botha to West Ridgeway, June 1906.*

> The Great Betrayal.
>
> *Heading in Milner's papers for 1906.*

THE year 1906 was one of conscious transition for the Transvaal.
The Boers looked forward with cautious optimism to a change in
British policy; the British were flustered and apprehensive. A change
was coming, that much was certain; but no one in the Transvaal,
from the High Commissioner downwards, knew what that change
was going to be. The Chinese labourers were to go, but it was not
certain how or when; it was evident that the Lyttelton constitution
would be amended but no one knew in what particulars. Rumours
spread on the Witwatersrand that the British Government had it in
mind to alter the franchise provisions, and by substituting population for voters as the basis of delimitation, to 'hand the country
back to the Boers'. Public meetings were held along the Witwatersrand, demanding that the principle of 'one vote, one value'—
regarded now as the last safeguard of British interests—should be
maintained, and a petition containing 41,000 names was sent to the
King. (Botha and Smuts publicly alleged that some of the signatures
had been obtained by misrepresenting the petition as one against
Chinese labour.) A further economic recession, which occurred at
this time, was popularly diagnosed as having been caused by un-
certainty about the Transvaal's future; there was much talk about
a flight both of settlers and capital. Churchill added to the prevailing
despondency among the British when he said in the House of
Commons that the property qualifications and the voters' basis for

constituencies in the Lyttelton constitution had led to the suspicion that 'something was intended in the nature of a dodge . . . artificially to depress the balance in one direction and to tilt it in another.'[1]

From the beginning of the year, Selborne pressed for a quick decision. If matters were delayed, it would not be possible for a legislative assembly to meet that year, he said, because it would be cruel to ask members to meet in Pretoria during the heat of the summer months. It would be 'very difficult' for him if he did not know before March what constitutional policy was going to be. There would be 'universal indignation' among the industrial and commercial community if there were any change from the provisions of 'one vote, one value', automatic redistribution of constituencies and biennial registration of voters.[2] On 29 January he once more pleaded for an announcement that the Lyttelton franchise should stay: 'There would be nothing less than a convulsion of political feeling if the British public here had definite grounds for believing that His Majestys' Government were contemplating such an alteration in the basis of the Constitution.'[3] A. B. Keith, a new and formidable recruit to the Colonial Office, minuted: 'It is curious that the Governor sends us nothing of the views of the other side, just as he never sent us officially the views of the miners as to Chinese labour.' Three days later, Selborne reported that there was danger of commotion among the British because of fears about the franchise: 'they regard it as a question of political life and death to them. You must remember that they have mainly grown to manhood under the heel of Krugerism . . . I am afraid of using language which His Majesty's Government may think exaggerated. I can only warn them in the most earnest words at my command of the consequences if they deliberately reject the unanimous opinion of the British in the Transvaal.'[4] A. B. Keith minuted: 'The British agitation seems rather

[1] 4th *Parl. Deb.*, vol. 155, c. 842. Churchill had read his Durham: cf. 'With respect to every one of those plans which propose to make the English minority an electoral majority by means of new and strange modes of voting or unfair divisions of the country, I shall only say, that if Canadians are to be deprived of representative government, it would be better to do it in a straightforward way than to attempt to establish a permanent system of government on the basis of what all mankind would regard as mere electoral frauds. It is not in North America that men can be cheated by an unreal semblance of representative government, or persuaded that they are outvoted, when, in fact, they are disfranchised.' *The Report and Despatches of the Earl of Durham* (1839), p. 221.

[2] C.O. 291/95. Selborne to Elgin, 6, 9 and 15 January 1906.

[3] Ibid.   [4] C.O. 291/96.

excessive. It may be doubted whether a Boer majority would perform any great iniquities, and whether the Boers have not really decided to settle down loyally under the British flag. A self-governing Colony conceded full powers of self-control is nearly in as good a position as a foreign State politically, and economically it is better off. The leaders of the Boers probably know this quite well.'

The British Cabinet did not decide on self-government for the Transvaal and the Orange Free State, until 8 February, and did not announce that decision until the speech from the throne at the opening of Parliament on 19 February. In the meantime, there was prolonged discussion, both in London and in the Transvaal, upon the form of government. In the Colonial Office, H. W. Just pointed out some of the constitutional difficulties which would have to be overcome.[1] In all other colonies, there had been an intermediate stage of representative government, which meant that the legislative assembly had been a party to the change when full responsible government had been introduced. In the Transvaal, the change would have to be made without concurrent local legislation. There was the additional complication in the existence of the Inter-colonial Council; if this were left in being, the railways and the police would be outside the control of the new legislature which would, in addition, find themselves burdened with charges to which they had not consented. He would like to see the Lyttelton constitution put into operation as a jumping-off point. 'The alternative is for His Majesty's Government to act arbitrarily and to assume to themselves unusual powers and to arrogate to themselves a knowledge and a capacity to judge, unsupported by and indeed in defiance of the judgement of the High Commissioner, Lord Selborne, who as long as he remains in South Africa and is not superseded, must be presumed to enjoy their confidence and to be accepted as their adviser.'

Graham was unimpressed by the argument that the British Government were acting arbitrarily: 'this country which has spent £200 million and sacrificed many lives in acquiring the new Colonies has a right to dictate its own terms in the grant of responsible Government.' He did not like the idea of responsible government at the present stage; but if it were to be given in a short time, it would be better to give it at once and on British terms. 'It would be of course without precedent, but the circumstances are without

[1] C.O. 291/95. Minutes on Selborne's dispatch of 15 January.

precedent.' Ommanney concurred that the British Government had a right to do as it pleased; 'but it may not be wise to exercise that right.'

In the Transvaal, the three main parties all desired a larger assembly than that provided for in the Lyttelton constitution. The Progressive Association wanted single-member constituencies, the Responsible Government Association preferred larger constituencies, returning from three to five members, but with no provision for minority representation. Selborne objected to multi-member constituencies, because he thought that under such a system the individuality of the country towns would be merged in Het Volk: '. . . from the point of political representation, it would absolutely destroy the individuality of the small towns of the Transvaal, such as Zeerust, Klerksdorp, Heidelberg, Ermelo, Krugersdorp, Boksburg, and many others.'

These towns, he hoped, would have a great influence under responsible government, because they contained a number of British citizens who would not be dominated by Het Volk and were not tied in any way to the mining interest. 'If the plan of multiple-member constituencies is substituted for that of single-member constituencies, the political influence of these towns would be annihilated; they will without exception either be absorbed into the domination of Het Volk or into that of Johannesburg . . . The multiple-member constituencies would give an undue advantage to the great organizations as against local influence and patriotism. I lay much stress on this objection.'[1] The Executive Council, he reported a week later, agreed with him, and had recommended that not only should the discretion of 10 per cent. in the delimitation of constituencies in the Lyttelton constitution be retained, but the Governor should be given a discretion to increase that margin whenever the delimitation commissioners should recommend it.'[2]

He thought that the new legislature should be bicameral, with a nominated second chamber. 'I admit the difficulty of finding eighty thoroughly satisfactory men for the two houses, but my opinion nevertheless is not shaken that in the particular circumstances of the Transvaal today and with reference especially to questions affecting Indians and Natives a second chamber may perform very valuable service and should be provided for *ab initio*'[3] The question of the

---

[1] Ibid. Selborne's dispatch of 22 January.
[2] Ibid. Dispatch of 29 January.   [3] Ibid. Selborne to Elgin, 30 January.

second chamber should not be left to be dealt with by the new Government of the Transvaal: its main purpose would be to safe-guard the interests of the non-White peoples and, if it were elected, it would reflect popular prejudices. He would search for moderate men as its members: if they were chosen from among the 'negrophilists' their influence would be discounted in advance.

There is no disguising the fact that, with rare exceptions, both Boers and British are prejudiced in this matter, and the result of prejudice is an almost complete absence of clear thinking as to what is involved. How many people, either Boer or British, have asked themselves this simple question: 'Am I prepared to lay down a hard and fast line and say that no coloured man or Native is ever to be allowed to rise above a certain line in the scale of civilization, no matter what natural gifts may have been given him, or am I not prepared to lay down such a hard and fast line? If the answer to the first question is in the affirmative, it is a deliberate avowal of policy which is not distinguishable from that of slavery, and there are very few who would not recoil in horror when confronted with the logical meaning of their answer. If, on the other hand, the answer is in the negative, then the question remains, 'Am I going to allow a coloured man or a Native to advance along the road of civilization by pure chance, or am I going to guide him on the right lines?'[1]

On the same day he telegraphed to Elgin, pressing his case for the representation of the small towns: he would like to see these, with Pretoria, holding the balance between the Witwatersrand and the *backveld*. 'These towns contain Boers of far better education than those of the country districts, while the British there are all men whose permanent home is in the Transvaal . . .'[2]

Selborne's correspondence with the Colonial Office was peculiarly one-sided. His warnings of the consequences of delay were acknow-ledged, but were received without sympathy. On 22 February, he reported that the banks had begun to call in their loans, and that applications for poor relief to the Rand Aid Association, the prin-cipal charitable body, had increased by one-third since the beginning of the year. A. B. Keith minuted that this reminded him of the financial crisis of 1903 which had forced the issue of Chinese labour.[3] On 5 March he received a deputation, introduced by the Mayor of Johannesburg, from thirty-seven public bodies, societies and associations on the Witwatersrand, which asked him to call the British Government's attention to the sad consequences of un-certainty.[4]

[1] C.O. 291/96. Selborne to Elgin, 2 February.   [2] C.O. 291/96.
[3] Ibid.   [4] C.O. 291/97.

II

The British Government were not to be hurried, and they wanted local advice from someone less identified with the *ancien régime* than Lord Selborne. In April, they sent out a committee of inquiry under the chairmanship of Sir Joseph West Ridgeway, a distinguished soldier and administrator who had been defeated as Liberal candidate for the City of London in the recent general election. Churchill described the committee as 'an imperial patrol' sent out to reconnoitre, not to commit the Government to action, but Ridgeway was instructed to make, if he could, a concordat among the Transvaal parties which could be submitted to London for ratification.

Ridgeway and his colleagues—Lord Sandhurst, Sir Francis Hopwood and Colonel D. A. Johnston—reached the Transvaal at the end of April, and during the next nine weeks they examined nearly 500 witnesses and received more than seventy deputations. They worked in private. Their relations with the Boers were friendly; General Botha, for the first time since his return from Europe in 1903, dispensed with an interpreter in official discussions and spoke in English. It is clear from their report that the members of the committee were searching for a means of distributing power evenly; it is also clear that by the time they left the Transvaal they were convinced that the central issue between Whites was not the hostility between British and Afrikaners, but of the relationship between the mining industry and the rest of the country: this was the argument which Smuts had used in his memorandum. The committee, in short, tried to find local agreement on a broad-bottomed administration which should be under the control neither of Het Volk nor of the Progressive Association. This attitude brought them into disagreement not only with Sir George Farrar and Sir Percy Fitzpatrick but also with Lord Selborne.

The representatives of Het Volk declared that they neither desired nor expected to achieve at once a position of predominance. The committee reported that:

Their leaders do not desire a Boer majority in this, the first Parliament. They are shrewd and sagacious men, and fully recognize the grave difficulties and responsibilities that would devolve upon a Boer ministry. They have, therefore, throughout these negotiations admitted that there should be a British majority, but they claim that that majority should not be so overwhelming as to reduce the Boer parliamentary party to impotence, and above all, that it should not be a Rand majority, fulfilling the dictates and carrying out the policy of absentee and other capitalists.[1]

Indeed, in the doubtful conditions of the time, the thought of a pure Het Volk administration must have appeared as embarrassing to Botha in some respects as it might appear advantageous in others. His party had been organized for defence, ostensibly against the 'money power', but also against 'Milnerism' and 'Jingoism'. Its cohesion was not yet fully knit; and although it officially repudiated racialism some of its leading members, notably A. D. Wolmarans and General Beyers, were obsessed with the memories of the war. The reunion of Afrikaners had been painfully and precariously achieved, and part of the basis of that reunion was that republicanism was still the cause, and England still the enemy, of the Transvaal patriot. One of the lessons drawn from the war was that a fresh disruption of the people—a *skeuring van die volk*—must be prevented at almost all costs. Already, it seemed to some Afrikaners, Het Volk had conceded too much in its alliance with the Responsible Government Association; there was some indignation in the Orange River Colony at this trafficking with the enemy. It was one thing to keep the Boers united for self-protection, bound together in a common hostility, quite another to preserve that unity if the Boer leaders were to assume power, with all its responsibilities and necessary compromises, and with an administrative machine designed by Lord Milner and manned by his chosen officials. Self-government had been promised, but the Boers were disposed to wait and see what the constitution would contain; in particular, they feared that the powers reserved to the Crown would be so extensive that real power would remain in London. As a body, Het Volk had not yet committed itself to accept what might be offered. Lord Selborne did not believe that Botha meant what he said, However, the test of sincerity came when the committee raised the issue of 'one vote, one value'; and sincerity seemed to be proven when Botha gave up his claim that constituencies should be delimited according to total population in return for the dropping of the property qualifications and the granting of manhood franchise.

To have settled the franchise by agreement was a notable success. However, the committee was hopeful of grounding British supremacy upon something less fragile than a parliamentary majority obtained at the polls.

[1] Ridgeway Report i, para. 27.

Although a British majority in the new Parliament is very desirable, yet it is not in a majority, which must be more or less uncertain, that the most effective safeguards of British supremacy should be sought. A British majority in the Legislative Chamber, which is mainly the offspring of a precarious political alliance between capital and labour, will be but an unstable and transient guarantee ... In our opinion, a more trustworthy security for British supremacy will be found in an upper chamber, the referendum, federation, the increase in the number of British families, especially of the agricultural class, and above all in a contented and prosperous community without distinction of race.[1]

The committee, in deciding upon the composition of the Assembly, was searching for a formula in the distribution of seats which would allow 'moderate men' to hold the balance between the principal antagonists. It hoped that it had found the answer in the influence of Pretoria. On Milner's estimate of 1904, there were in the capital 5,700 British and 1,400 Afrikaner voters; but the British there were no zealots. The committee quoted with approval a statement made in 1905 by the chairman of the Transvaal Political Association (which had kept its identity in Pretoria): 'We have on one side Het Volk and on the other side the Progressives. Gentlemen, you and I cannot join Het Volk and we will not join the Progressives ... [because] that organization has been captured by ... the capitalists of the Rand ... If you stand firm in Pretoria, the first Cabinet that will be formed will be a coalition Ministry into which much of the best of two sections will be taken.'[2]

The voters' roll drawn up under the Lyttelton constitution contained 46,000 names for the Witwatersrand. Het Volk objected to this being taken as an authentic record; the figure, they said, was higher by 3,000 than that given by the census, and they charged the Progressives with having inflated the roll with the names of men who had left the country, were dead, had never existed, or were otherwise ineligible. (When asked why they had not challenged the roll earlier, they replied that they were a poor party and unable to afford heavy legal costs.) The committee, holding that justice must not only be done but be seen to be done (and manifest justice in this instance coincided with their professed purpose), decided to set aside the roll and to rely instead upon the census: on those figures, the Witwatersrand and the country districts were counterbalanced. The figures showed 43,196 for the Witwatersrand and 41,118 for the country, with 7,170 for Pretoria. But if the semi-rural district of

---

[1] Ibid., paras. 39–40.   [2] Ibid., para 15.

Krugersdorp on the western fringe of the Witwatersrand were regarded as belonging properly to the countryside, the total for the Witwatersrand was reduced to 41,797 and that for the countryside raised to 42,517. There, it seemed, were the elements of a compromise. The committee proposed to the parties that there should be a legislative assembly of sixty-three members, twenty-nine from the Witwatersrand (excluding Krugersdorp), five from Pretoria, and twenty-nine from the rest of the Transvaal.

It was calculated that the scheme . . . would give the British party a majority of five, and possibly eight . . . The calculation was made on the following basis: In [sic] the Rand the British would have 29 members (either Progressives or Responsibles); Barberton . . . would also return either a Progressive or a Responsible; and in Pretoria . . . the British party expected to win four, if not five, seats. The Progressives were also confident at that time that they could win seats in Potchefstroom town and Pretoria district, and perhaps two or three other country towns.[1]

Het Volk and the Responsible Government Association accepted this proposal; and the committee therefore thought it certain that the 'British party' would make a clean sweep of the Witwatersrand. General Botha had persisted with his *nolo episcopari* and pledged that, if the Progressives accepted this proposal, Het Volk would not contest any seats outside Pretoria and the country districts. But what was the 'British party'? To the Progressives that term, in politics at least, could properly be applied to none but themselves. Their leaders gave a provisional acceptance and then, after an interview with Lord Selborne, refused. Selborne, as he explained later to the Colonial Secretary, thought that the census figures for 1904 were now too low for the Witwatersrand, and he was sceptical of the committee's electoral forecast: as a former whip in the House of Commons, he said, he knew more about elections than anyone else in the Transvaal. 'I have studied the question deeply and I am convinced that except in Pretoria, Witwatersrand and the Barberton district, no British candidate will get in for any seat.'[2]

Selborne's intervention was regarded in London with disfavour, and the Cabinet discussed his recall.[3] It was decided that he should stay, but he was rebuked in a dispatch which reminded him that a colonial governor who disagreed with a committee appointed by the

[1] Ibid., para. 98.   [2] C.O. 291/99. Selborne to Elgin, 19 May 1906.
[3] Spender, op. cit., ii. 240.

Secretary of State should make his protest to London, and not take countervailing action of his own. 'His Majesty's Government', the dispatch concluded, 'view with regret the procedure adopted and its results.'[1]

The Progressives plainly had no faith in Het Volk's promise to abstain from electioneering on the Witwatersrand, did not wish to see Pretoria holding the balance of power, and regarded the Responsibles as political renegades. These sentiments, however, would have been embarrassing to express in public; and the Progressives based their rejection of the committee's proposal on the contention that the census figures for the Witwatersrand were too low by 13,000. They reached this conclusion by taking the number of men who had come of age since 1904, and then adding an estimated number of immigrants, based on the average increase between 1890 and 1904: if this ratio were applied to the years 1904 and 1905, they said, the figure of potential voters should be 56,000. But extrapolation is always questionable; and it could be pointed out that there had been spectacular bursts of expansion of the Witwatersrand which had not been repeated, and that the Progressives' calculations made no allowance for the exodus which, by common repute, had occurred during the past two years. The committee, Het Volk and the Responsibles all refused to admit the accuracy of this estimate; and the Progressives then asked that a new voters' roll should be drawn up before a decision were taken. 'The Progressive Association were firmly convinced that they would largely benefit if a new voters' list were prepared, and they believed that this result would probably give the Rand a representation far exceeding the rest of the Transvaal, and thus more than compensate for the evils of the long delay which the preparation of a new list must necessitate.'[2]

To wait for a new list would mean a delay of at least six months. After a great deal of discussion, most of it fruitless in results, the committee made up its mind upon a second partition, which gave thirty-three seats to the Witwatersrand (excluding Krugersdorp), six to Pretoria, and thirty to the rest of the Transvaal. Het Volk and the Responsibles agreed, with reluctance; the Progressives protested and, when their protest was disregarded, sent a deputation to London to urge, without success, that an additional seat should be given to the Witwatersrand. The committee reported, with a certain

1 C.O. 291/99. Elgin's dispatch of 16 June 1906.
2 Ridgeway Report I. para. 70.

weariness, that: 'The settlement which we have proposed is a fair compromise . . . It should ensure a British majority, if only the British will, on this critical occasion, work together as a united party, but should the Labour Party desert the Progressives at the poll, or should the Progressives persist in the intention which is imputed to them of opposing the election of men like Mr. E. P. Solomon, Mr. Cullinan, manager of the Premier Diamond Mines, and others, whose patriotism is above suspicion, the result cannot be by any means certain.'[1]

Hence, the committee was, more than ever, 'emphatically in favour' of a second chamber, nominated in the first instance.

The Legislative Assembly about to be created will be inexperienced in Constitutional and Parliamentary ways. Moreover, owing to the close division of parties, it is possible that some crucial measure may be carried by a majority of two or three votes. The position of the supreme Government in the case of this and other questionable legislation would be delicate and difficult. Each side would look up to it as a court of appeal—as the arbiter who is to deliver his award by the exercise or non-exercise of the right to veto, and each side would raise its voice in angry protest against undue interference, when the decision happened to be unfavourable. A Second Chamber would, to a great extent, remove this danger, and indeed we would suggest that the Imperial Government should reserve to itself the right of appealing to the electorate *en masse* by Referendum, as regards any legislation or question which seems to it to be sufficiently important or doubtful.[2]

Furthermore, it argued, a second chamber would provide a place in the legislature for men who were sympathetic towards the non-Whites. There the committee approached the dilemma of Article VIII of the Terms of Surrender—that self-government for Whites might involve injustice to the rest of the population. They avoided the dilemma by denying that it existed. They observed, indeed, that Milner's administration had neglected the non-Whites, and that although Native taxation had increased from £110,000 in 1898 to £653,000 in 1905 'little or nothing has been done for the amelioration of the Native population.'[3] But, they suggested, better times were on the way; and they quoted the opinion of Sir Godfrey Lagden, the Commissioner for Native Affairs, that imperial intervention would probably do more harm than good, but that 'during the past few years there has been a wholesome change in public opinion on Native questions. That opinion is moving in the right direction, and

[1] Ibid., para. 78.   [2] Ibid., para. 101.   [3] Ibid., para. 140.

is tolerant in character.' No evidence was quoted for this contention. The committee reasoned, however, that benevolence and self-interest alike would make for fair treatment: the Native, it said, was 'indispensable in the social as well as the industrial economy of the two Colonies. If he were ill-treated he might leave the Colony, and certainly he would not migrate into it.' It was to be hoped that 'the question of the representation of Natives will sooner or later be dealt with in a liberal spirit by the new legislatures.' Indefinite hope was all that the committee could offer. Its recommendation was firm: 'We are convinced that any attempt to dictate a policy to the new Legislature would be bitterly resented, and that the best and wisest policy as regards the self-governing states which are about to be created is to trust to their sense of justice.'[1]

Finally, the committee expressed its opinion that the greatest hope for improvement in South Africa would be found 'in a Con-federation on the same general principles as those on which the Dominion of Canada and the Commonwealth of Australia have been founded.'[2]

In short, the Ridgeway Committee reassured the Colonial Secretary that untrammelled self-government would be good for relations between British and Afrikaners, and would be more favourable to the non-Whites, in the long run, than any system with safeguards operated from London. Selborne disagreed with the first contention, but concurred reluctantly with the second. When asked whether a definite sum of money should be reserved in the proposed Letters Patent, for expenditure on Native welfare, he replied that such a provision would be resented in the Transvaal as demonstrating an unnecessary distrust in the Whites. On 4 June he wrote to Elgin: '. . . on the whole I consider that the interests of the Natives will be best consulted if questions affecting their betterment are left to be settled under the sense of duty and responsibility which I am sure will actuate the Parliament of this Colony.'[3]

In the main, the Colonial Office agreed that indigenous populations could not effectively be protected by clauses written into a constitution. Indirect sanctions were discussed, such as reserving part of the colonial revenue for direct expenditure on non-Whites: the precedent were not encouraging. Such expedients had been tried, and had failed, in Natal, New Zealand and Western Australia. Lambert minuted: 'My own view strongly is, if I may reiterate it, that when

[1] Ibid., para. 146.   [2] Ibid., para. 107.   [3] C.O. 291/99.

once you give self-government all these devices are necessarily worthless . . . Certainly our previous experience in the Transvaal has not been happy—under the Pretoria Convention there were plenty of safeguards, all worthless as far as the native was concerned, and the precedents in responsibly-governed colonies are in the same direction.'[1] Elgin concurred: it would be best, he said, to take a stand on 'the necessity of preserving all legitimate rights and property as they now stand.'[2] The Colonial Office would do its best, in other words, to see to it that the lot of the non-White was not conspicuously worse under self-government than it had been under the Crown. Further than that, it would not go. The dilemma, in short, was unavoidable: to enact elaborate precautions for the protection of the non-Whites might, indeed, unite British and Afrikaners, but unite them in common hostility to the British Government; to attempt to reconcile Whites through self-government, while retaining British supremacy, involved abandoning the non-Whites to the mercy of the local legislatures. The Liberal Government of 1906 was faced with the same dilemma which Milner had stated in stark terms in 1897.[3] But, by 1906, the issue had already been prejudged. The Liberal Government, found itself bound by Article VIII of the Vereeniging agreement, and confronted by unanimity of counsel from South Africa, including that of two High Commissioners and its own committee. From all aspects, it seemed that without good relations between British and Afrikaners there was no way to protect the coloured races except by continuing the direct rule of the Crown, and a continuance of Crown government was, *ex hypothesi*, impossible. Once the premise was accepted that the primary objective was to find a means by which white men in South Africa should live contented both with each other and with the Empire, the Liberal Government (in 1906 as when it passed the South Africa Act in 1909) had no choice.

Elgin followed the precedent set by Lyttelton in accepting the

---

[1] C.O. 291/113. Minute of 17 August 1906 on a memorandum by F. E. Garrett, suggesting that the Governor should be empowered to convene an advisory council, partly elected and partly nominated, of 'leading natives and experts on native affairs', to consider legislation. This council (which had some analogies with that set up under the Glen Grey Act) would, Garrett thought, strengthen the hand of the Governor and allow him to exercise 'the mediating influence which is at present exercised from Downing Street, necessarily at a less plastic stage of the Acts in question and usually at the instance of agencies or persons who are not in touch with South African opinion nor responsible to anyone in South Africa.'
[2] C.O. 291/95.   [3] See above, p. 11.

South African definition of 'native' as referring to any coloured person. On 13 June 1906, Dr. A. Abdurahman, president of the African Political Organization, sent from Cape Town a petition from Cape Coloureds, asking for political rights for Coloureds in the Transvaal, and pointing out that the Vereeniging agreement referred 'only to aboriginal natives, and not to such coloured subjects as Your Majesty's petitioners claim to represent.'[1] Churchill was questioned in the House of Commons on whether the Government had repudiated the definition of 'native' adopted by the South African Native Affairs Commission of 1905[2]—'aboriginal inhabitants of Africa south of the Equator, including half-castes and their descendants by natives'—and, if so, precisely what meaning they did attach to the word.

> *Mr. Churchill*: His Majesty's Government have been advised that the adoption of the definition of the word 'native' by the . . . Commission in the interpretation of the Vereeniging Agreement would be regarded as a breach of the spirit of the agreement by the other parties to it.
> *Mr. Rees*: Is the hon. Gentleman aware that the application of this term to British Indians causes natural and justifiable indignation?
> *Mr. Churchill*: I can quite understand that.
> *Mr. Cox*: The hon. Gentleman has not answered the latter part of my question.
> *Mr. Churchill*: I believe the precise meaning attached to the word 'native' is native of any country other than a European country . . .
> *Mr. Myer*: Does that apply to the Japanese?
> *Mr. Churchill*: Certainly.[3]

An answer in this sense was sent to Dr. Abdurahman.[4]

However, the West Ridgeway committee had gone a long way towards reassuring and conciliating the Transvaal Boers. Botha, in a personal letter to West Ridgeway of 2 June, wrote:

> From the first meeting we felt convinced—and our conviction has been deepened since—that you and your colleagues were determined to do what was fair and just between the old and the new population of the Transvaal . . . We told you that our aim was not to secure political predominance for the older population, but only to safeguard abiding interests of the permanent population of the land which, in the peculiar circumstances of the Transvaal, do admittedly require very careful safeguarding . . . The Boer people are anxious for co-operation but only on a basis of justice and fairness. However wretchedly poor and abject their lot is today, they still retain sufficient self-respect to refuse to co-operate on any other basis.

[1] C.O. 291/112.   [2] The Lagden Commission.
[3] 23 July 1906.   [4] C.O. 291/112.

The Milner Constitution, which had the trail of distrust all over it, was deeply resented by them, and their resentment would have found very grave expression but for the restraining influence of their leaders . . . There is only one medicine that could cure this country of its deep-seated ills—and that is plain, honest, straightforward meting out of equal justice to all. The pity is that the partisan spirit has been so consistently displayed in high places that people have almost come to despair of justice or fair dealing from that quarter . . .[1]

The committee was, in its own opinion, far from leaning backwards to be charitable to the Boers. In his final memorandum, West Ridgeway estimated that his franchise proposals would produce a British majority of from five to ten, provided that the British would work together. He would, he said, guarantee this, 'and I have no objection to the fact being stated on my authority.'[2]

III

In the Orange River Colony, the committee found fewer problems. There was no chance, by any exercise of electoral mathematics, of contriving a British majority there; but the committee reported, comfortably, that racial antagonisms except in a few districts were on the wane. It found, to its surprise, that there was wide support for Selborne's suggestion that the constitution of the Republican Free State should be modified and restored, and it reported that a majority both of British and Afrikaners would be found in favour of such a proposal if a referendum were held. But decisive opposition came from the leaders of Oranje Unie, the party which was the counterpart of Het Volk. Abraham Fischer, the leader was 'strongly, even vehemently' against the proposal: an elected president and an appointed governor, he said in effect, were clean different things, and to give to the executive head of the administration power to appoint members to the executive council at will would be a denial of responsible government. Nevertheless, the committee recommended that a plebiscite should be held upon this issue. It would have liked, it added, to have recommended that elections should be held under some form of proportional representation, but it had been unable to find anyone of any standing in the colony to agree with it.[3]

The committee presented its report at the end of July; the Letters Patent for the Transvaal were issued on 6 December. In the intervening period, discussion in the Colonial Office turned for the

[1] C.O. 291/114.　　[2] C.O. 291/112.　　[3] C.O. 291/114.

most part on the nature of a second chamber, and its composition; on what, if anything, could be done to protect non-Whites; and on the status to be given to the Dutch language. These were old questions. Selborne, throughout the year, had pleaded for the discouragement of Dutch, arguing that it was a foreign language to most Boers, and that the vernacular—the *taal*—had no literature. The *taal*, he said, was 'no danger' to English, and for that very reason the 'Boer intelligentsia who still look for a United States of South Africa' wished to substitute Dutch, which could be developed as a rival.[1] Churchill disagreed; in fact, he argued that, in language as in politics, the British should hope for victory through tolerance and innate superiority. He minuted on Selborne's dispatch:

In all these sort of petty-burning questions wisdom indicates the line of least resistance. I am for complete bilingual equality. I do not think that High Dutch—a foreign language as Lord Selborne calls it, not understood by the mass of the Boer people, not rooted in the soil—would be likely to oust the dominant literary and commercial medium of speech, even if that were intrinsically a less powerful language, instead of being the most flexible, forceful, widespread and magnificent of modern tongues. No devices however costly and inconvenient will in the present age accomplish such a resolution. I do not think many artificial stimulants will be demanded, once it is known that they will not be refused.

Upon the other hand, if the Boers do not make a point of complete bilingual equality in its most pedantic forms, I would not suggest inconvenient methods to them. Let us follow calmly and trustfully the line of least resistance . . . But if further recognition of the *taal* or of High Dutch (or of Japanese or Volapuk) is vehemently demanded by the Dutch in South Africa to their own detriment and at their own proper expense, I would not under any circumstances offer any resistance to their wishes.[2]

In the main, the British Government accepted the West Ridgeway committee's recommendations, but it rejected the proposal to hold referenda as an unprecedented constitutional innovation in British possessions. There was to be an assembly of sixty-nine members and a second chamber, to be known as the legislative council, of fifteen, to be nominated in the first instance by the Governor with the approval of the Colonial Secretary; the Transvaal legislature was empowered, after not less than four years, to provide for the election of future legislative councils. The Intercolonial Council was to cease its functions if either colonial legislature decided that it should

[1] C·O. 291/116.   [2] C.O. 291/98.

do so. There was a specific prohibition upon 'any conditions of employment or residence of a servile character', and the administration of the native territory of Swaziland was transferred from Lord Selborne in his capacity as governor to Lord Selborne in his capacity as high commissioner. Otherwise, there were no exceptional restrictions upon the power of the legislature, except for the usual provision that acts 'whereby persons not of European birth may be subjected or liable to any disabilities or restrictions to which persons of European birth or descent are not also subjected or made liable' were subject to disallowance by the Crown.

There was to be manhood suffrage for Whites only, biennial registration of voters, and automatic redistribution of constituencies by three commissioners to be appointed by the Governor-in-Council. These commissioners were given a wider discretion than that laid down in the Lyttelton constitution: in drawing electoral boundaries, they were to give 'due consideration' to the existing boundaries of municipal and magisterial divisions; to the community or diversity of interests of the local population; to means of communication; and to physical features. At their discretion, they were empowered to vary the electoral quota by 15 per cent. upwards or downwards. At the elections of 1907, the average constituency on the Witwatersrand contained 1,616 voters, that in the countryside 1,414: the largest constituency contained 1,770, the smallest 1,086. These provisions were extended to the Orange River Colony, and carried into the Act of Union. As they were devised, they represented one more attempt to secure British or 'moderate' representation by permitting the commissioners to give parliamentary seats to the medium-sized country towns, which were thought to contain a substantial number of voters who were dominated neither by Het Volk nor the mining industry.

Speeches in the Legislature might be either in English or Dutch, bills and votes and proceedings were to be published in both languages, but English was to be the language of record. This provision was another defeat for Milnerism. There was some discussion on whether the use of Dutch might be at the permission of the presiding officer, or granted as a right: it was pointed out that permission, once requested, could hardly be refused; and that to place Dutch on an inferior footing would be to encourage the representatives of Het Volk to use it, as a matter of pride, on every occasion.

IV

The elections to the assembly were held on 22 February 1907. The pact between the Responsible Government Association (rechristened the National Association) and Het Volk had been extended to an understanding that, if the combined parties were in the majority, the premiership should go to Sir Richard Solomon, who had resigned from heading the Legal services of the Transvaal to join his two brothers as Nationalist candidates. The Progressives selected their most powerful debater, Sir Percy Fitzpatrick, to oppose Richard Solomon in Pretoria. Selborne once more laid himself open to the charge of partisanship. It was critically important to the Progressives to dominate the Pretoria seats, to tilt the balance which West Ridgeway had hoped would be kept in equilibrium by 'moderate' men. In November, Fitzpatrick announced that he would make three public speeches in Pretoria, with the avowed object of 'bringing about a better understanding' between Johannesburg and Pretoria. The electoral object seemed plain enough; and it was, therefore, indiscreet of Selborne to commend Fitzpatrick's mission to the mayor of Pretoria in a formal letter, which began: 'Nothing has troubled me more in Transvaal politics than the absence of good feeling between Pretoria and Johannesburg. To me the difference that exists between the two communities, and which I should scarcely exaggerate if I called an attitude of marked hostility, is most mischievous to the country, and the effect on both communities is evil.'[1] The intervention was ill-received, and the explanation regarded as naïve, among Fitzpatrick's political opponents. The *Transvaal Advertiser* of 5 November accused the High Commissioner, obliquely, of electioneering in the Progressives' interests and, more directly, wanted to know how he 'was induced to put this kind of veiled affront upon our intelligence.' Selborne reported the incident to the Colonial Secretary, who let it pass in silence.

Personal considerations, Selborne wrote as the campaign began in earnest in the new year, 'operate as usual in the direction of fissiparousness as far as the British and in the direction of solidarity as far as the Boer section of the community is concerned.' Thirty-one independent candidates, almost all British, presented themselves, and the Labour sects, united for the occasion, fought both the Pact and the Progressives on the Witwatersrand. By contrast, Het Volk

[1] C.O. 291/114.

was demonstrating a monolithic quality. On 31 December, Selborne reported:

> The reports from the various constituencies illustrate . . . the rigid discipline which exists in the Association of Het Volk, the implicit obedience of the subordinate branches to the Head Committee, and the autocratic nature of the Head Committee's control. It is stated that, according to the statutes of Het Volk, nomination meetings must be attended by at least one member of the Head Committee, and General Botha and Mr. Smuts have been touring the country directing the nominations.
>
> At Heidelberg, for instance, General Botha, after holding a private meeting with the members of the local committees, simply announced to the people the name of the candidate who had been chosen for one division of the district, informed them that the nomination of the candidate for the other division had been left to the Head Committee, and appealed to them to support the nominee whoever he might be.[1]

It was regarded in Downing Street as a foregone conclusion that the Pact would win. This gave a double importance to the nominations to the Legislative Council. Churchill minuted on 13 February: 'I am of opinion that in view of the certainty of a Het Volk–Nationalist majority in the Lower House, it is important that there should be a clear majority of British (I do not say Progressive) in the Second Chamber; and I would instruct Lord Selborne accordingly. The nominated Second Chamber was always intended to be a safeguard of a temporary character.'[2] Selborne was searching diligently for candidates for the Legislative Council who were known to be sympathetic to non-Whites. The search was not easy. In the first list of twenty-seven candidates which he submitted to the Colonial Secretary, only five could be said to be of this disposition; and his list was criticized as containing names without weight— only Lionel Phillips, of Selborne's first list, appeared in the *Anglo-African Who's Who*, and Lionel Phillips refused nomination.[3] Selborne continued to send suggestions, and *curricula vitae*, to London, where Churchill insisted that the final choice should rest with the Colonial Secretary. The final choice contained only three men who were not wedded to the doctrine of the 'white man's country'—A. S. Raitt, who represented Labour, and two members of the 'kindergarten', Lionel Curtis and Richard Feetham.[4] 'I regret', Selborne telegraphed, 'that I have not been in a position to find

---

[1] C.O. 291/115.   [2] Ibid.   [3] Ibid.
[4] Curtis's benevolence did not, at that stage, extend to Indians.

more ex-burghers more sympathetic to natives. They are rare enough among British and cannot be found among Boers.'[1]

The results of the election were received by the 'British party' with horrified surprise. The total electorate was 105,338; of these 54,972 were on the Witwatersrand. Het Volk won thirty-seven seats, five of them on the Witwatersrand. The Progressives won twenty-one, the National Association six, Labour three and Independents two. Het Volk won every rural seat except Barberton (which went to an Independent with Progressive sympathies). The votes cast (excluding those in ten constituencies in which the Het Volk candidate was returned unopposed) were:

Het Volk	24,123
Progressives	17,635
Independents	8,255
Nationalists	6,025
Labour	5,216

In every respect, Het Volk had demonstrated the power of its appeal and the superiority of its organization. The percentage poll for the country was 67·5. The average for the Witwatersrand was 65·1, for Pretoria 68, and for the country districts 72·5. Well might Smuts exclaim: 'We are in for ever!'[2] 'Next perhaps to Mr. Winston Churchill', commented the *Johannesburg Star*, 'the politicians who are most to blame for the absence of a British majority from the first Legislature of the Transvaal are the brothers Solomon.'

The most conspicuous, and by far the most important, casualty of the election was Sir Richard Solomon, beaten by Fitzpatrick in Pretoria (South Central) in a three-cornered fight. Lord Elgin flatly refused to invite a defeated candidate to form a ministry. The premiership was offered at once to Louis Botha. He formed a cabinet of four members of Het Volk; himself, Smuts, J. de Villiers and J. Rissik; and two Nationalists—E. P. Solomon and H. C. Hulls.

Thus, unexpectedly, had the premiership dropped into Botha's lap, and many Boers were disposed to regard the event as the gift of Providence. The *volk* had been led, if not into the Promised Land, at least to the upper slopes of Mount Pisgah. Neither Botha nor Smuts drew philosophy or purpose exclusively from the Old Testament. In his first speech as Prime Minister, Botha promised the British

---

[1] C.O. 291/115.   [2] Quoted in Thompson, p. 226.

that their interests would be safe in his care, and that 'the old population . . . were actuated by motives of deep gratitude, because the
King and the British Government and people had trusted the
Transvaal people in a manner unequalled in history by the grant
of a free Constitution. Was it possible for the Boers ever to forget
such generosity?'[1] It is impossible not to feel, when considering
Botha's conduct then and in the future, that one is witnessing one
of the rarest phenomena in politics—a profound and enduring
change of heart.

So simple an explanation cannot, however, be applied to the
complex mentality of General Smuts. To Smuts, the victory of
Het Volk gave him the chance of gratifying a smouldering ambition,
and at the same time of drawing Transvaal politics out of narrow
circles of *campanilism* and prejudice. No less clearly than Milner, he
saw that the centre of gravity of South African politics lay in the
Transvaal. Federation was in the air; but would not a closer union
still sooner or later draw South Africa into the orbit of a Transvaal
redeemed from Milnerism, and made safe for Afrikanerdom? From
the victory of Het Volk onwards, Smuts's mind turned away from
the thoughts of federation to thoughts of the union of South Africa—
one land from the Limpopo to Cape Agulhas, and guided from the
Transvaal.

[1] Thompson, p. 32

CHAPTER NINE

CONCLUSION

THE Anglo-Boer War was a seminal event in South African history.
A study of the events of the conflict, and of the period of reconstruction in the former republics under Lord Milner, may provide
the key to some of the riddles which have puzzled inquirers into the
politics of contemporary South Africa, especially the politics of
Afrikaner nationalism. Why, it may be asked, did the war for so
long form part of the groundwork of current controversy? How was
it that the Orange Free State, which James Bryce had praised in
almost fulsome terms in the 1890s, as a model republic where racial
animosity among Whites scarcely existed, became the cradle of a
xenophobiac nationalism? Why was it that so many Afrikaners
simultaneously feared that they would be swamped by the indigenous
non-White peoples, and at the same time were reluctant to admit
immigrants from Europe in large numbers? How was it that the
Afrikaner people, in previous times noted for the individuality and
resistance to discipline, should have become dominated by the drives
towards *volkseenheid* and *gelykstelling*?

In great measure, these attitudes were developed as a reaction
to the policy of anglicization which Milner attempted, and failed to
achieve. Afrikanerdom was not broken in the field. It had been
strained almost to the limits of cohesion; but the fibres had held
together. In the event, the memory of the war, carefully nurtured
as it was, did more to unite Afrikanerdom than Kruger had ever
succeeded in doing. The war gave to Afrikaners throughout South
Africa common victims to mourn, common injuries upon which to
brood, a common cause in the restoration of republicanism and, in
the tragic figure of Kruger, dead in exile, a martyr around whom
myths could be woven. Moreover, the manner and result of the
peace negotiations in Pretoria and Vereeniging confirmed the
authority of the commando leaders—the 'bitter-enders'—as the
unquestioned leaders of the Afrikaner *volk*. During the prolonged
resistance, the political hierarchy of the Boers had been transformed;
a new elite had appeared. The Krugerites had been pushed into the

background, and in their place had arisen men of youth and competence, who had achieved political influence through military ability, and whose authority over their followers reflected the tight discipline of the commandos of 1902, not the quasi-anarchic organization of 1899. In 1902, Botha was 39, Hertzog was 36, Smuts was 32.

One shrewd observer noted this at once. On 21 July 1902, Merriman wrote to Bryce:

The old Boer—the so-called 'takhaar'—of whom Paul Kruger was the ido and the most prominent representative, has practically disappeared as a factor. He it was who by his impracticable attitude forced the progressive section into the attitude that led up to hostilities and brought on the suicidal ultimatum. When actual hostilities began he did not bear the brunt of the fighting. All or nearly all the prominent leaders were either progressive farmers like de la Rey, de Wet, Botha [and] Kemp or educated men from the towns like Steyn, Hertzog, Smuts and others. The soul of the fighting force consisted of young men and progressive farmers, many of them well-to-do, in some cases rich men. The takhaar when he surrendered became a 'National Scout' in many cases. Now this has a very important bearing upon the future . . .[1]

Lord Rosebery had once expressed the hope that the Boers would go directly from their commandos into the British Empire. They did so, unreconciled and under their own leaders. Only the eye of hindsight can discern in the attitude of the Boer leaders at the end of the war a desire to shake hands and be friends with their former enemies.

This attitude has been misinterpreted by some students of the period. One recent historian has written: 'Immediately upon the cessation of the fighting, Botha, with the able assistance of Schalk Burger, began the task of reconstructing Anglo-Boer friendship with a view to the foundation of "a Greater South Africa". The first of the Boer leaders to see this vision, Botha used the term in a parting address to his military staff at the close of the war, while to the Wakkerstroom commando, when ordering them to lay down their arms, he declared: "Tomorrow begins our great task of building a South African nation." '[2]

The nuances of the Afrikaner political vocabulary are not always easily expressed in translation. 'People', 'nation', and 'South

[1] Bryce PP.
[2] G. B. Pyrah, *Imperial Policy and South Africa, 1902–1910* (1955), p. 138.

Africa' are sometimes interchangeable terms; they may all be embraced within the concept of Afrikanerdom. The regeneration to which Botha immediately looked was that of a *volk* which the war had almost shattered; the magnanimity that he preached extended first to his own people—to the 'hands-uppers' and the National Scouts. Indeed, Botha's notable political achievement, perhaps, was that of knitting together the torn fabric of Afrikanerdom, immediately after the war, so that by 1906 the Boer party in the Transvaal— Het Volk—had acquired a monolithic solidarity.

Two themes dominated white politics in South Africa during the fifty years after the Peace of Vereeniging. One was the attempts to reconcile the Afrikaners and those of English speech. One might say that, in almost each instance, the price of reconciliation was paid by the non-White peoples. The terms of the Peace of Vereeniging excluded 'natives' from the franchise in the former republics. The compact of union, in 1909, brought together Whites, but introduced a colour bar into Parliament. The pact between General Hertzog's Nationalist Party and the largely English-speaking Labour Party in 1924 extended the colour bar to industrial employment. Fusion between the parties of Hertzog and Smuts in 1934 involved the removal of the African voters of the Cape Province from the common roll. The war-time coalition between the United, Dominion and Labour Parties produced restriction upon ownership of land by Indians. Finally, the reunion of the parties of Hertzog (then led by his *fidus Achates*, Havenga) and Malan in 1948 led to the removal of the Coloured voters of the Cape from the common roll.

The second movement, sometimes running parallel to the politics of reconciliation, sometimes coming into conflict with it, may be described as the attempt by Afrikaner leaders to unite their own people in a single political organization. For Afrikanerdom did not remain monolithic and vengeful after the war. The grant of self-government to the Transvaal and to the Orange River Colony— Campbell-Bannerman's 'act of magnanimity'—did divide Afrikaners between those, like Botha and Smuts and, later, Hertzog, who were prepared to accept imperial membership, and those who sought for a restoration of republicanism. It is worth remembering that Johannes Strijdom was the first prime minister of South Africa who was able to govern without a coalition. It may be argued that Campbell-Bannerman gave to white politics in South Africa nearly half a century of moderation.

INDEX

Abdurahman, Dr. A., 205.

African, 177; voters removal from roll in Cape, 215.

African Political Association, 205.

Afrikaner Bond, 3, 14, 15; urges Kruger to make concessions, 18, 40, 54–6; refuses to follow Schreiner, 69; denounces war, 71, 103; opposes Chinese labour, 162.

Afrikaner Nationalism, 3; Milner's views on, 78–9; British Army encourages, 86, 171; politics of, 213.

Afrikaner Party, 165, 172.

'Afrikanerdom', 3–4, 39; Milner determined to break, 53, 86, 92, 95, 132, 173, 189; in war, 213, 215.

Afrikaners, sympathy of Cape, 3, 4, 6–7, 9, 11, 14; dislike of British, 31, 48, 50; Milner doubts loyalty of Cape, 51, 53; South African English press and, incensed by Milner, 54; disarming of, 54; detention under martial law, 55; Cape, 68; concentration camps mythology, 110, 134, 144, 169, 173–4, 176–7; on Chinese labour, 183, 190; Unity, 198; 'Volkseenheid and gelykstelling', 213; political vocabulary, 214–15.

Albert, annexed to Republic, 54.

Alberts, J. J., votes against Resolution at Assembly, 153.

Aliwal North, 47; annexed to Republic, 54, 109.

Amery, L. S., 32, 34–5, 41; on war aims, 73, 123, 139.

Anglo-German Agreement, 15.

Article VIII, see Vereeniging.

Asiatics, 170, 173, 178.

Asquith, H. H., 11, 39, 45, 177.

Assembly of the People, 141–54.

Association of Coloured Peoples of the Witwatersrand, 'Article VIII', 179.

Austin, Alfred, 31.

Badenhorst, C. C. J., votes against Resolution at Assembly, 153.

Bailey, Abe, 172.

Balfour, Arthur, 7, 34, 44; on peace moves, 129; resigns, 182; Transvaal British alarm at resignation of, 188; and Policy of Magnanimity, 189.

Banishment Proclamation, 104–6.

Baring, Sir Evelyn, 9.

Barkly East, 50, 114.

Barkly West, Annexed to Republic, 54.

Basutoland, 49, 101.

Bester, A. J., votes against Resolution at Assembly, 153.

Bethulie, 108.

Beyers, General, and Assembly of the People, 143–4; and Chinese labour, 163; violent harangues, 174, 198.

Bigge, Sir Arthur, 44, 95.

Birkenstock, C., 142.

'Bitter-Enders', 91, 173–4; leaders of Afrikaner Volk, 213.

Bloemfontein, 157.

Blood River, 173.

Boer, Boers, 2, 5, 7, 9; ultimatum, 26, 28, 30–1, 38–9; supremacy, 40; commandos invasion and superiority of arms, 43; victories, 44, 49; Governments and 'hands-uppers', 85; two Presidents protest at farm burning, 88, 101; volunteer for British Army, 126, 130, 134, 136, 140; army unbeaten, 151; and Treaty of Vereeniging, 154, 155; return of organized politics, 158; and reconstruction, 159–60; and importing of Asiatics, 161; representative, 163, 164; and self-government, 165–7; census, 168–9; Congress, 171; and failure of Milnerism, 172–7; and responsible Government, 181; distrust of, 183; and self-government, 184, 188–9; new elite of, 213–14.

Boer Commissioners, put forward basis for negotiations, 145; appoint Hertzog and Smuts to work with Milner, 146–7.

Boer Remedies, 107.